W9-BUJ-649

Arnulfo L. Oliveira Memorial Library

WITHDRAWN
UNIVERSITY LIBRARY
THE UNIVERSITY OF TEXAS RIO GRANDE VALLEY

LIBRARY
THE UNIVERSITY OF TEXAS
AT BROWNSVILLE
Brownsville, Tx 78520-4991

Frances Burney
Dramatist

Frances Burney Dramatist

Gender, Performance, and the
Late-Eighteenth-Century Stage

Barbara Darby

THE UNIVERSITY PRESS OF KENTUCKY

LIBRARY
THE UNIVERSITY OF TEXAS
AT BROWNSVILLE
Brownsville, Tx 78520-4991

Publication of this volume was made possible in part by a grant from the National Endowment for the Humanities.

Copyright © 1997 by The University Press of Kentucky

Scholarly publisher for the Commonwealth,
serving Bellarmine College, Berea College, Centre
College of Kentucky, Eastern Kentucky University,
The Filson Club Historical Society, Georgetown College,
Kentucky Historical Society, Kentucky State University,
Morehead State University, Murray State University,
Northern Kentucky University, Transylvania University,
University of Kentucky, University of Louisville,
and Western Kentucky University.
All rights reserved.

Editorial and Sales Offices: The University Press of Kentucky
663 South Limestone Street, Lexington, Kentucky 40508-4008

01 00 99 98 97   5 4 3 2 1

Library of Congress Cataloging-in-Publication Data

Darby, Barbara, 1966-
    Frances Burney, dramatist : gender, performance, and the late-eighteenth-century stage / Barbara Darby.
        p.   cm.
    Includes bibliographical references (p.   ) and index.
    ISBN 0-8131-2022-5
    1. Burney, Fanny, 1752-1840—Dramatic works.   2. Feminism and literature—England—History—18th century.   3. Women in the theater—England—History—18th century.   4. Women and literature—England—History—18th century.   I. Title.
PR3316.A4Z6424   1997
823' .6—dc21   97-19459

This book is printed on acid-free recycled paper meeting
the requirements of the American National Standard
for Permanence of Paper for Printed Library Materials.

Manufactured in the United States of America

Contents

List of Illustrations and Figures vi

Acknowledgments vii

Note on Texts and Abbreviations ix

Introduction 1

1. Gender and the Stage 7

2. Censored Women: *The Witlings* 22

3. Politicized Bodies and the Body Politic:
   Edwy and Elgiva and *Elberta* 43

4. The Daughter's Tragedy:
   Hubert De Vere and *The Siege of Pevensey* 82

5. "Choice" and Evaluation: *Love and Fashion* 108

6. Family Matters: *A Busy Day* and *The Woman-Hater* 130

7. A Context and Overview:
   Burney and the Late-Eighteenth-Century Stage 165

Conclusion: Really a Genius for the Stage 193

Notes 204

Index 227

Illustrations and Figures

Illustrations

1. First page of the manuscript *The Witlings* 26
2. First page of the manuscript *Love and Fashion* 116
3. Frank and Miss Percival in *A Busy Day* 133
4. Eliza, Margaret, and Cousin Joel Tibbs in *A Busy Day* 136
5. Mr. and Mrs. Beverley in *The Gamester* 184

Figures

1. Analysis of Act 2 of *The Witlings* 31
2. Actantial Model of *The Siege of Pevensey* with Adela as Subject 99
3. Actantial Model of *The Siege of Pevensey* with De Belesme as Subject 100
4. Triangular Representation of Adela's Position in *The Siege of Pevensey* 101

Acknowledgments

This book has been written with the professional, financial, and emotional support of a large number of individuals who remind me without doubt that while writing is a solitary activity, it does not occur outside a community of important people. I am above all pleased to acknowledge my debt to Peter Sabor, who introduced me to Burney in the first place. I had the pleasure of watching him complete his edition of Burney's plays, and he has served as a model for me of how to combine scholarly excellence with a warm personality and a sense of humor. H. Grant Sampson offered me numerous helpful suggestions when he first read this manuscript, for which I thank him. Brian Corman gave me the necessary encouragement to pursue the refinement of this topic and of my research generally. Maggie Berg is both a dear friend and a mentor. Janice Farrar Thaddeus has gracefully shared with me her thoughts on Burney and other matters, both in person and on the "net." Her encouragement meant a great deal to me as I developed my own view of Burney's work. Marta Straznicky and Natalie Rewa presented me with important questions to consider at significant points in my research. Parts of this book have been presented at eighteenth-century studies conferences, which gave me an opportunity to share my work with colleagues at early stages.

I thank Francis Mattson, curator of the Henry W. and Albert A. Berg Collection at the New York Public Library, for permission to do research in this collection. Wayne Furman and Rodney Phillips of the Office of Special Collections granted permission to reprint Burney material and Philip Milito provided the photographs of the manuscripts. The other librarians in this institution were also most helpful. I would also like to acknowledge the Astor, Lenox and Tilden Foundations in connection with the Berg Collection material. Photographs for *A Busy Day* are reprinted by permission of Bob Willingham and Alan Coveney of the Show of

Strength theater company. The photograph of Sarah Siddons and John Philip Kemble is courtesy of the British Museum. I received a generous grant for a research trip to New York from the Rita Catherall Travel Scholarship, administered by Ann Saddlemyer at the University of Toronto. Funding for research was also provided by the Social Sciences and Humanities Research Council of Canada, the Alberta Heritage Scholarship Fund, and the Department of English and the School of Graduate Studies at Queen's University, Kingston, Ontario.

I thank the editors of the *Journal of Dramatic Theory and Criticism* and *English Studies in Canada* for allowing me to reprint the material on *Edwy and Elgiva* and Burney's views of motherhood that first appeared in these journals.

Most of this book was written in Kingston, a place of much professional and personal development for me. I thank my many friends who spurred my intellectual pursuits and gave me relief from them. Unlike Eliza Watts, I have been blessed with a loving and supportive family. I would like to recognize the support I have always felt from my parents, Alice and Dennis; my sister and brother-in-law, Sandra and John; and my grandmother, Winogene. Gemini, LC, and Misty watched the process from comfortable chairs. Finally, I thank Anthony Stewart for his love, encouragement, and humor. To him I dedicate this work.

Note on Texts and Abbreviations

Throughout this study, all references to Burney's plays are to *The Complete Plays of Frances Burney*, edited by Peter Sabor, with Geoffrey M. Sill and Stewart J. Cooke, 2 vols. (Montreal and Kingston: McGill–Queen's University Press, 1995), cited by act, scene, and line number where these designations are available. Unless otherwise noted, all references to Sabor are to this edition as well. The comedies are printed in volume 1 and the tragedies in volume 2; volume numbers have been provided only where this may be unclear. I have not referred to *The Triumphant Toadeater* because of a lack of evidence that it is Burney's (see Sabor, 2:311).

Several abbreviations are used when Burney's letters and journals are discussed. *The Journals and Letters of Fanny Burney (Madame d'Arblay)*, edited by Joyce Hemlow el al., 12 vols. (Oxford: Clarendon, 1972-1984), is designated as *JL*, followed by volume and page number. *The Early Journals and Letters of Fanny Burney*, edited by Lars E. Troide et al. (Montreal and Kingston: McGill–Queen's University Press, 1988-), is designated as *EJL*, followed by volume and page number. Modern editions of some journals and correspondence are as yet unavailable. In these cases (generally in reference to the tragedies), I have used Charlotte Barrett's edition of *Diary and Letters of Madame d'Arblay*, 6 vols. with Austin Dobson's preface and notes (London: Macmillan, 1904-1905), cited as *DL*, followed by volume and page number. References to unpublished material in the Henry W. and Albert A. Berg Collection, New York Public Library, are cited as *BC* followed by folder number or title. Throughout, all emphases are original unless otherwise noted. For all plays except Burney's, dates listed are for first performances unless otherwise noted.

Introduction

In a letter of October 1799, Charles Burney Jr. writes triumphantly to his sister Frances that Thomas Harris, manager of Covent Garden Theatre, is delighted with her new comedy, *Love and Fashion*. He refers to the new play in the siblings' code of secrecy: "Huzza! Huzza! Huzza! Mr. H. admires the Table—& will bring it into use in the month of March!—" Charles closes his letter, in which he urges Burney to come to London to meet with Harris, by telling her that Harris "is surprised, that you never turned your thoughts to this kind of writing before; as you appear to have really a genius for it!—There now!" (*BC*, Scrapbook, "Fanny Burney and family. 1653-1890"). *Love and Fashion* was not to reach the stage, partly because of the death of Burney's sister Susanna, which rendered the production of a comedy improper in the eyes of Burney and, more notoriously, in the eyes of her father. However, while Dr. Burney was very clear on the matter of entirely abandoning the production of the comedy, Burney herself was less sure about this. Passionate in her defense of her work, she writes at this time to her father about her ambition: "I have all my life been urged to, & all my life intended, writing a Comedy" (*JL*, 4:394-95).[1]

These epistolary communications contain some of the perplexities that surround Frances Burney's efforts as a dramatist. Her success in the genre was predicted by many of the more notable figures of the London literary and theatrical world. In addition to Thomas Harris, who was said to be "in love" with the heroine of *Love and Fashion,* Hester Lynch Thrale, Samuel Johnson, Arthur Murphy, Richard Brinsley Sheridan, and Richard Cumberland all encouraged Burney in her playwriting. This encouragement started in 1778, after the publication of *Evelina.* Burney reports Hester Thrale telling her that "You seem to me to have the right & true talents for writing a Comedy,—you would give us all the fun & humour we could wish, & you would give us a scene or 2 of the pathetic kind that would set all the rest off. If you would but *try,* I am *sure* you would

succeed, & give us such a Play as would be an Honour to all your Family"
(*EJL,* 3:133). Burney's success as a dramatist was, however, limited by this
need to bring "honour to all [the] Family" and her first play, *The Witlings*
(1779), was suppressed by Dr. Burney and Samuel Crisp. The movement
of *Love and Fashion* toward the stage was also halted and Burney does
not seem to have shared her other comedies, *A Busy Day* and *The
Woman-Hater,* with anyone.

As Burney's letter to her father also indicates, she had strong opinions
about her work for the theater, which included these four comedies, three
complete tragedies—*Edwy and Elgiva, The Siege of Pevensey,* and
Hubert De Vere—and the incomplete tragedy, *Elberta.* By the time *Love
and Fashion* was withdrawn from production in 1800, Burney (1752-
1840) was a well-established novelist, as the author of *Evelina; or, The
History of a Young Lady's Entrance into the World* (1778); *Cecilia; or
Memoirs of an Heiress* (1782); and *Camilla; or, A Picture of Youth*
(1796). (*The Wanderer; or, Female Difficulties* was published in 1814.)
The tantalizing question that remains is where her career might have gone
had her comedies reached the stage. The manuscripts that survive bear testimony to the importance of drama in Burney's *oeuvre.* After the suppression of *The Witlings,* Burney wrote to Samuel Crisp that "there are *plays*
that *are* to be saved, & *plays* that are *not* to be saved!" (*EJL,* 3:349). Her
own plays were saved, at least privately, and Burney edited nearly all of
them at different times in her life. As a very old woman she reread many of
them and made comments for revision. Ambitious cast lists envisioning the
leading performers of her day in several of her plays also survive. As a
journalist and letter writer, Burney often dramatizes scenes of daily life
and visits for her correspondents. Numerous scraps of paper among
Burney's materials in the Berg Collection at the New York Public Library
preserve small notes for dialogue, bits of character development, and short
scenes that never made their way into the finished plays, but that indicate
an abiding interest in writing for the stage. In one scrap, a drama is proposed that will "Illustrate the varieties of Poverty—":

> Labour—sweetened by rest
> Privation—recompensed by ease
> Temperance—enjoyed by Health—
> & Spirit, in every exertion, & every
> sacrifice, rewarded by
> Independence . . . .
> [*BC,* Miscellaneous Pieces of Manuscript, 1772-1828, folder I]

This fragment could be an early sketch for a dramatic version of *The
Wanderer.* What these two-hundred-year-old fragments and complete

manuscripts offer to us is a picture of a dramatist often frustrated but also equally persistent in her scripting of ideas into scenes, characters, and dialogue.

Despite the encouragement by theater professionals, Burney's own inclinations, and her numerous compositions in the genre, Burney's plays remained for the most part only in manuscript until very recently. The one play that was produced during her lifetime, *Edwy and Elgiva*, received dismal reviews and closed after one night, but there is no convincing evidence that this indicates any particular lack of talent on Burney's part. The play was not rehearsed properly, Burney was unable to make revisions to it, and the performance (21 March 1795) was marred by imperfect acting. Ellen Donkin suggests that much of the failure may, in fact, be laid at the foot of the company at Drury Lane and its manager, Richard Brinsley Sheridan.[2] Had Burney's comedies been produced, she might have redirected her career entirely toward the stage, as she perfected her craft and enjoyed the monetary rewards that accrued to dramatists. Twentieth-century productions of *A Busy Day* have been very successful. A review of the 1993 performance by the Show of Strength theater company in Bristol suggests that the play is a "comic masterpiece that deserves to immediately decorate the repertoire of [the] Royal National Theatre" and that "Burney's true metier was the stage."[3] Who knows how a contemporary audience might have responded? The idea is intriguing.

It is the purpose of this book to place Burney's plays in a context that acknowledges their importance to the writer, substantiates other critics' arguments (especially those of Margaret Anne Doody and Peter Sabor) in favor of carefully reading the drama, and contributes to the ongoing feminist analyses of eighteenth-century works by women. As I argue, late-eighteenth-century women writers used the stage and its conventions to analyze the position of women in their society and their gender-specific experiences of such institutions as the family, government, and marriage. Social critique emerges from the plays by female playwrights not only through their depictions of female experiences that mirror those of women in the society around them—experiences of submission and constraint—but also through their efforts to portray alternative modes of existence for women both on and off the stage. That Burney's plays did not reach the stage does not repudiate the possibility that she, too, envisioned her drama as having such a political function. As I add my voice to those of the other approving readers of Burney's drama, I hope also to provide compelling arguments for appreciating the plays that have been largely condemned by Burney's critics: her tragedies.

This study seeks to build upon the existing treatments of Burney's plays in two significant ways. The first lies in the effort to produce a sustained feminist critique of Burney's representations of women and of women's issues in her drama, treating it not as tangential to her work as a novelist, but as an integral element of her creativity. A majority of her central characters are female, and the plots, situations, and themes that she explores are all focused on issues of concern to women. While male protagonists figure prominently in *Edwy and Elgiva* and *Hubert De Vere*, the plight of the central female character takes precedence in these plays as well. Institutions and practices depicted by Burney—marriage, the family, financial management, government, public scrutiny, and punishment—are all part of a larger atmosphere in which gender is the primary determinant of the degree and kind of participation individuals are allowed in the organization and power structures of the society they live in. Lurking behind this analysis, of course, is a consideration of the extent to which women at the end of the eighteenth century were granted autonomous subjectivity. Burney's drama explores this question and scrutinizes basic assumptions about the nature of the division between the sexes and its effect on people. This analysis of Burney's drama expands our sense of the variety in Burney's treatment of women's issues. By dealing with these hitherto largely neglected texts, I suggest that the genre may have provided this writer with important possibilities for the representation and treatment of gender-related issues.

The second dominant and, I think, distinctive focus of this study is an attention to the manuscripts' dual nature as texts for reading and analysis, and as scripts for performance. Burney's plays are not casual, dramatized variations on the themes and stories found in her novels. She was clearly attentive to the demands of writing for the stage, with its concomitant generic particularities of embodiment, movement, and blocking, the elements of both space and time that distinguish this genre from prose fiction. The dramatist's use of space and methods of representation have a unique semiotic function, a tenet that has been incorporated into this feminist reading of the plays. I also analyze significant revisions and changes Burney made as she altered characterization, plot, and approaches to the *mise en scène*, speculating on the purpose of the changes in terms of their contribution to Burney's treatment of women's issues.

The neglect of Burney's drama is peculiar given the significant interest she has garnered, especially from feminist critics, in the last decade. Burney scholars have a large body of quite provocative critical work to draw upon in this respect. A portrait of a conflict-ridden Burney emerges from Margaret Anne Doody's critical biography, and the artist who is torn between paternal adoration, rebellion, a desire for fame, and a need for propriety is also found in the criticism of Katharine M. Rogers, Kristina Straub, Julia Epstein, and Joanne Cutting-Gray. Each writer acknowledges the challenge of contextualization when evaluating early modern women writers and their feminist sensibilities.[4] While these readings of Burney clearly differ in emphases and opinions, they are consistent in their suggestion that Burney's identity and works are characterized by ruptures and divisions, the simultaneous pull of conservative and radical ideologies, the contradictory strategies of rebellion and apparent submission: in effect, the author "Burney" is changeable and her texts contradictory and multipositional. Rogers writes of "the conformity that [Burney] consistently professed and the individualist protest that continually appears."[5] Straub considers the "mixed and contradictory *bricollage* [*sic*] of ideological assumptions" in the fiction.[6] Epstein suggests that criticism has helped construct two different "Burneys," and she emphasizes, against the "prudish snob" and comic artist, the "masked simmering rage of a conflicted but self-conscious social reformer."[7] Cutting-Gray describes Burney's use of the nameless woman as a source of antipatriarchal redemption, although she emphasizes that Burney's heroines search for a "legitimating patronym to lend them substance."[8] Doody devotes chapters to the drama, but her interest lies in the "life in the works," so her observations have a strong psychological and biographical leaning. The work of Rogers, Straub, Epstein, and Cutting-Gray provides many fascinating insights into Burney's literary achievements that could as easily be applied to the drama, but which are not. At other times, some generalizations made by these critics about Burney's view of women's issues are proven inaccurate or at least narrow sighted when her drama is taken into account. I argue for the necessity of reading the plays as well as the novels before such generalizations are attempted.

This book has been organized in a fashion that I hope will be of use for those people reading Burney's plays for the first time as well as for those who are familiar with them and come to them with perspectives other than my own. I have dealt with each play separately but invite comparisons between them throughout. The chapters are organized to represent the rough chronological order in which Burney composed her plays, except in the case of the tragedies, which I have discussed thematically. I refer throughout to the recent edition of *The Complete Plays of Frances Burney*, edited by Peter Sabor with Geoffrey M. Sill and Stewart J. Cooke. Three of Burney's plays, *The Witlings*, *Edwy and Elgiva*, and *A Busy Day*, have been previously published. Parts of act 4 of *The Witlings* were transcribed by Constance Hill in *The House in St. Martin's Street*. The play has been edited in full by Clayton J. Delery and has been published by Katharine M. Rogers in *The Meridian Anthology of Restoration and Eighteenth-Century Plays by Women*. *Edwy and Elgiva* was edited by Miriam J. Benkovitz in 1957. *A Busy Day* was published by Tara Ghoshal Wallace in 1984; her 1975 master's thesis is "An Introduction to Fanny Burney's Comedies."[9] The manuscripts for all of Burney's plays are extant in the Berg Collection of the New York Public Library. Additional manuscripts of *Edwy and Elgiva* are at Emmanuel College, Cambridge, and in the Larpent collection at the Huntington Library, Los Angeles.

I have repeated details about the composition of each play that can be found in the biographies by Joyce Hemlow and Margaret Anne Doody and in Sabor's invaluable headnotes to each play. These biographies and Sabor's edition provide a very important background for all of my own work on Burney's plays. Janice Farrar Thaddeus's excellent insights into Burney's life and works will be another substantial addition to Burney studies. In addition to Rogers, Straub, and Epstein, I return to several other sources throughout this discussion of the plays. These include book-length studies by Michael E. Adelstein, D. D. Devlin, and Austin Dobson; a frequently cited article by Hemlow, "Fanny Burney: Playwright"; and doctoral dissertations on Burney's plays and novels by Marjorie Lee Morrison and Elizabeth Yost Mulliken.[10]

Another scholarly debt must be paid to those critics who have offered scholars a wide range of information on and opinions about women's position in the eighteenth century. Of particular value to my own work have been studies written or edited by Alice Browne (*The Eighteenth Century Feminist Mind*), Leonore Davidoff and Catherine Hall (*Family Fortunes: Men and Women of the English Middle Class, 1780-1850*), Bridget Hill (*Eighteenth-Century Women: An Anthology*), Vivien Jones (*Women in the Eighteenth Century: Constructions of Femininity*), Gary Kelly (*Women, Writing, and Revolution, 1790-1827*), Felicity Nussbaum (*Torrid Zones: Maternity, Sexuality, and Empire in Eighteenth-Century English Narratives*), Mary Poovey (*The Proper Lady and the Woman Writer: Ideology as Style in the Works of Mary Wollstonecraft, Mary Shelley, and Jane Austen*), Katharine M. Rogers (*Feminism in Eighteenth-Century England*), and Susan Staves (*Married Women's Separate Property in England, 1660-1833*).[11] This study could not have been written without the foundation provided by the ground-breaking work of so many critics I have not listed in the field of eighteenth-century literary and feminist studies.

In addition to placing Burney's plays in a dual context of feminism and performance, I hope to provide my readers with an appreciation of the variety of thought-provoking and intriguing situations she offers in her drama. My wish is that my readers will be encouraged to take their response to Burney's plays in directions beyond the scope of this book and thus further give Burney her due as a dramatist.

1

Gender and the Stage

Critics in the area of feminist studies and performance theory explore the ways in which drama and performance are related to notions of gender and gender-related behavior and attitudes. This is a particularly compelling area of investigation because performance has so often furnished theorists with a metaphor for describing the differences between men and women. Greek drama, after all, provided Freud with a narrative on which to model a theory of gender development and differentiation. The concepts of spectatorship, objectification, and the regulation of movements or bodies in a social space, the typical rules of which are preexistent or predetermined, all suggest that the place of women in the theater parallels the dynamics of patriarchal society as a whole. Indeed, because theatrical space is often seen to mimic social space so minutely, some critics feel that the representation of female experience on the stage can only replicate the real relations of people offstage, by remaining within the purview of the phallocentrism that constructs a masculine gazing subject and frame. The question asked repeatedly is whether woman exists on or off the stage only as a represented object, or whether she might speak for and of herself.

Responses to this question vary, of course, with the varied approaches that feminist dramatic critics take toward the ways in which female playwrights work within, or attempt to move beyond, an ideology of phallocentrism. The relationship between the tools available to the female dramatist and the potential for new and experimental uses of them is a persistent topic of discussion. As Barbara Freedman writes, "[g]iven the reliance of theatrical narratives on the discovery of identity or place in relation to others, on various forms of the socialization process, the task of rethinking theatre may indeed require an Oedipus Wrecked. Yet a feminist theatre need not deny the limits of language, the place of images, the tyranny of gazes and roles, or the misrecognitions and displacements that attend them, as it goes about the work of reviewing them."[1] The varied and wide-ranging topics reviewed and revised by feminist critics of drama include questions about genre and narrative, the gendered nature of theatrical representation and spectatorship, theater history, images of women on the stage, acting styles, and the work of female playwrights and individual professional theater groups.[2] Female playwrights tackle the problem of representing woman-specific experiences in a similarly varied manner by, for instance, focusing on female figures; redressing the masculinist biases in narratives about heroism; reenvisioning how female figures can occupy space; or, as Hélène Cixous writes, by giving "back to the theatre its fortunate position, its *raison d'être* and what makes it different—the fact that there [in theater] it is possible to get across the living, breathing, speaking body."[3] That the body represented can be a specifically female body, one that encounters and endures the world in gender-specific ways, is one of the central assertions of a feminist dramatic criticism and praxis.

I emphasize from the outset that when I use the term "feminist theater," I do not understand modes of representation, genres, or plays to be feminist in an inherent way, as some critics have suggested about comedy or domestic situations, for example,[4] but rather that feminist theater includes plays in which either the method of representation or the subject matter (or both) draws attention to gender as a category of subjectivity that unmistakably influences female participation in social institutions and relations and female access to physical, intellectual, and emotional self-determination. Nor do I feel that feminist drama need necessarily be dependent on the sex of the writer. Where subject matter is concerned, Rosemary K. Curb's label "woman-conscious" is relevant. She describes woman-conscious drama as that which features "multiple interior reflections of women's lives and perceptions."[5] Hélène Keyssar's definition of "feminist theater" also underlies my own approach to Burney's plays, which are plays that are characterized by "the creation of significant stage roles for women, a concern with gender roles in society, exploration of the texture of women's worlds and an urge towards the politicisation of sexuality."[6]

Because this study is feminist in its outlook, it is fitting that I also offer a brief discussion of my use of the term "feminist." Underlying this approach to Burney is a materialist feminist understanding of gender and sexuality, one that sees both as socially constructed, historically specific, and therefore alterable. I rely on Jill Dolan's words to clarify my position: "[f]eminism begins with a keen awareness of exclusion from male cultural, social, sexual, political, and intellectual discourse. It is a critique of prevailing social conditions that formulate women's position as outside of dominant male discourse."[7] In a materialist context that emphasizes the variable experiences of women based on their social circumstances, their sexual orientation, their culture, or the time in which they lived, gender can be seen as an ideological construction that interprets and divides the sexes, and in dividing them relegates women to a submissive and subordinate position to men and describes the behaviors that are associated with a notion of femininity.[8] Burney's works depict just such a view of gender: her varied female figures and their experiences of a division of the sexes suggest that she sees femaleness and femininity as patriarchally defined categories that limit women's participation in the discourses described by Dolan. Even when Burney represents a role that is rooted in biology, that of mother, she questions the extent to which the ideals associated with mothering are "natural," inherent to women, or acceptable as standards for judging women who have children.

A feminist analysis of a body of dramatic work argues implicitly that we understand the theater to be an institution that has social and political significance because of its simultaneous reflection and creation of particular perspectives and ideologies. The theater has been construed as an especially effective genre for the transmission of ideas about gender not only because of its public prominence, but also because of its artificial, framed nature. The physical body on the stage, the stage space, and all other elements of dramatic production (gesture, lighting, costumes, movement, etc.) exist in an iconographic atmosphere because of the stage context, signifying not just the object or activity on the stage, but emerging as signifiers of social relations generally or of power imbalances between groups of people or individuals.[9] Spaces, bodies, positions, and movement, as they are represented on the stage or implied in a text, are all subject to a feminist analysis: "[s]ocial conventions about the female gender will be encoded in all signs for women. Inscribed in body language, signs of gender can determine the blocking of a scene, by assigning bolder movements to the men and more restricted movements to the women, or by creating poses and positions that exploit the role of woman as sexual object. Stage movement replicates the proxemics of the social order, capitalising upon the spatial relationships in the culture at large between women and the sites of power."[10] Feminist dramatic theory attends to *how* figure and action are presented on the stage, to *what* is represented, and to the biases in conventional forms of representation and conceptualizations of genre and subgenre.

If the theater can be used to examine an existing social order, it can also be used to imply new and different ways not only of depicting objects on the stage, but also of envisioning the people, relationships, and uses of power beyond the stage. In Sue-Ellen Case's terms, the theater is a "laboratory" in which repressive practices can be "exposed, dismantled and removed."[11] Playwrights can represent oppression, critique the forces that enact it, and depict liberation from various forms of confinement as well as they can undertake to alter the gendered biases of representational modes themselves. Although for some critics theater is antagonistic to feminist reconceptualization because of its grounding in preexistent patriarchal languages, narratives, and dualities (between the subject and object, seer and seen, male and female), for others, the potential for theater to alter conventional views about gender is strong; the possibility that Oedipus can be wrecked and replaced is explored theoretically and practically by playwrights and theorists. As Dolan suggests, a materialist feminist dramatic theory approaches the theater as an ideological institution, a cultural forum that can promote social roles that maintain the economic and political ends of the dominant culture (or sex), because traditional theater is governed by an ideology that "has promulgated dangerous assumptions about social relations."[12] These social roles and relations, however, can be changed *because* they are constructed rather than unalterable givens. Janelle G. Reinelt writes that women's experience might exist within a prevailing patriarchal hegemony, but at the same time, those who depict it can recognize that "there is stage space to represent the gendered subject up against the limits of current gender constraints. Further, the representation of the subject-in-process practicing resistance, exploding the strait jacket of gender through doing the 'work' of self-inscription on stage, before an audience, is both theoretically and practically a vital, imaginative, political act."[13] Feminist dramatic representation can escape from the persistent restraints of phallocentric ideologies if it "can serve not only dominant but also counter-hegemonic discourses—if it can access novelty."[14]

In this study of Burney's drama, I have drawn on the provocative body of feminist dramatic and performance theory, which I have only outlined above, in two main areas. Simply put, these are in my analysis of Burney's subject matter and figures and her method of representing her ideas; I undertake a study of her content and form. I label Frances Burney's drama "feminist" because her plays offer numerous instances of how a woman writer could envision drama and the stage as important sites for depicting, analyzing, and reformulating the sexual ideologies in place at the end of the eighteenth century. Such ideologies were, of course, not static over the course of Burney's long life (1752-1840); nonetheless, a division between the sexes was evident in all facets of English economic, legal, educational, artistic, and social life. Acceptable femininity was deemed to include a narrow range of male-determined and male-regulated, familially based roles (mother, wife, and daughter) and a similarly narrow range of behavior. The band of tolerance for deviations from these roles widened or narrowed over time. These variously defined female roles are predominant in

Burney's plays and she questions the submissiveness, passivity, and punishment that these positions forced on women. At the same time as Burney examines what might be considered women's typical experiences of such institutions as marriage, for example, she offers alternatives to passivity, showing the living, breathing, speaking female figure in the process of making her own decisions and evoking her own set of standards for behavior. The world of female difficulties explored in Burney's plays includes financial insecurity, romantic conflict, familial disintegration and reunion, public scrutiny, marriage, motherhood, pain, and death. This body of plays is thus concerned with and contributes to what Vivien Jones describes as a "discourse of femininity" and the "culturally defined category" of "'women' . . . which women had to negotiate and to suffer."[15] In her depiction of action, conflict, and resolution, Burney uses established dramatic conventions and techniques in a manner that literally brings to front and center issues of gender. At the same time, we can read in Burney's dramatic practice other examples of the masculinist biases of conventional dramatic representation, instances of the exposure of these biases, and, to some extent, the revision of them. My feminist analysis of the formal aspects of Burney's drama includes attention to her use of genre, narrative, and the semiotic function of the physical and aural components of drama: stage space, dialogue and silence, entrances and exits, and gestures.

What, then, is the texture, to use Keyssar's vocabulary, of the women's worlds explored by Burney in her drama? Her content is undeniably focused on female figures who are involved in actions that are highly gender conscious. In the plays, conflict develops specifically because of the way in which femininity is defined and how this definition in turn influences female and male figures. There are always male figures in close proximity to the female figures in these plays and the initial conflict of the action may not be immediately specific to women. However, a related conflict motivated by a debate about social roles, gender, and female duty is unfailingly prominent. For example, in each tragedy, the overarching situation is based on a political struggle between men—Edwy and Dunstan, De Vere and De Mowbray, William and Chester, or Arnulph and Offa—but this conflict invariably and inexorably seeks to play itself out on the female figures close to these men: Elgiva, Cerulia, Adela, and Elberta. The heroines are evaluated based on notions of a wife's, mother's, or daughter's proper duties; the expression of their sexuality is judged and regulated; and their active participation in determining the uses to which their bodies and their individualities are put is resisted or chastised. In the comedies, similarly, a female figure always finds herself subject to a dilemma because of socially determined hierarchies that dismiss female desire, security, and happiness in favor of upholding the prejudicial ideals of familial duty, filial submission, or class integrity. Cecilia is thus rejected because she has lost her fortune, Hilaria and Eleonora are evaluated as morally degenerate because they are thought to seek their own financial and physical security, and Eliza must endure the inner divisiveness of wanting to be a dutiful daughter and yet feeling shame about the parents to whom she should demonstrate her duty. The problems of these individual figures are all dictated by a larger context that expects female inferiority and demands passivity and obedience where marital, familial, or financial matters are concerned.

Burney's plays thus meditate on the ways in which people are caught in a larger, preexistent social web of power relations that almost invariably subject female to male figures, the lower to the upper class, and colonized, marginalized peoples to imperial centers. I suggest above that Burney depicts "typical" female experience, but any set of familiar experiences includes variations of them as well. In her drama, figures occupy different social positions and, requisitely, enjoy different degrees (and kinds) of authority when it comes to speaking for themselves, dictating the actions of others, or acting on their own behalfs. Her upper-class figures include both men and women who demean those beneath them, and the person at the bottom of any scale of authority is not a woman, but a male Indian servant in *A Busy Day*, a man whose social insignificance is signified in his nonappearance on the stage. The complexities of class, race, and gender are thus shown to intersect in Burney's plays. However, while her female figures do not *uniformly* lack at least a modicum of social power, they are never exempt or protected from forms of control that in turn subject them to others. The degree of influence female figures enjoy over others or over themselves varies with their class and their access to money or education, but more often than not their position is ultimately a subordinate one and the figures with unchallenged power and authority tend to be patriarchal Englishmen, heads of households and of communities who uphold exacting communal standards for behavior, choice, contrition, and the resolution of conflict.

Burney's plays provide excellent opportunities for a feminist reconsideration of the biases of traditional perceptions of tragic and comic narrative, conflict, and resolution. For example, as Allardyce Nicoll's view of tragedy so neatly expresses (see chapter 3), discussions of tragedy often lean towards the Aristotelian and masculine in terms of definitions of heroism and the types of "elevated" conflicts that are said to prompt our admiration. Particularly in an eighteenth-century context, the designation of tragedy is often reserved for plays that show the trials of good leadership or individual integrity as they affect male figures who, unlike female figures, have access to a public persona and a coherent sense of "self." Requisitely, tragedy is seldom considered to focus on the domestic or private trials of women. The heroes of Burney's tragedies—Edwy, Arnulph, Hubert, and De Belesme—are quite typical in their vacillation between their inclinations as leaders or as political subjects and their personal desires. The enduring suffering of the female figures in these plays, by contrast, is private rather than public, and emerges less from a disjunction between two morally or civically significant alternatives, than it does from an inability to enact choice at all, to move freely, or to create the values by which they would act and be judged. A tragic narrative that would conventionally see the trial of a solitary leader against tremendous forces is disrupted in Burney's plays by a concentration on the personal and the private, on scenes behind doors that are usually closed. Female suffering, rather than male heroism, is emphasized, and female figures who might typically be dramatically peripheral to the action are made prominent.[16] These plays suggest that an expanded notion of the range of late-eighteenth-century tragedy should be contemplated when plays of the period are studied.

Feminist theorists argue that narrative patterns in general are conventionally biased towards the masculine and that, within narrative patterns, the female is often relegated to peripheral positions or to components of narrative that serve to advance or impede the progress of male figures.[17] Burney's plays at different points participate in, foreground, and challenge this sort of gendered aesthetics. As my discussion of tragic narrative implies, male heroism often is created in an atmosphere that discourages female participation, or that presents female elements as alternatives to or obstacles in the way of public authority. Elgiva is used as a barrier to Edwy's construction of himself as king and is the bodily space over which Dunstan exercises his power to punish. However, while Burney recognizes and depicts the tendency for female figures to be used in this manner, she also depicts the ramifications of such use and abuse. Burney calls attention to (and is critical of) the result of the intrusion of the public into the private—the torture of Elgiva—and she refuses to limit the heroine to the peripheral position to which she is relegated by the historians who also write about her. In the tragedies, the use of women in a political economy that sees them as the space on which to enact physical coercion is dangerous and literal, as women are exchanged as prisoners or are held as hostages and sacrificed bodily to male pursuits of power. Burney asks us to think critically about the forces that enact such oppression and the stories that are told about them.

Marriage plots, so familiar to comedy, tend especially to rely on female figures who are exchanged between male constituencies and through whom figuratively pass money or social status that will be transmitted from the woman's father to her husband, or from a father to child or grandchild.[18] Burney addresses the processes by which women are constructed as passive objects rather than as subjects motivated by their own desires. She also examines the consequences of envisioning female figures merely as currency, or spatially, as vessels through which are transferred patrilineage and legitimate inheritance, family fortunes, and community moral standards. The construction of Hilaria as a cipher of Valentine's moral outlook and Ardville's pride is dramatized, for example, in *Love and Fashion*. Again, Burney does not allow the restricted position of women to go unnoticed, but instead concentrates on the female figure's experience of passivity or manipulation. The heroines of the comedies are depicted as caught within sexual, financial, and marital economies in which their worth is evaluated quantitatively as they pass between families or suitors. Burney displays onstage the exile, psychological turmoil, helplessness, and confinement of these figures because of such a patriarchal economy.

Both tragedy and comedy, especially comedy with highly sentimental elements, tend to rely on stock resolutions. Such typical endings in late-eighteenth-century plays might include a tragic mad scene or comic closure that involves the uncovering of identities, the restoration of lost emotional ties, and the recognition of virtue that triumphs over adversity. These endings can be used in order to call attention to just such conventional devices of closure and the larger issues they gesture toward. There are moments at the ends of Burney's plays when the conventional is disrupted by an antagonistic refusal of a narrative in which women are mere spaces narratologically or aesthetically. I argue that, in the tragedies, the conventions of the mad scene or death scene are made to serve a political end in that they offer a moment of accusation toward the figures who enact physical brutality on female bodies. In *Edwy and Elgiva* and *Hubert De Vere*, the suffering woman returns to the scene of the crime, forcing a statement of responsibility from her antagonist and finally, as a corpse, displaying publicly the signs of physical coercion. Although the tragedies end with a pronouncement of masculine authority (all but *Elberta* end with a male voice), these endings challenge the "naturalness" or acceptability of narratives and processes that envision the female as the excessive, marginal, or negligible. It is in this respect that Burney accesses novelty, to use Reinelt's term. Her tragedies draw attention to the severe damage and suffering that the physical manipulation of women entails. While a male voice ends the play, the female body is the focus of attention.

The resolutions of Burney's comedies are often ironic, given the values that are exposed throughout the action of the plays (an emphasis on finance rather than inner worth, dependence rather than self-reliance, or prejudice rather than tolerance). Resolutions come about through the subordination of female interests to male authority, whether the authority is found in Censor's blackmail (*The Witlings*), Valentine's moral scrutiny (*Love and Fashion*), or Sir Marmaduke's greed (*A Busy Day*). These comic endings, however, often show the necessary masking of severely tried relationships, masking that points to the artificial nature of resolution itself. In *The Woman-Hater*, for example, the resolution typical of sentimental comedy—the outpouring of emotions, recognition of virtue, and the reunion of family members—comes with a concomitant implication that marriage and familial relations suppress women intellectually, emotionally, and physically. The play foregrounds the wife's and daughter's obedience to the husband, the father's privilege of marital choice for the daughter, and the male prerogative of accusation. The threat of family violence lingers within the Wilmots' enclosed circle and the joy proclaimed at the end of the play is forced, and challenged by Joyce's celebratory emancipation from Mr. Wilmot. In the comedies, female turmoil is less severely physical than it is in the tragedies (though here, too, it has physical components). Turmoil persists in the silencing of women by their families, the threats to female safety that misogyny portends, or the demand that women have no autonomous social existence beyond the family or marriage. Progress toward satisfying resolutions is jarred by female figures who announce dissatisfaction or trepidation about their future unhappiness, were they to exist temporally beyond the play's ending. At other times, female silence or absence signals such dissatisfaction, as the suppression of the female self that patriarchy might demand is enacted before us.

There are other forms of rebellion, dissatisfaction, or unassimilated chaos depicted in the plays in addition to the female corpse or the closing verbal statements of the female figures of each play. Burney uses the stage as a vehicle for altering in subtle yet significant ways an ideology about female submissiveness, for example. While these plays are not, of course, outside ideology, they do enact what Cixous describes as a scratching at or tearing away of the ideas about female inferiority that mold people conservatively.[19] Burney's drama contains some of her most revolutionary and novel depictions of female experience, in that she *shows* female figures who make self-directing choices and demonstrate a certain degree of agency, control, and resistance against the inadequacies of family life or marriage that are presented to them. In *The Woman-Hater*, Joyce's exuberant refusal of her father's book learning and her joy in dancing and singing is one obvious example of a challenge to male-determined, repressive modes of female existence. Eliza's calls for the humane treatment of her Indian servant (*A Busy Day*) and Mrs. Wheedle's insistence on the financial requirements of working women (*The Witlings*) are instances of attention being paid to what might be the otherwise presumed or forgotten issues of sexual, class, or racial inequality. The potential political power of such embodied rather than narrated resistance is significant, even if Burney's plays did not reach the stage; Burney attends to the experiences of the "living, breathing, speaking body" that suffers prejudice and an inadequate acknowledgment of its needs and desires.

I would like finally to discuss this issue of how Burney uses the qualities of drama that differentiate it from prose fiction or poetry: its basis in physically embodied figures, visual and aural cues for the audience, a real experience of time, and a stage space in which to depict movement. Her scripts demonstrate an attention to the technical side of production. She timed several of her plays and made comments about the pacing of various acts and the effectiveness of different figures' presences on the stage. Her notes for revision include emendations that are specific to performance: elaborations to the descriptions of sets, additional uses of music, or specific directions for blocking. The Gothicism present in her tragedies and in the late comedies assumes a use of lighting and scenery that would communicate the exaggerated gloom and confinement of this mode of drama. Her ambitious casting enlists the resources of the most prominent players of her day, which suggests that she was familiar with the acting styles that were popular and therefore most likely to contribute to a production's success.

It is important at this point to consider the challenge of reading Burney's drama with an eye toward the potential physical realization of the cues we are supplied with by her manuscripts. These dramas have an intriguing status. They are scripts clearly intended to be performed, but for the most part they did not reach the stage. Furthermore, Burney was writing at a time when a playwright's control over the production of a script was limited. As Donkin describes in *Getting into the Act*, the contemporary system of theater management was particularly harsh for female playwrights, who were forced to develop their own strategies for success, as Elizabeth Inchbald did, or were simultaneously encouraged and regulated by a managerial father figure like David Garrick, as were Hannah More and Hannah Cowley. Any or all of Burney's suggestions about sets, entrances or exits, gestures, or space could and likely would have been subject to alteration by the theater manager or the actors and actresses involved in the production. I thus recognize that I am placing a heavy emphasis on intentionality when I imaginatively extrapolate from the scripts the staging possibilities Burney might have considered. I have tried to fend against too much hypothesis by focusing attention on the actual details about space and movement in the manuscripts. For instance, Burney often indicates gestures or blocking with the use of intradialogic (implied in the dialogue) as well as extradialogic (present in the script) stage directions. Her work would have been altered on the stage, but, in the absence of this range of interpretation, we can cautiously consider the efforts she took to guide readers' (the hypothetical viewers') responses to her drama in particular directions through her use of dialogue, the amount of time she devotes to different figures and situations, or her arrangement of figures in an imaginative space.

In terms of the physical dynamic of Burney's drama, I ask three questions about the spatial, visual, and aural/oral cues in the plays: How do female figures move about the stage and who controls the space they enter? How often and how significantly do they participate in determining the action or dialogue? What use of gesture does Burney make? I have broken the plays down scene by scene in order to answer such questions. This method of analysis reveals, for example, that there are times when female figures are on the stage for an extended length of time, but are present only as observers or as the observed, not participating in the dialogue or action at all. Cecilia is present in the second act of *The Witlings* and is the subject of discussion but participates in it only rarely. Cerulia's body, the focus of the closing scene of *Hubert De Vere*, is obviously silent, but its presence is all-important, because it calls attention to the use made of her in political machinations. Elgiva's corpse has a similar function, and Burney's dialogue in both plays draws repeated attention to the body and the traces it bears of suffering and neglect. The act of watching this damaged body is made self-conscious as well. Entrances and exits are also significant: female figures are frequently introduced into or led from the scene by male figures who control their movement or permit or deny their access to the represented space, which the male figures thus maintain in their purview. Gestures further indicate ideological constructions of femininity. At the close of *The Woman-Hater*, Wilmot and Eleonora join Sophia's hand to Jack's in order to signal their future marriage. This is one of Wilmot's first gestures of physical contact with Sophia after seventeen years, and indicates not only his immediate assumption of paternal, patriarchal power (as her kneeling to him does as well), but also the lack of choice Sophia has where the match is concerned. This joining of hands contrasts with Eleonora's earlier cowering at her husband's feet, or her terrified scream at finding him nearby.

The approach I take to Burney's plays—considering them as literary texts and as scripts for performance—has been comparatively rare where late-eighteenth-century drama is concerned. This neglect is regrettable (though certainly not uniform), given that feminist approaches to drama have revolutionized studies of the work of earlier periods, such as Renaissance or Restoration drama.[20] Criticism of late-eighteenth-century

LIBRARY
THE UNIVERSITY OF TEXAS
AT BROWNSVILLE
Brownsville, Tx 78520-4991

drama has been slow to make sustained analyses of the theater as a political, ideologically controlled and controlling institution. Important exceptions include discussions of censorship, revolutionary politics, the craft and profession of acting, and the composition of eighteenth-century audiences. Early and recent histories of eighteenth-century drama tend to concentrate on established authors, providing accounts of acting styles, theater dimensions, lighting, seating configurations, attendance and performance details (runs, benefit nights), and, most frequently, plot summaries of the works of major playwrights.[21] Discussions are divided by subgenre, but, again, the influence of earlier writers or continental writers on style and genre is emphasized, along with plot summaries of representative works and discussions of audience "taste."[22] It is difficult to garner from most studies a general view of the ideological undercurrents in the dramatic work of this period.

This lack of political criticism is difficult to reconcile with the volatile nature of a theater environment that was perceived in its own time as a site for contesting views of the distribution of power between classes, genders, races, and social groups generally. Arthur Murphy is said to have observed that the "theatre engrossed the minds of men to such a degree . . . that there existed in England a *fourth estate*, King, Lords and Commons and *Drury Lane Playhouse*."[23] The theater was considered to have a strong influence on the public's perception of how society was ordered and governed: theaters were closed during times of crisis and content was strictly controlled through licensing. The Lord Chamberlain's Examiner of Plays (between 1778 and 1824, John Larpent) consistently censored political, sexual, and religious references during a time when revolutionary fervor made for "close links between theatrical innovation and political change."[24] The late-eighteenth-century theater featured increasingly blurred genres and spectacles that included opera, melodrama, farce, parody, burlesque, the Gothic, and the musical, all of which threatened the more decorous notion that tragedy and comedy were clearly distinguishable domains. This, too, had political overtones. Jeffrey N. Cox, in the introduction to his anthology of Gothic drama, argues that artistic flux was seen as symptomatic of general social instability. It was thus, as he notes, that Edmund Burke could find in the language of drama an apt metaphor when he figured the French Revolution as a "tragi-comic scene." As if the Revolution were an extension of a demand for new stage pageantry, Burke wrote that people were disenchanted by the idea of "[a] cheap, bloodless reformation, a guiltless liberty," demanding instead a "great change of scene; there must be a magnificent stage effect . . . a grand spectacle."[25]

Playwrights then, as now, responded to their society's prevailing attitudes toward any number of political or social issues by confirming or questioning the values of the world around them. In the eighteenth century, a play was only lucrative for the author if it survived to the third night's performance, the night of the author's benefit. Writers devised strategies for coding unpopular ideas (or popular, but unofficial sentiments), including the displacement of criticisms about contemporary events or political decisions onto the historic past or into foreign settings.[26] A process of mutual creation and recreation of values, behaviors, and ideals has always been ongoing as drama is written, produced, reviewed, and produced again. That Burney's plays did not reach the stage (save *Edwy and Elgiva*'s one performance) clearly means they did not participate directly in this process, yet her writing was informed by this social and professional atmosphere. This atmosphere included, for instance, a patriarchal social order that is reflected in such dramatic conventions as the emergence of a long-lost, benevolent male patron or the reunion of a fragmented nuclear family at the end of a sentimental drama. It included the threatened and exposed heroine of Gothic drama, which echoed the rage for Gothicism in the novel and prompted discussions of gender as it related to a novel-reading public. And Burney also recognized this atmosphere to include the dominance of an actress such as Sarah Siddons, who, as Donkin suggests, had a powerful effect on how femininity was perceived in the late eighteenth century.[27]

That Burney and her contemporaries were writing in years that have subsequently fallen through the cracks of traditional periodization has likely been one cause for the neglect of the drama written or produced between 1775 and 1800. The emphasis on poetry in romantic studies contributes to this problem and one often encounters the proposal that the theater began to decline into Victorian melodrama and farce at the end of the eighteenth century. Cox discusses a "dramatic ideology" that relegates late-eighteenth- and early-nineteenth-century drama to an unexplored gap: "[f]irst, there is what we might call the 'peak phenomenon': a small number of great figures are seen as speaking to one another across the ages, from the rare mountaintops of dramatic excellence. . . . The rest of dramatic history is largely condemned to silence. The second underlying tenet might be termed the 'culture gap': canonized plays are presented as having more in common with their great precursors and descendents than with the dramatic and theatrical cultures within which they were created."[28] Burney's plays fall in just such a gap in dramatic history. The steadily increasing regard for late-century novelists, particularly women novelists, has not been matched by a similar increase in studies of late-eighteenth-century drama by women. Burney's own work as a novelist and letter writer may have further pushed her drama out of the limelight.

These comments about neglect are not, however, intended to obscure the important studies of eighteenth-century drama that have contributed to my own understanding of the field. Ellen Donkin's *Getting into the Act: Women Playwrights in London 1776-1829* features chapters on Frances Brooke, Hannah More, Hannah Cowley, Sophia Lee, Elizabeth Inchbald, Burney, and Joanna Baillie, and includes an excellent discussion of the business of theater production in the late eighteenth century. *Curtain Calls: British and American Women and the Theater, 1660-1820*, edited by Mary Anne Schofield and Cecilia Macheski, includes essays on Margaret Cavendish, Elizabeth Inchbald, Sarah Siddons, Katherine Philips, Aphra Behn, Elizabeth Griffith, Hannah Cowley, Hannah More, Catherine Trotter, Mary Pix, and others. It closes with a useful enumeration of the works by female dramatists and how their published and performed numbers compare to the number of works by other female writers of the eighteenth century.[29] However, these studies lack an overview of how issues of gender and sexuality influenced the subject matter and the manner of representation we find in this period.

Similarly, Nancy Cotton's earlier work, *Women Playwrights in England c. 1363-1750,* tends to view feminist theater as a matter of content only. Aphra Behn, as Astrea, and Katherine Philips, as Orinda, are juxtaposed as representing commercial (improper) or noncompetitive feminine interests, respectively. For Cotton, neither writer succeeded in dramatizing "feminine perceptions," for these women were caught between the bind of writing as a man, or writing as a man thought women should write.[30] Cotton discusses the progress these women made from the early work of nuns to the Restoration theater of wit and to a high public profile for the female playwright. Susan Carlson's *Women and Comedy: Rewriting the British Theatrical Tradition,* on the other hand, shows how comic heroines are "constrained by comic structures and fractured by social and cultural processes encoded in the plays." Carlson's thesis is that women play significant roles in comedy, but "the genre does more to reduce than to enlarge female power."[31] The eighteenth-century examples Carlson uses include *The Way of the World* and plays by Behn, but her book is fraught with sweeping generalizations. Her conclusion, that comic plays either depend on or are disruptive of a status quo, is dissatisfying.

Paula R. Backscheider's *Spectacular Politics: Theatrical Power and Mass Culture in Early Modern England* is a notable addition to the field, providing an intriguing discussion of various types of performance and public spectacle, including playhouse drama, pageants, pantomimes, and ceremonies. She explores how public and popular texts (in a broad definition of the term) became "effective or even important hegemonic apparatus[es]," and she asks "what kinds of literature can function effectively in hegemonic processes, and what characteristics those that function most powerfully have."[32] Social order and values are reconfigured by these texts,

Backscheider argues, which reflect and mold predominant ideas about sex, gender, class, and race in early modern society. She concentrates on texts that served to "assimilate change and reestablish ideological, and therefore social, stability" in a time of crisis, that resolved "tensions and ambiguities, named and confined the Other, and confirmed or helped create a new moral order with an idealized English self-image."[33] Her discussion of the late century's drama is focused on Gothic drama and she explores its construction of femininity. My own argument about Burney's use of the Gothic modifies Backscheider's assertion that these texts support hegemony rather than subvert it. Backscheider writes that the Gothic's "formulaic structure and its concluding harmonious tableaux created symbolic order and momentarily gave the illusion of a kind of unity and wholeness that seemed applicable to the individual and the national life."[34] I emphasize instead the possibility that the Gothic's abundant representations of disorder, punishment, and chaos may not be fully incorporated into "concluding harmonious tableaux"; such is the case in Burney's Gothic drama, in which the mangled female body lingers on the stage as a sign of disarray that may reemerge at any time.

Burney's dramas range widely, mixing historical and Gothic tragedy, sentimentalism, farce, satire, and mock-Gothicism. In studying them, I bring to the surface the strategies she uses as a dramatist, how she builds on the genre's foundation in space, time, and spectacle as she examines social institutions (courtship, marriage, government, the family) and women's participation in them. She represents the various positions women find themselves in, and from which they struggle to emerge, as daughters, wives, mothers, political pawns, and courted prizes. Feminist dramatic theory asserts that theater can "accommodate the presence of women in the art, support their liberation from the cultural fictions of the female gender and deconstruct the valorisation of the male gender."[35] Using the genre to her own ends and creating through it politicized responses to her society, Burney examines the forces that construct ideas of femininity and female behavior and suggests alternatives to stereotypical notions about women. This is evident in the stories she dramatizes, in the figures who enact them, and in the techniques she uses to represent on the stage the female experience and the relationship of women to men and to social institutions.

2

Censored Women
The Witlings

The problems of inevitable social interdependence preoccupy most of Burney's novelistic heroines. Evelina seeks the familial legitimation that will secure financial and social status and is perpetually requesting others' help, although the sincerity of her pleas has been debated.[1] Cecilia suffers from bad advice and the mismanagement of her money by male guardians; her desired romantic match is marred by an inheritance clause that asserts her father's power over her from the grave. Camilla is plagued by debts that are foisted upon her by others and suffers from an absence of caring advisors. In *The Wanderer*, Juliet's position as a person displaced and unacknowledged forces her to seek the social ties that will legitimize her or at least ensure her subsistence. In *The Witlings*, Burney explores the often antagonistic relationship between the desire for individuality and independence, on the one hand, and social interdependence that is influenced by inequalities of gender, class, and education, on the other. Money and approval—the latter often contingent on the former—are shown to determine all aspects of social life, including one's place in a community, freedom of choice, and physical movement. Burney suggests in this comedy that individual reputations, money, and the acceptance that both can garner are controlled ultimately by male figures. *The Witlings* depicts the triumph of censorship and subjugation over independence, and it is women who are publicly censored or confined financially, physically, and intellectually. While the play's romance and "Esprit Party" plots are for the most part separate, they share this common concern with the vagaries of reputation, "worth," and dependence.

It is not surprising that a work exploring on multiple levels issues of socialization, exposure, and publicity would be the first to follow Burney's own appearance in the world of the literary elite after the publication of *Evelina* in 1778. The success of her first novel thrust an apparently

unwilling Burney into the center of literary activity in London, largely because of her father's encouragement. Admiration for *Evelina*'s comic dialogue and theatrical style led many people to advise Burney to try her hand
at writing a play. As Hemlow writes, "the spirited entrances of fops and
affected young ladies, the lively idiomatic dialogue, the shifting locale of
the action—both in form and content resembled lively scenes in the
comedy of manners."[2] Samuel Johnson, Hester Thrale, Arthur Murphy,
Sir Joshua Reynolds, Edmund Burke, and Richard Brinsley Sheridan were
all family friends, and Murphy and Sheridan in particular expressed an interest in Burney's next project being a play. Samuel Crisp urged her on,
but cautioned her against becoming the author of "*such* Freedoms as
Ladies of the strictest Character would make no scruple, openly, to laugh
at" (*EJL,* 3:187). Hester Thrale was hopeful that Murphy would aid
Burney with her play and that "Johnson should write [her] Prologue, &
Murphy [her] Epilogue" (*EJL,* 3:244). Sheridan (who managed Drury
Lane Theatre at the time) also agreed, jokingly at first, with Reynolds's
demand that he accept a comedy by Burney "*Unsight unseen,*" to which
Sheridan is said to have answered "*Yes* . . . with quickness,—& make her
a Bow & my best Thanks into the Bargain!" (*EJL,* 3:235). Burney observed to her sister: "if I *should* attempt the stage,—I think I may be fairly
acquitted of presumption, & however I may fail,—that I was strongly
pressed to *try* by Mrs. Thrale,—& by Mr. Sheridan,—the most successful
and powerful of all Dramatic living Authors,—will abundantly excuse my
temerity" (*EJL,* 3:236). Her excitement at the prospect is betrayed when
she confides that, after speaking with Sheridan and Reynolds, "I actually
shook from Head to foot! I felt myself already in Drury Lane, amidst the
Hub bub of a first Night" (*EJL,* 3:234).

The resulting work—ironically, as it would turn out—is *The Witlings,*
in which public image is molded by forces that include gossip, art, and finance. A draft of the play was completed by May 1779 and read by the
Burney family and Arthur Murphy.[3] The conversations Burney reports in
her letters reveal a bevy of consultants, including Thrale, Crisp, Johnson,
and Murphy, who indicated that her play would probably be successful.
Murphy is said to be "quite charmed with [the] second act,—he says he is
sure it will do, & *more* than do" (*EJL,* 3:286). The letters also relate the
displeasure that came eventually from Crisp, Dr. Charles Burney, and
others, including Hester Thrale, who noted that "none of the scribbling
Ladies have a Right to admire [the play's] general Tendency" (*EJL,* 3:268,
n. 18) and that Lady Smatter was probably an imitation of herself (*EJL,*
3:279). Crisp was concerned about the play's resemblance to Molière's *Les
femmes savantes*—a resemblance Burney protested as coincidental (*EJL,*
3:345)—and both Crisp and Dr. Burney feared that the witlings were

identifiable contemporaries who would retaliate against such sharp satire.[4] Specifically, Lady Smatter, who holds a literary "Espirit Party," was seen to resemble Elizabeth Montagu, the famous Bluestocking, who published *Essay on Shakespeare* in 1769. Lady Smatter does remark that Shakespeare "is too common; *every* body can speak well of Shakespeare!" (IV.102-3).[5] Crisp advised Burney to change her subject matter from "the invidious, & cruel Practice of pointing out Individual Characters, & holding them up to public Ridicule" (*EJL*, 3:353). He tells Burney that she must instead allow nature to be her guide, and rather than sit to "*Fagging*, & Labour," she should compose as if inspired by the muses rather than by a desire to be a professional (*EJL*, 3:352). The serious objections that came from her two "daddies" prompted Burney to observe that she had "but little hope of ever writing what you will both approve" (*EJL*, 3:343). The "fatal knell" was tolled for *The Witlings* in August 1779, the reasons for giving up the play "for-ever & for-ever & for-ever" noted not as Burney's, but as her father's (*EJL*, 3:345).

It would seem that the complete rejection of *The Witlings* came as a surprise to Burney, and she suggests in a veiled way that one of her father's main concerns was the protection of his reputation, not her own: "yet any *general* censure of the *whole*, & the *Plan*, would cruelly, but certainly, involve *you* in it's severity" (*EJL*, 3:346). Burney claims to give up any opinion she has of her own work in favor of that of her father, who has "finished [the play], now,—in *every* sense of the Word,—*partial* faults may be corrected, but what I most wished was to know the general effect of the Whole,—& as *that* has so terribly failed, all petty criticisms would be needless. I shall wipe it all from my memory, & endeavour never to recollect that I ever writ it" (*EJL*, 3:347). In this letter of circa 13 August 1779, Burney both accepts and rejects the advice she receives, mentioning her surprise at the condemnation, given the "warm approbation" of Thrale and Murphy (perhaps a reminder to Dr. Burney that others might know better than he). She admits to having desired success. Rather than give up writing, she will "exert [her]self to the utmost of [her] power in endeavours to produce something less reprehensible" (*EJL*, 3:347). The affair ends with Burney's apology for having troubled her father and for "the kind pain which . . . must attend [his] disapprobation" (*EJL*, 3:348). It is telling that Burney felt she must aim not to *please* her father, but to *displease* him as little as possible.

Burney's letter to Crisp of circa 13 August 1779 is less deferential and more sarcastic. She writes of her belief that the daddies' "Hissing, groaning, catcalling Epistle" was sent with sorrow and affection. Her claim that she is pleased to have the truth from her family and close friend is, however, mitigated by her understated confession that she is "somewhat disconcerted" by the criticism (*EJL*, 3:350). Burney was in later years to annotate her letters from her father and Crisp regarding this affair. She sarcastically writes of "Dr. Burney's *critique* on a MS. comedy called The Witlings, sent for his verdict" (*EJL*, 3:345). The letter to Crisp is identified as "F.B.'s Answer to a severe criticism upon a MS. Comedy submitted to the perusal of her two dear Daddys—native & adopted: after the same play had been highly commended by Mrs. Thrale & Mr. Murphy" (*EJL*, 3:348). These notes suggest a lingering resentment that questions the original decisions made apparently on her behalf about the play's viability.

Only one manuscript of *The Witlings* survives, in the Berg Collection. The fair copy in Burney's hand consists of 165 pages in five notebooks, with few corrections or alterations to the text. Sections marked for possible deletion confirm that Burney's main concern was to edit the material relating to the Esprit Party. For example, in act 1, a long passage in which Beaufort condemns the Witlings' false learning is so marked, as well as a passage in act 4, when the Esprit members discuss Censor's admission to their number. These deletions may be a response to Dr. Burney's and Crisp's objections to the play's satire.

While Burney did abandon the distinct text of *The Witlings* and turned her attention to *Cecilia*, character sketches, scraps of dialogue, and plot outlines survive which reveal that Burney returned to these characters and incidents later, perhaps as she began work on *The Woman-Hater*.[6] Other scraps that do not directly relate to *The Woman-Hater* describe characters who either became "witlings" or emerged from them. One set of characters includes a Mr. Objection, Mrs. What, Mrs. Compliant, Mrs. Cant, and Mr. Literal (perhaps a forefather of Litchburn in *Love and Fashion*), another an "oppressed Chief," his children, an agent Messenger, and "Mrs. Wheedle, a Milliner" (*BC*, V). Burney also developed allegorical characters: Mr. Laconic; Mr. Dry (*BC*, IVa); Sir Splendido Sposo; his wife, Lady Splendida Sposa; Miss Megrim; Mrs. Teiser; Miss Tant Mieux; and Miss Tant Pis; along with the more familiar Codger, Jack, Mrs. Sapient, Lady Smatter, and Miss Voluble (*BC*, IVb). At some point, Burney drew up a cast list which included Dignitatas (John Philip Kemble), his son (Charles Kemble), Jack (John Bannister), "Daughter to Dignitatas" (Maria Theresa De Camp), Miss Megrim (Dorothy Jordan), and Mrs. Sapient (Maria Ann Pope). Burney proposed the use of each of these actors again in *A Busy Day* and *The Woman-Hater*. Some of these characters are well developed in sketches, others much more shadowy. The reappearance of so many witlings in *The Woman-Hater* confirms Sabor's argument that Burney was hesitant to relinquish these creations completely.[7] Of course, the heroine reappears in an altered form in *Cecilia* as well.

First page of the manuscript *The Witlings*. Courtesy of the Henry W. and Albert A. Berg Collection, New York Public Library, Astor, Lenox and Tilden Foundations

Society is depicted in *The Witlings* through multiple plots that represent a thwarted and restored romance, a literary party, and the activities of a millinery shop. The heroine and hero, Cecilia and Beaufort, are to be married, but the news that Cecilia's banker has been ruined leads Lady Smatter, Beaufort's aunt, to demand that he break the engagement rather than marry an unportioned woman. Lady Smatter distances herself from Cecilia, and Beaufort's friend, Censor, tells him to placate his aunt by appearing obedient to her, an action Cecilia interprets as abandonment. Lady Smatter, meanwhile, is distracted from Cecilia's plight by her position as the head of a literary club. Her Esprit Party is notorious for the collective ignorance of its members, who include the toadying plagiarist-poet Dabler, Mrs. Sapient, and Beaufort's stepfather, Codger. Despite protestations to the contrary, the main aim of Lady Smatter's club is to provide its members with a forum for mutual flattery and would-be authority rather than knowledgeable literary analysis. Censor resolves the conflict between Beaufort and his aunt, and between the lovers, by supporting Cecilia financially and blackmailing Lady Smatter into approving the marriage. He threatens to tarnish her reputation with lampoons and ballads, a possibility she cannot tolerate. The play's action begins and ends in the shop of a milliner, Mrs. Wheedle, and the home of Mrs. Voluble, who rely on the literal and figurative fortunes of the upper class for their livelihood as purveyors of hats and gossip, respectively.[8]

The Witlings presents to us a variety of dependencies: the milliners' need for business, Cecilia's need for Censor's intercession, and Dabler's reliance on the interest of Lady Smatter.[9] The five acts feature a variety of physical locales, each suggestive of a form of reliance or economy and, requisitely, the requirements that these economies demand of participants. Act 1 is devoted to the business world of the millinery shop, where material goods are sold and gossip is exchanged for attention.[10] This is undeniably a place of work, and the work continues while those not immediately concerned with work mill around the place. The conversation in the shop reflects basic economic principles: everyone has something for sale, the price varies with availability, and the ability to pay monopolizes others' attention. Mrs. Wheedle is a capable saleswoman who is able to draw most people who enter her shop into her business; even the haphazard Jack, Beaufort's half-brother, pauses to look at the goods. His accident-prone movements are indicated by an intradialogic stage direction when Miss Jenny comments that he has "tumbled and tossed the things about like mad" (I.379).

Mrs. Wheedle is a good businesswoman, as well as a cheat, a liar, and a flatterer. She peddles her wares no more or less than the other characters do their own immaterial goods. She offers last year's materials as *au courant*, ignores customers who are not socially prominent, and fawns to her customers' weaknesses. The entrances and exits that contribute to the stage business and busyness are indicative of the financial and social hierarchies that govern the exchange of goods in the shop. Over the course of the act, two footmen enter on behalf of their employers, but only one succeeds in commanding Mrs. Wheedle's attention and she leaves the stage with him. Such departures and the dialogue gesture to a world beyond this space and show that *non*entrance and absence are as indicative of privilege as presence. Those who can send emissaries, of course, signify status by not appearing in person.

One of the privileged customers of these women is Miss Cecilia Stanley, whose patronage of the shop establishes a chain of influence that traces Cecilia's financial worries through to the milliners, because they depend on her expenditures for their livelihood. Cecilia is, for the working women, very pragmatically seen as a source of income. It is thus appropriate that she is introduced almost exclusively in terms of her money. As an orphaned "young Lady with a Fortune all in her own Hands," about to be married to Beaufort (I.73-74), Cecilia is both a source of income to the shopkeeper who is filling her bridal order and a source of pride and financial security for Lady Smatter and Beaufort.

The information about Cecilia comes from Mrs. Voluble, who enters Mrs. Wheedle's shop in order to peddle her wares as well: she exchanges information in an effort to be the center of attention. Burney combines dialogue and blocking in a fashion that indicates the disjunction between Mrs. Voluble's dramatic function and her social status in the shop. We receive essential expository information from this figure, but within the shop she is easily ignored. Her stories are general enough in content that this speaker does not require a specific auditor, but any auditor at all. She speaks to Mrs. Wheedle about Cecilia, and with Wheedle's exit, turns successively to Miss Jenny and Miss Sally and Miss Polly, who serve the purpose she demands: an acknowledgement only that she is being heard. The frequent exchange of auditors, however, indicates yet another type of hierarchy, as listeners are identified in turn as their importance to the shop decreases. When Mrs. Voluble enters initially, she remarks upon the different women: "Mrs. Wheedle, how do do? I'm vastly glad to see you. I hope all the young Ladies are well. Miss Jenny, my dear, you look pale; I hope you a'n't in Love, Child? Miss Sally, your Servant. . . . I don't think I know that other young lady? O Lord yes, I do,—it's Miss Polly Dyson! I beg your pardon, my dear, but I declare I did not recollect you at first" (I.33-40). Mrs. Wheedle's health is inquired after, Miss Jenny is remarked upon, Miss Sally is merely acknowledged, and Miss Polly nearly ignored. Like nonentrances, nonrecognition indicates status as well.

This subtle use of dialogue defines the figure who speaks and those spoken about. The strongest mark of distinction between Burney's figures lies in how they participate conversationally with others. Mrs. Sapient, who enters later, offers us a series of tautological statements that result in no conversational increments. Her observations, such as "there is a wide difference between fiveteen and fifty" (I.252), indicate that she has nothing to contribute to the gossipy economy, but she occasionally stumbles upon a serious comment on the action, as when she notes that "the real value of a Person Springs from the *mind*, not from the outside appearance" (I.300-301). The play shows instead the relentless inversion of this moral. Cecilia, of course, suffers from others' beliefs that her value springs from her pocketbook. Lady Smatter is vulnerable because she is intellectually vain, though her mental spring is truly dry. Mrs. Sapient, however, cannot be taken seriously as the spokesperson for the drama's moral—as Beaufort's final speech must similarly be dismissed—because she speaks while "*turning quick to the Milliners*" and inquiring about her hat's trim (I.303). Conversation is used throughout act 1 to individuate figures' social rank and their attitudes. Mrs. Wheedle wants to make a sale, Mrs. Voluble wants to indicate that she knows *of* people of rank ("though I have not the pleasure of knowing her Ladyship myself, I know them that do" [I.193-95]), and Censor must insist on his superiority over the crowd. The only straightforward request for information that we hear is finally that of Bob Voluble, who asks his mother what is for dinner. For this quite blunt but necessary inquisition, he is chased off the stage and insulted as "idle, good for nothing, dirty, greasy, hulking, tormenting—" (I.479). A question about bodily sustenance is treated here as an indication of vulgarity.

The social significance of Mrs. Wheedle's shop is marked by who appears in it and who does not, and figures are then further distinguished based on their conversations. The shop is also shown to be a gendered space when Beaufort and Censor express their ill feeling about being in the place at all. They are waiting for Cecilia in this "foreign environment,"[11] which allows Censor to reveal his gender-specific view of work, conversation, and habit. The bits of lace and caps "in this Region of Foppery, Extravagance and Folly" are dismissed by him as ineffectual female weapons that he scorns as being beneath his reasonable self (I.129-30). The women, too, are dismissed because of their linguistic habits, which for Censor are specific to their sex. Mrs. Voluble "will consume more Words in an Hour than Ten Men will in a Year; she is infected with a rage for talking" (I.158-59). Mrs. Sapient is "more weak and superficial even than Lady Smatter" (I.215), who is *very* weak indeed. By contrast, Jack, who is arguably as shallow as Mrs. Sapient, garners Censor's attention, perhaps because he attempts to display traits that often characterize a conventional distinction between masculinity and femininity: he acts and moves and almost *does things*. Censor's view of the women and their inferior conversational tendencies gestures towards an elitism that elevates classical learning and reason (male prerogatives) over the gossip of the working women's world. Tellingly, Censor addresses a vast majority of his speeches to Beaufort directly, or combines curt responses to the women with a scornful quip to his male companion. When asked about Dabler, he responds to but does not really answer Mrs. Voluble: "Mr. Dabler?—O, yes, I recollect.—Why, Beaufort, what do you mean? did you bring me hither to be food to this magpie?" (I.152-53). This type of dialogue implies blocking that might depict Censor and Beaufort as an island of "rational" or "serious" conversation in this shop, surrounded as they are by women and their "idle chatter." The irony, of course, is that the "idle chatter" occupies those who work for a living, while Censor and Beaufort merely observe work and comment loftily upon it.

Jack brings act 1 to a close by finally appearing with news of Cecilia's nonappearance. He requires three entrances and eighteen speeches to get this information out, however, and we hear that he was given his commission more than two hours earlier. Cecilia's shadowy presence in the play—she does not appear in the first act at all—is an important device.[12] Initially discussed only in the conversations of others, and then more often than not standing silently when she is on the stage, this dramatic figure's occupation of the stage space mirrors many women's social insignificance. Apparently less important as a physical body than as an assurance of monetary reliability, Cecilia's "presence" in act 1 is akin to financial credit: neither has a tangible existence but both nonetheless circulate between people and are necessary for their contracts with others. Cecilia's reputation and social status are intact while her finances are guaranteed, but she must also be governed by a sense of feminine propriety that initially bars her from appearing in the milliner's shop because Lady Smatter cannot chaperone her. Unlike the nonappearing elite, who proclaim their status by dispatching their servant-proxies, Cecilia's nonappearance communicates her necessary submission to Lady Smatter's whims. Her unfortunate emissary is Jack, who is nearly incapable of delivering messages accurately, or in good time. The heroine is, throughout the play, entirely dependent on others either for ease of physical movement or for basic communication. Her money initially, it would seem, does not necessarily grant her the freedom to do as she pleases.

The second act is set in Lady Smatter's home. Like the place of business, this locale indicates social status and, more importantly, is occupied by those who are deemed to have the qualities Lady Smatter requires. This is where we hear of Cecilia's misfortune, and it is from this space that she

Figure 1. Analysis of Act 2 of *The Witlings*

scene #	1	2	3	4	5	6	7	8	9	10	11	12	13	14	15	16	17	18	19
Lady Smatter	53	25	on	43	on	44	50	9	6	14	50	50	on	on	50	100	100	50	
Cecilia	47	25	on	3	on	on	on	2	18									50	100
Beaufort		50	on	10	on	6	on	5	13				50	33	50				
Servant			100		100		50										on		
Codger				43	on	10	on	28	19	14	on	25	on	66					
Dabler						40	on	42	1	on	25								
Mrs. Sapient								14	4	43	25	25	50						
Jack									38	29	25	25							

Act 2 has been broken into French scenes. I assume the servant exits after each appearance (scene 3, 5, 7, 17). An empty cell indicates the figure is offstage. "On" indicates the character is onstage but silent. The numbers indicate an approximate percentage of speech contributed by each figure present in the scene.

is exiled. Act 2 also introduces the witlings of the club and the rules of their interaction, which reward obsequiousness and punish the straightforward and the literal. Cecilia's first onstage appearance finds her with the most authority she ever achieves in the play, but even this is presented as tenuous and deferential. She converses with Lady Smatter about the aunt's literary pursuits, during which she voices in ambiguous terms her evaluation of these activities. A series of veiled insults placates Smatter and shows Cecilia is not without convictions, but her circuitous announcement of her opinions denies her any real verbal force. Of course, it *is* strange that, as Cecilia says, Smatter's research is unsuccessful, as it is ironically true that Smatter's "desire of celebrity is too well known for [her] motives to be doubted" (II.26-27). Cecilia *is* unqualified to join the Esprit Party, because she does not flatter insensibly as its members do. Later, Censor insults Cecilia in her absence by suggesting that he means "not seriously to suppose the Girl is wise enough" to wish for Beaufort's absence, and he feels that she does not really know her own mind (IV.656-61). Throughout the play, the heroine's verbal and physical acts are ineffectual, dictated by others, or simply assumed.

Burney's use of space in act 2 offers a physical parallel to Cecilia's verbal inabilities. Cecilia appears on the stage along with Beaufort, Codger, Dabler, Mrs. Sapient, and finally Jack, who arrives at midpoint, but she is a presence only and is perhaps even less significant in the flesh than she was in conversations in act 1, because we have nothing more to learn about her. She speaks very little, especially once the witlings' repartee begins. Figure 1 represents Burney's distribution of dialogue among the figures onstage.

This chart visually indicates a number of components of act 2. For instance, the triangular shape of the plotted dialogue shows the staggered entrances and exits of characters in the act. The largest congregation of figures occurs in the middle of act 2, when Cecilia's bad news is revealed, so that her troubles are publicized immediately. The entrances and exits also show Cecilia's departure in scene 9, reappearance in scene 18, and then her solitary position onstage in the last scene. Because act 2 concerns the very serious news that Cecilia has lost her fortune, her absence (scenes 10-17) is significant. If we include in this analysis of dialogue those scenes when each figure is silent except for the servant (3, 5, 7, 17), it is clear that Cecilia is onstage for 11 scenes, but speaks in only 7 of them, and she speaks only once in scenes 2, 4, and 8 (25, 3, and 2 percent of the dialogue, respectively). In scene 9, when Cecilia's bankruptcy is revealed, she still speaks less than Codger or Jack, who argue between themselves. Lady Smatter speaks throughout the act, and Mrs. Sapient and Jack speak the entire time they are onstage. Other figures speak infrequently in some scenes (Codger is often ignored, for instance), but only Dabler's participation in a scene dips below Cecilia's: he speaks once in scene 9 (1 percent of the dialogue) and not at all in scene 10. While this type of analysis does not attend to the relative substance or duration of individual speeches or the difference between direct speech and asides, for example, it does offer an overview of the dialogue patterns in the act. Burney often concentrates dialogue between two characters while others look on or participate minimally, and Cecilia is most often the onlooker or is present only as a topic of conversation, rather than as a producer of it.

Jack's interruption of the proceedings occurs in scene 9, when he brings bad news. This new information is obviously of primary importance to Cecilia, but after Jack's hurried entrance, when he announces, "I'm come on purpose to tell you some news" (II.345-46), no less than seventy discrete exchanges between figures take place before the news is spoken. Between Jack's announcement and the disclosure of the news, Codger and Jack have a long interchange about the respect due to one's elders, during which Jack makes as if he is leaving three different times. Even after Cecilia manages to draw his attention back to the subject at hand, her circumstances, she must ask Jack nine questions and interject several gasps of apprehension before she finally is told the news. The failure of Cecilia's banker is at last mentioned inadvertently, when Jack defends himself from an accusation and "accidentally" blurts out his information. "Real" information is repeatedly lost in discussions that come to no real resolution, and Cecilia is marked again and again as a silent observer or an ineffectual interrogator.

Once Cecilia has learned of her misfortune, her place in Lady Smatter's house becomes physically and metaphorically tenuous. She is led from the scene under Beaufort's power because her nerves cannot support the news, and the drawing room is confirmed as a space controlled by Lady Smatter. The lost money prompts Lady Smatter to acknowledge the embarrassment of Beaufort's marrying an unportioned woman. The aunt announces her own interest in the affair when she says, "here is an End of *our* marrying her!" (II.494-95, emphasis added). Beaufort understands the relationship between space and respect and urges his aunt to "go to Miss Stanley" (II.532). When Lady Smatter offers instead to "send for her here" (II.537), as one might command a servant, Beaufort asks, "Surely your Ladyship will go to *her*?—at such a Time as this, the smallest failure in respect—" (II.538-39). Cecilia, however, is *sent for*, and Lady Smatter announces that while her home is open to Cecilia (but only begrudgingly), she no longer occupies it as Beaufort's fiancée. Instead, Cecilia is urged to seek other resources. The scenes that follow reveal that she in fact has no resources at all, except for Censor's sympathy and his hatred of Lady Smatter. Cecilia's lost status means she is literally out of *place*. She refuses to follow Lady Smatter to her room—symbolically left alone on the stage—but she has no fixed destination herself: "without fortune, destitute of Friends, ruined in circumstances . . . where can the poor Cecilia seek shelter, peace or protection?" (II.651-53). This lack of any reassuring space or contact continues throughout the play. Cecilia's refusal to accept Lady Smatter's insincere and insulting charity prompts her departure from the house, ironically one of her few assertive actions; that Beaufort does not believe Cecilia could have left on her own initiative underscores her reputation for passivity.

The departure of Cecilia and her avowal to Lady Smatter to "converse . . . no more" (II.649) begins a retreat into silence and failed communication, as she becomes nearly incapable of speaking for herself. She is thrust into the linguistic equivalent of being unable to appear in Mrs. Wheedle's shop without a chaperon. Cecilia arrives at Mrs. Voluble's apartments, and finds the woman in a space that announces itself as the home of indiscretion and a lack of privacy: Voluble is secretly rummaging through Dabler's manuscripts when Jenny, and then Cecilia, arrive. It is Bob who reminds his mother repeatedly that she should not be in Dabler's room, to no avail. Mrs. Voluble manages to gain all of Cecilia's private information and immediately communicates it to Jenny and Bob. The announcement of the misfortune serves no dramatic function (we already know the news), but it does define the atmosphere on the stage as one of gossip, indiscretion, and opportunism. Cecilia's distraction is dismissed as the musing of a lover, of a "sort of a pet," or of a touched head (III.547-49). She feels herself invaded by others' inquiries and is subject to interpretation and speculation. Although she wants "a few minutes private Conversation" (III.413), she is increasingly unable to make herself heard over the constant interruptions and questions of those already present. Desiring to be "quite private" and to be talked to "no more" (III.517, 522), she says, "I know not what I say!—I can talk no longer;—pray excuse my incoherence" (III.526-27). She asks that she might "recover [her] composure in silence" and the women do as they are told, conversing "as if [she] was not here" (III.533-34). Their conversation, however, makes public property of Cecilia's personal worries. The heroine's silence is juxtaposed with the world that goes on despite her troubles.

Cecilia requires intervention, which appears in the form of Censor. He attempts to bring a message from Beaufort to Cecilia, but, true to all the important communiqués in the play, he is interrupted. It is Mrs. Voluble who again intrudes, prompting Censor to comment metatheatrically that "Surely this Woman was sent to satirize the use of Speech!" (III.733-34). Cecilia remains doubtful of Beaufort's attachment to her, which reminds her of her *displacement* as she desparately seeks out a place to stay. She says distractedly to Mrs. Voluble: "O for a little repose!—leave me to myself, I beseech you! I can niether speak or listen to you;—pray go,—pray—alas, I know not what I say!—I forget that this House is yours, and that I have no right even to the shelter it's Roof affords me" (III.768-71). Cecilia's physical and vocal position in these settings is integral to the representation of her excision from social comfort.

Cecilia's inability to communicate persists to the end of the play and she is later unable even to request a pen and ink from Mrs. Voluble (V.87-131). This dialogue indicates that Cecilia's speech is purely locutionary; it does not achieve the second or third levels of a speech act.[13] The desired illocutionary (referring to the status of the statement made) and perlocutionary (referring to the statement's effect) components of her speech are absent: the request or command she tries to make produces no appropriate response from the listeners. Burney presents Cecilia's removal from social acceptance as a removal from speech and contact with those who might help her. Although Cecilia remains a target of gossipy information, she has no control over her place in this society.

Cecilia's fate is left hanging when the scene changes to the Esprit Party in act 4; this change is a subtle but effective way to emphasize the waiting Cecilia endures before her troubles are solved, because the audience experiences the delay as well. The party demonstrates a unique set of conversational and social rules. The commodities exchanged here are witticisms, bought with compliments no matter how paltry the product. Lady Smatter has asked earlier "where can be the pleasure of reading Books, and studying authors, if one is not to have the credit of talking of them?" and this is the use to which she puts her "learning" (II.24-25). Burney presents in the literary witlings a set of people who seek to imitate the responses of an educated class of readers. While their effusions are indeed laughable, they also more seriously imply the commonly held view that an understanding of poetry and criticism is a mark of refinement, status, education, and leisure. Imitation of mannerisms is an important theme that Burney explores further in *A Busy Day* and *The Woman-Hater*. Although the witlings lack the classical learning that would supply them with accurate attributions and "taste," they nonetheless understand the form of literary clubs, if not the content of them. Poetry and criticism, for Smatter, provide a sort of social cachet ("there is something rather elegant in a Taste for these sort of amusements" [II.117-18]) and an opportunity to indulge in the rapture that she feels should properly accompany poetry. While the formal rules of the club forbid mere flattery, this is all that takes place. Language, emotion, and fawning become goods to be exchanged between the friends who agree on the real, rather than written rules of the game. Lady Smatter and Mrs. Sapient thus respond simultaneously to Dabler's poetry with cries of "O elegant! enchanting! delicious! / O delightful! pathetic! delicate!" (IV.63-64). Codger speaks and hears literally and without pretension, so he is barred from participation in the conversation. The art of ignoring what people say, in favor of attending to what they actually mean, is quite a challenge. Dabler, for instance, asks Codger to "Speak sincerely, for [he] hate[s] flattery," but he will only converse with those who admire him (IV.132). His poetic absurdities are offered up along with his pirating of others' works and his modest (but true) denial of his abilities. In a set piece that underscores the play's themes, the late-arriving Censor challenges Dabler's ability to write extempore verse by proposing the themes of self-sufficiency, war, the abuse of time, and slander.[14] Of course, the unoriginal Dabler cannot oblige.

Censor's intervention in the lovers' trials and the Esprit Club allows him to invoke his own set of elite standards and marks him as a character able to make himself heard effectively. It becomes clear that he has a stronger interest in punishing Lady Smatter for her pretensions to the learning that he feels is his exclusive purview, than for her dismissal of Cecilia from want of sympathy. He has had a long-standing dislike of her, and Cecilia's misfortune seems to serve almost as a pretext for his vengeance: "Heavens, that a Woman whose utmost natural capacity will hardly enable her to understand the History of Tom Thumb, and whose comprehensive faculties would be absolutely baffled by the Lives of the seven Champions of Christendom, should dare blaspheme the names of our noblest Poets with Words that convey no ideas, and Sentences of which the Sound listens in vain for the Sense!—O, she is insufferable! . . . Folly torments because it gives present disturbance,—as to want of feeling,—'tis a thing of Course" (III.176-87). Censor is *the* guardian of a literary and cultural heritage that Lady Smatter threatens. The little learning of the witlings is a humorous thing, and our own laughter at those who seem harmless enough may prompt us to question the severity of Censor's viewpoint . . . or to feel equally condemned by him for our lack of outrage. We are left questioning how dangerous these witlings really are, as we examine the inequalities of class and gender that permit Censor to reign over everyone intellectually and, by extension, morally.

Censor views the witlings from the same gendered and classist plateau from which he surveys Cecilia's financial woes. His assurances to Cecilia that Lady Smatter will welcome her home establish him as the final authority in the play. He is distinct from the other figures in many ways, acting as he does the part of a monitor or commentator and dismissing the other figures and their interests.[15] His role as the source of resolution—and the "punisher"—demonstrates the difference gender lends to male and female action and authority.[16] Censor thrives on the hope that he represents a masculine ideal. He accuses Beaufort of exposing himself to "a ridiculous and unmanly situation" when he goes to the milliner's, saying that he, unlike Beaufort, is "a *Free* man, and therefore . . . allowed to have an opinion of [his] own, to act with consistency, and to be guided by the light of Reason" (I.94, 122-24). He is generally dismissive of all the other figures, but female figures garner more than their share of his scorn. Codger receives a measure of sympathy from Censor, who pities the silencing of the old man, and Jack, despite Censor's criticism of his rambling, is enlisted to help blackmail Lady Smatter. Mrs. Voluble, by contrast, is condemned as a "prating, intolerable Fool" who circulates scandal, Mrs. Sapient as "weak and superficial," and Lady Smatter as "insufferable" (I.156, 215, 200). It is significant that Censor illustrates his opinions about these women with allusions to the "noblest Poets," including Spenser and Pope. Although Lady Smatter acts as a censor herself, determining Cecilia's acceptability to her family, she, too, is severely subject to another's authority. In her case, she is censored and censured by Censor, who threatens her with infamy if she refuses to do as he says. When the witlings leave her home, dissatisfied with Censor's insults, he puts his plan in place, speaking the language of metatheater when he asks if Beaufort, a "noble fellow," will be "suffered to ruin himself" (IV.672). He then enlists the aid of Jack (with the threat of a caning) in his scheme to upset Lady Smatter's power over Beaufort.

Censor's blackmail of Lady Smatter does more than comment on the uses and abuses of literature, abuses for which Lady Smatter is certainly indictable.[17] It underscores the unequal distribution of power between male figures who have control over personal reputation and instruments that can influence it, like the press and public gathering places, and the female figures who are therefore at their mercy. Certainly, it is the case that Burney satirizes both male and female pretensions to learning—Censor does threaten to expose Dabler's inability to write extempore verse—but the censuring of Lady Smatter seems particularly severe and tinged with the sort of violence that characterizes Captain Mirvan's attacks on Madame Duval. Censor's intimidation of Dabler is private (he "*takes him aside*") and he does nothing once he enlists Dabler against Lady Smatter (V.671). The blackmail against Lady Smatter in the final act involves the initial humiliation of her in front of the assembled group and a warning about future public degradation. Further, while the blackmail of Dabler concerns threats only, Lady Smatter is encouraged to believe she is *already* a laughingstock, because Jack claims already to have heard the verses against her at a public house. Her shame would seem to be widespread rather than private. One cannot help but recall the passage from a letter Burney wrote to her sister following the eager reception of *Evelina*, when she was invited into the literary circle at Streatham: "But pray for me, my dear Susy, that Heaven may spare me the Horror irrecoverable of personal abuse.—Let them Criticise, cut, slash, without mercy my *Book*,—& let them *neglect me*,—but may God avert my becoming a public Theme of Ridicule" (*EJL*, 3:163).

Censor's assumption of social and literary authority does make him "a Witling of sorts, composing verses for his own purposes—and his verses will have to be suppressed, or censored too, after this private hearing."[18] However, the act of blackmail suggests that Censor's concern is not so much that literature be maintained on a worthy plane, but that it might be put to ends that are useful for him and that demonstrate his control over the problems of Cecilia, Beaufort, and Lady Smatter. His blackmailing verses, in fact, constitute an *ad feminam* attack on Lady Smatter's appearance and what has become a stereotypical topic of female vanity, her age.[19] Jack enters, singing a ballad that jokes about Lady Smatter in Bedlam:

> She has ta'en such a Dose of incongruous matter
> That Bedlam must Soon hold the Carcase of Smatter
> . . . .
> I call not to Swains to attend to my Song;
> Nor call I to Damsels, so tender and young;
> To Critics, and Pedants, and Doctors I clatter,
> For who else will heed what becomes of poor Smatter.
>   with a down, down, derry down.
> . . . .
> This lady with Study has muddled her head;
> Sans meaning she talk'd, and Sans knowledge she read,
> And gulp'd such a Dose of incongruous matter
> That Bedlam must soon hold the Carcase of Smatter.
>   with a down, down, derry down. [V.745–82]

The female body is literarily degraded with the poison of false learning and a reputation is publicly sullied. Even Dabler notes how differently public exposure affects men and women: "we men do not suffer in the World by Lampoons as the poor Ladies do;—they, indeed, may be quite— quite ruined by them" (V.741-43). Censor reminds Lady Smatter that his "*power*" is strong (V.827). As if to prove his point, he physically bars her from leaving the room, and he finally reduces her to tears (V.819, 842). Censor succeeds in swaying Lady Smatter—who does not have much choice in the matter—by appealing to her desire for flattery and she agrees reluctantly to Beaufort and Cecilia's marriage.

Cecilia's financial worries are proven inconsequential by the close of the play, because Censor is able to restore her to financial and social favor and her ruin is not as severe as first supposed. Burney comments on the relative importance of money to people in different social stations by contrasting Cecilia's sense of confinement when her money seems to be gone with the financial concerns of the working-class figures, who, with the exception of Bob, are all women. The real gulf that separates these characters from Cecilia and Beaufort is shown in the manner in which Burney has them discuss their situations. The workingwomen understandably regard Cecilia's class-biased effusions on dependence as verbal posturings. The women who overhear Cecilia's lamentations dismiss her as "talking to herself" and having "a mighty way of Musing" (V.99, 100). It is symbolic that the women who gather at Mrs. Voluble's encourage Cecilia to substitute sustenance for words, calling to her repeatedly to "Eat a morsel first," as if to remind her of money's function in gaining necessities rather than the intangibility of social station (V.115). The mingled comments on Cecilia and the roast beef are oddly appropriate, for possession of the roast beef depends in some way on the heiress's repossession of her fortune, for those whose income is the payment they receive for services rendered. Mrs. Voluble attempts to make parallels between Cecilia's misfortunes and the "bad things of one Sort or other [that] are always coming to pass" when merchants face bankruptcy, a comparison that is completely lost on Cecilia (V.124). Mrs. Wheedle reminds Cecilia that she expects no more from her than the payment of her account, and the thought of such "dunning" leads Cecilia to make the somewhat absurd suggestion that a beggar is "not more powerless and wretched,—a tortured and insulted Heart is all that I can call my own!" (V.146-48). Burney walks a very fine line with her satire here. Cecilia's language is exaggerated and her suffering does not endure, but her situation is, for her, severe; she is truly shocked by this sudden change in her prospects and she desperately begins to seek a job. She has, however, *because* of her privilege, no real skills with which to help herself and in this respect, she has fewer options for self-reliance than her working-class female counterparts. We must feel some sympathy for her, though her own sense of sorrow for herself is comically exaggerated.

Both Cecilia and Beaufort make overstated pronouncements about their love and their tragedy, pronouncements undermined by the acknowledgement that ultimately neither has to give anything up.[20] Beaufort has to gasp for breath when he speaks to Censor of his fondness for Cecilia: "Hasten, then, to the sweet Sufferer,—tell her my Heart bleeds at her unmerited distresses,—tell her that, with her fugitive Self, peace and Happiness both flew this mansion—" (III.242-44). Beaufort's separation from his beloved prompts his hatred of the "chains" of dependence that bind him, but his desire for the independence of self-employment is never more than a verbal alliance he constructs between himself and the "toiling Husbandman, and laborious mechanic" (III.262-63). For Cecilia as well, verbal protestations are never actually replaced by the need to work for a living, something she has a great difficulty imagining. She resolves in the face of her tragedy to "submit to [her] fate . . . should servility and dependance be [her] lot," without stopping to consider the class-based distinctions between the fate she "submit[s] to" rather than "chuse[s]" and the fate of the working class (V.265-66). Burney reveals how relative the concept of dependence is; the resolution of the play supports this distinction by contrasting a falsely self-important moral with the real, material dependence of the workingwomen. Cecilia is brought back into the social circle to devote herself to Lady Smatter's service and Beaufort takes the opportunity to muse that "Self-dependance is the first of Earthly Blessings" (V.951-52). He proposes that he and Cecilia (who are neither independent nor self-directing) might be an example for others. Beaufort, who has not acted on his own behalf at all, assumes the role of moralist in the play's final speech, but he is the least effectual of all of the witlings, the thinking but static parallel to Jack, who is all action and no thought.

In the final act of the play, Mrs. Sapient, who fears an encounter with Dabler, with whom she is infatuated, is hidden in Mrs. Voluble's closet with broken dishes. Her hiding place, however, is not kept private and she is exposed to ridicule. This position, a confinement that is open to public knowledge and scrutiny, can be seen as representative of the position of each of the women in the play. Cecilia, Mrs. Wheedle and the milliners, Lady Smatter, and Mrs. Sapient are confined in various ways—by finances, the media, or a closet—that render them incapable of complete self-direction and at the same time expose them to the masculine eye of public scrutiny and evaluation. Although in Mrs. Sapient's case a façade of secrecy and privacy is maintained, her simultaneous presence and absence in the closet expose her to the public degradation of her character by Lady Smatter, against which she cannot protest effectively.[21] There are no spaces of privacy or protection for the women in this play.

Burney announces on her title page for *The Witlings* that the play is by "A Sister of the Order." In placing herself in this world of the witlings, where reputations and security are contingent on male authority, she ironically predicted the fateful suppression of her play by her two daddies. This first mature and public attempt at representing figures embodied on a stage, performing for an audience, is obsessed with instances of social interaction that enact power for some and subjugation for others via flattery, gossip, literary pursuits, and financial exchanges. Despite Cecilia and Beaufort's longing for the contrary, this is a definitively unidealized world of misplaced priorities, all of which favor the upper class in general, and Censor in particular. He can count on Lady Smatter's desire for fame as much as he can count on Beaufort's willingness to be directed and Cecilia's unwillingness to take herself completely out of Beaufort's reach. Doody suggests this is all a part of the play's concern with independence: "[s]elf-sufficiency means not being a parasite socially, not cheating intellectually, but having a mind and life of one's own and being willing to 'act vigorously.' . . . But Burney sees how much we are all affected by cultural climate and commonplaceness. . . . She has presented in her light comedy issues that have no solution. At the end of the play, nothing has really altered. . . . People go on as they do. It's a big world, full of shops and money and intellectual and social fashions, and nothing alters that big world."[22] There are severe limitations placed on people's abilities to "act vigorously." These limitations include both social station and gender, for all attempts to act individually are ultimately judged by Censor, as his name suggests, who claims authority as the play's only free man and rational thinker.

It is ironic that this exploration of gender, finance, and public reputation would remain confined to Burney's family and close friends, for the play asserts that the private and secret are elusive, that independence is difficult to achieve, and that public identities are as numerous as there are people to express opinions about themselves or others. Charles Burney and Samuel Crisp effectively proved to Burney that her gender and her own susceptibility to the whims of public scrutiny made her dependence on others unavoidable. Burney responded to Crisp's cautions about comic freedom by observing her own sense of confinement as a female artist: "Every word you have urged concerning the *salt & spirit* of gay, unrestrained freedom in Comedies, carries conviction along with it,—a conviction which I feel in trembling! should I ever venture in that walk publicly, perhaps the want of it might prove fatal to me. . . . I would a thousand Times rather forfeit my character as a *Writer*, than risk ridicule or censure as a *Female*" (*EJL*, 3:212). Burney's talents were returned to the novel. Her next literary work was *Cecilia* (1782), in which the heroine of *The Witlings* reappears and suffers similar trials (the manipulation of her through the use of her money) on a scale that extends far beyond the scope of a dramatic comedy. Cecilia's novelistic counterpart is pushed finally to madness by others' interference, a topic Burney would explore in her tragedies. Characters and objects of scrutiny that appear in *The Witlings* reappear in other works as well, specifically *The Woman-Hater*, as does a concern established in this first play: the lot of individuals (particularly women) who are caught in predetermined definitions of their function in a social network, where individual action and a discrete identity are difficult to achieve without a radical challenge to existing social structures. Only in *The Woman-Hater* is such a challenge comparatively successful, and the challenge is effected by a woman's control of her own language and the labels by which she is known.

The witlings are included and excluded from communities on the basis of their money or their contributions to the stock of gossip, information, or flattery. The momentarily threatening restrictions of their physical movement and expression of ideas are alleviated (but never eliminated entirely) as they are drawn back into their communities and their relationships. Mrs. Sapient can emerge from the closet, but she remains an object of ridiculing laughter. In the tragedies, Burney explores much more serious forms of restriction. Confining and threatening actions—imprisonment, torture, hostage-taking, and seclusion—are shown to be particular to women and affect them in ways that are lasting and often mortal. The stage is used to depict literal, physical confinement that parallels but intensifies the less tangible, but still serious sources of conflict for the female figures in the comedies.

3

Politicized Bodies and the Body Politic
Edwy and Elgiva and Elberta

Burney's tragedies—*Edwy and Elgiva, Hubert De Vere, The Siege of Pevensey*, and *Elberta*, all written between 1788 and 1791 and revised later—present the important critical challenge of rethinking the established contexts for these plays. They have been condemned for their occasional inelegance in an age not known for successes in the genre, or recuperated as little more than the therapeutic creations of a troubled woman. Morrison writes that the tragedies "could not even be classed as mediocre." Burney was "working in a field for which she had absolutely no talent and in which she could do no more than follow conventions." Such statements, echoed by almost all critics who have read the tragedies, do little to encourage interest in these plays.[1]

While Burney's tragedies are not merely personal in reference, it is difficult to overlook the resonance they have with the experiences of the decade of their composition. Doody remarks that it was the "most troubled period of [Burney's] life" and Hemlow suggests that the years leading to Burney's miserable tenure in court were marked by "[d]isappointed love and wild love, manifested in scenes as pathetic, lurid, or tender as those of eighteenth-century drama or romance . . . ."[2] Although the novelist's success with the publication of *Cecilia* (1782) outweighed even the approving reception of *Evelina*, she was not to begin writing again until 1788.[3] The intervening years saw a disappointing involvement with George Cambridge, which ended without ever really beginning (1783), the deaths of Burney's longtime "daddy" Samuel Crisp (1783) and friend Samuel Johnson (1784), the gradual dissolution of her close friendship with Hester Thrale, and the departure of all of her siblings from the family home.[4] The solution for the single and aging Burney's financial future was found satisfactorily (for all but Burney herself) in an appointment as the

Second Keeper of the Robes in Queen Charlotte's court in July 1786. Her position in the court is well documented as miserable and was envisioned by her as an unhappy, enforced marriage performed largely to please her father. She writes to her sister Susanna in a journal: "I was now on the point of entering—probably for ever—into an entire new way of life, and of foregoing by it all my most favourite schemes, and every dear expectation my fancy had ever indulged of happiness adapted to its taste—as now all was to be given up. . . . I am *married* . . . I look upon it in that light—I was averse to forming the union, and I endeavoured to escape it; but my friends interfered—they prevailed—and the knot is tied. What then now remains but to make the best wife in my power? I am bound to it in duty, and I will strain every nerve to succeed" (*DL,* 2:380-82). This royal favor was to confront Burney with a variety of experiences: her father's delight in this public honor, her own horror at her inevitable removal from happiness, the physical demands of the job, the possible attachment to Colonel Digby, the madness of the king, and the confinement of his family and court at Kew. It is of little surprise that the plays she wrote while in the queen's service focus on the uneasy and often enforced mingling of the personal, the filial, and the sociopolitical.

Burney's account of the composition of her tragedies is interwoven with her first-hand experience of the king's illness. She writes in October 1788: "in mere desperation for employment, I have just begun a tragedy [*Edwy and Elgiva*]. We are now in so spiritless a situation that my mind would bend to nothing less sad, even in fiction. . . . [I]t may while away the tediousness of this unsettled, unoccupied, unpleasant period" (*DL,* 4:118). At this time, Burney was called upon to nurse an anxious queen, which demanded self-denial and physical hardship. When the king grows worse, she writes, "[e]ven my melancholy resource, my tragedy, was now thrown aside; misery so actual, living, and present, was knit too closely around me to allow my depressed imagination to fancy any woe beyond what my heart felt" (*DL,* 4:155).[5] She returned to her by now "long-forgotten tragedy" in 1790, an activity which "does not much enliven, but it soothes" (*DL,* 4:362, 365). A rough draft was finished in August 1790.

Upon completing her first tragedy, Burney began to write two others, *Hubert De Vere* and *The Siege of Pevensey*, in August 1790. She refers to herself in the third person:

> the author finished the rough first draft and copy of her first tragedy. What species of a composition it may prove she is very unable to tell; she only knows it was an almost spontaneous work, and soothed the melancholy of imagination for a while, though afterwards it impressed it with a secret sensation of horror, so like

real woe, that she believes it contributed to the injury her sleep received about this period.

Nevertheless, whether well or ill, she is pleased to have done something at last. . . .

. . . [S]carce was this completed, . . . when imagination seized upon another subject for another tragedy. [*DL,* 4:413]

Burney's physical and emotional stability were to deteriorate rapidly after this, and in October 1790 she drew up her petition for the discharge of her duties. This was not presented to the queen until December 1790, and Burney's attendance was prolonged for months after that.

The final month before Burney's "release" was also occupied with writing. She began her fourth tragedy, *Elberta,* in June 1791:

[s]o melancholy indeed was the state of my mind, from the weakness of my frame, that I was never alone but to form scenes of "foreign woe," when my own disturbance did not occupy me wholly. I began—almost whether I would or not—another tragedy! The other three all unfinished! not one read! and one of them, indeed, only generally sketched as to plan and character. But I could go on with nothing; I could only suggest and invent.

The power of composition has to me indeed proved a solace, a blessing! When incapable of all else, that, unsolicited, unthought of, has presented itself to my solitary leisure, and beguiled me of myself, though it has not of late regaled me with gayer associates. [*DL,* 4:478-79]

Her long-awaited discharge in July 1791 brought an end to an undoubtedly distressing five years, when filial obedience and obedience to the monarchical authority both contributed to distress that was mental, emotional, and physical, a failure of strength and spirit.

Reading Burney's tragedies, with their heritage of negative evaluations and their strong biographical resonances, provides an excellent opportunity for a shift in critical direction that will bring into prominence elements of these otherwise dismissed plays. This feminist reading attends especially to the female figures in these tragedies and the ways in which Burney depicts tragic circumstances. These plays are coherent and quite compelling works. Burney's dramatizations of the physical and emotional traumas of women meditate quite overtly on gender and how ideas about behavior and one's place in social hierarchies are influenced by it. In a word, the female figures in these plays suffer *because* they are women and because of the submissive status to which this relegates them. Confinement and manipulation are shown to be pervasively emotional, intellectual, and especially physical. Burney uses the stage as an effective vehicle for her depiction of these myriad types of containment. The female figures of Burney's comedies are restrained with respect to their marital choice, their financial control, and their self-definition. Burney's tragedies represent a substantially different view of female confinement than that in the comedies, displaying figures who suffer bodily anguish because of their personal and political relationships with fathers, suitors, or husbands. As daughters, wives, and mothers, these female figures assume a value because they can be used by politically mobile men to manipulate other men. Women are thus imprisoned, ransomed, exiled, tortured, or killed by enemies who rely upon their adherence to prevailing notions of obedience, sexual decorum, and submission to men.

Burney's tragedies are thus of interest not only for their compelling view of female suffering, but also for the perspective they offer on the larger issue of just what situations, characters, and conflicts female dramatists considered "tragic" at the end of the eighteenth century (see chapter 7 as well). Dramatic literary histories have done little to pursue the complex relationship between gender and genre in this period, no doubt partially because of the prevailing general scorn for late-eighteenth-century tragedy. Richard W. Bevis describes the picture of tragedy at the end of the eighteenth century as "confused" and suggests that tragic dramatists returned to "Congrevian tragicomedy and heroic themes. . . . Many plays contain elements that can reasonably be called 'classical', but they are accompanied by appeals to pathos, and piteous touches are as likely to occur in a classical or heroic play as in a domestic one."[6] Matthew H. Wikander suggests that pathos came to dominate history plays as well. He concludes that Restoration and eighteenth-century history plays tend to "localize and domesticate history" and to show the "escapism of pathetic tragedy," which presents the victimization of monarchs for whom "passion is wholly antipathetic to power."[7] Allardyce Nicoll is more dismissive, writing that "[i]t is not to be denied that the image of tragedy during the latter half of the eighteenth century makes but a sorry picture." He adds, "[i]n all, or in nearly all [tragedies of this period], we note the same uninspired features, we note the same continual decline."[8] Pathos is out of fashion now and perhaps suggests to too many critics what is stereotypically considered to be feminine emotionalism. It is not, I think, a dramatic quality we should dismiss, given its prominence at the end of the eighteenth century.

A feminist dramatic criticism of late-eighteenth-century tragic drama must negotiate with these negative views of the genre and seek to counter the prevalence of notions about the "hero" and Aristotelian rules, which seem antagonistic to drama that is a forum for gender issues.[9] The critical neglect of gender-specific experimentations in the genre raises the question of the extent to which tragedy is seen normatively as a masculine and male-dominated genre: the leader of a community, usually male, comes into conflict with other men, or must choose between his position of authority and his personal desire, usually for a woman. Such a narrative inevitably creates woman as a negative alternative to honor, patriotism, or courage. Bevis describes Nicoll as the "master" of eighteenth-century dramatic theory.[10] Although dated, Nicoll's views in *The Theory of Drama* are representative of a critical tradition that discourages feminist analysis. Nicoll describes the necessity to tragedy of universality, a prominent and flourishing tragic hero, extrahuman forces, a sense of fateful inevitability, symbolism, and a general tragic spirit. Tragedy is "stern and majestic," and the audience gains pleasure from "a feeling of awe allied to lofty grandeur." This pleasure flows from the purgation of emotion and the witnessing of a "lofty nobility" and "heroic grandeur" which are somehow universal. In suffering the misery of human existence, "quiet resignation" and "calmness in face of death" are distinguishing features of the tragic hero.[11]

The forceful component of Nicoll's evaluation of tragedy is his view of the figure of the hero. He is said to act because of conscious or unconscious error, often against forces more powerful than himself, as he is torn between conflicting duties or confronted by antagonistic circumstances. This exclusively masculine version of a protagonist is most subject to a feminist critique. Nicoll writes that "tragedy differs from comedy in being often almost entirely masculine," and while he notes that "masculine" and "feminine" are terms with different connotations for different times, he continues with the assertion that "tragedy almost invariably stresses the masculine at the expense of the feminine elements" because of "the hardness and sternness which we have already noted in the highest tragic art." Whatever feminine element is present in tragedy "does not often have any great influence on the development of the play directly, although indirectly, by influence on the mind of the hero, it may have much." Central figures of great tragedies are all men or atypical women. On the other hand, "'she-tragedies,' as sometimes they have been called, have rarely an atom of tragic greatness, although some of them are affecting. . . . They never reach that sternness of majesty which is an inevitable concomitant of this highest type of literature. It is this insistence on the feminine, and, along with the feminine, the pathetic, which has marred the plays of Fletcher, Webster, and Ford." Nicoll concludes that "[t]he feminine in high tragedy, we may repeat, must either be made hard, approaching the masculine in quality, or else be relegated to a position of minor importance in the development of the plot."[12] The language of this discussion is strongly masculinist and does not consider the importance of a dramatic practice that has different emphases besides the "hard" and "lofty."

The alternative version of tragedy that I am proposing is one that is less concerned with the public, the majestic, or the lofty (ideas linked conventionally with the masculine) than it is with the emotional, domestic, and personal. Certainly, Burney's tragedies all feature heroes and male-centered conflicts between passion and duty or bravery. I do not mean to indicate that a woman-conscious tragedy is exclusively about female figures. However, Burney does shift her lens onto the "alternative" character in tragic stories, the female figure who suffers along with or sometimes *instead of* the tragic hero. Burney's tragedies are insistently focused on the female, the feminine, and often the feminist. This does not, however, produce a "she-tragedy" about exalted female nobility or tragedies featuring villainous temptresses. Rather, Burney portrays female victimization that results from untenable alternatives; her emphasis is on destruction rather than noble suffering. Her revision of the tragic formula from a female point of view ought not to make the claims of her own formula irrelevant or uninteresting.[13]

Burney's tragedies exemplify composition in a time of generic flux, incorporating elements of Gothic, classical, and historical tragedy, she-tragedy, and melodrama in a version of tragedy that focuses on gender as a source of oppression and physical suffering. The relationship between Gothicism and gender is intriguing. In *Seven Gothic Dramas 1789-1825*, Cox discusses the ideological force of a form that contradicts standard histories of drama because it closed the gap between high and low art, was linked with poetry and the novel, and was specifically antirealistic. He emphasizes the Gothic's representation of the uncontrolled and unassimilated, the antirational, and the antimoral, writing that "the Gothic drama could be used to stage a protest—both aesthetic and ideological—against convention and containment, against generic and political hierarchy."[14] Discussions of Gothicism are highly suggestive for feminist analysis, because the conventions of terror, entrapment, and the quest for freedom (what Cox calls the Gothic's revolutionary ideology) underlie many representations of female experience, dramatic or otherwise. Epstein writes that the Gothic is a "literature of entrapment and engulfment, a literature that inscribes closure as at once stifling, inevitable, and necessary and that thematizes and textualizes the twin creations of domesticity and subjectivity as deriving from female intensity."[15] However ambiguous the term "female intensity" is, Epstein is correct to consider the Gothic as gendered. Eve Kosofsky Sedgwick, in *The Coherence of Gothic Conventions*, discusses Gothic fiction in ways that are suggestive for a feminist analysis of drama as well. She writes that the Gothic represents ". . . the position of the self to be massively blocked off from something to which it ought normally to have access," a separation of an isolated, inside sphere from that outside it, spheres that are joined through violence or magic.[16] The mechanisms that separate the spheres Sedgwick describes (the isolated and the desired beyond it) are seen by Burney as clearly gender-specific and the violence that overcomes separation does so in ways that tend to destroy female autonomy or existence. Gothicism appears in Burney's plays in a range of forms, from extreme villains and male figures who strike a pose and declare their mental turmoil, to raving women and atmospheres of claustrophobia: churchyards, monasteries, ruined caves, and castles. Each individual use of Gothic devices is relevant to Burney's larger contemplation of gender-specific experience.[17]

The conceptualization of space, freedom, and choice is related to Gothicism and is the element of Burney's tragedies on which I concentrate. Women are "caught" (literally and metaphorically) between men when the political, popular, and moral authority of one man over another becomes displaced onto or reenvisioned as parental, moral, or marital control of a woman. Burney's use of stage business inscribes ideological forms of control in physical, spatial terms, as does her representation of the relationship between power and pain. As Elaine Scarry notes, a major step in making torture effective is "the translation of all the objectified elements of pain into the insignia of power, the conversion of the enlarged map of human suffering into an emblem of the regime's strength."[18] In Burney, the female body is the location of the insignia and is constantly under siege. Coercion includes being led astray (physically, morally, and emotionally), unwillingly exchanged in marriage, seduced, starved, imprisoned, taken hostage, exiled, hamstrung, or murdered. The terrorism is emotional, spiritual, psychic, and physical. The goal of these varied punishments remains constant (the subordination of one man to another), but the brunt of this authority is felt by the female figures.[19]

While the exchange of women between men in these plays is directed ultimately at securing political power, this exchange inevitably takes place in an economy that is sexual as well. Female sexuality, subject as it is to the sanction and control of male authority (religious, familial, marital), emerges as a tool of political power. Gayle Rubin's discussion of kinship systems is relevant here. She notes that the social worth of women (the "presents") is a function not of any intrinsic value but of their place in an economy: ". . . it is the partners, not the presents, upon whom reciprocal exchange confers its quasi-mystical power of social linkage."[20] In Burney's tragedies, the forms of social linkage are usually antagonistic and political. While Burney emphasizes exchanges between disputing men, kinship is frequently an issue, where marital alliance or the maintenance of a "pure" lineage requires the control of father over daughter. In the case of *Edwy and Elgiva*, kinship is invoked as a taboo that justifies the removal of

Elgiva from one man's power to another's. As Rubin notes, the exchange of women is only part of a larger system of social organization ("sexual access, genealogical statuses, lineage names and ancestors, rights and *people*") that "specif[ies] that men have certain rights in their female kin, and that women do not have the same rights either to themselves or to their male kin."[21] Women are easily integrated into political relationships between men because the force of male power builds so easily on female subordination to male desire and authority.

Sedgwick's discussion of male homosocial desire in *Between Men* is a useful addition to Rubin's anthropological and psychoanalytic theories of female oppression. Sedgwick concentrates on the spectrum of relations between men and the position women occupy as the capital exchanged between them. She argues that "the status of women, and the whole question of arrangements between genders, is deeply and inescapably inscribed in the structure even of relationships that seem to exclude women—even in male homosocial/homosexual relationships. . . . [I]n any male-dominated society, there is a special relationship between male homosocial (*including* homosexual) desire and the structures for maintaining and transmitting patriarchal power."[22] Whether the relationships between men are erotic or antagonistic, Sedgwick suggests that homosocial desire and homophobia serve to define and alter heterosexual relationships, particularly those that can be geometrically illustrated by the triangle (usually two men, one woman), as it is described by René Girard in *Deceit, Desire, and the Novel* (1972). She adds to Girard's triangular configuration of desire an interrogation of the sex and gender positions of the people at the points of the triangle. In Burney's tragedies, the exchange of women between men is rarely homoerotic (although there are overtones of this), but it *is* a function of the homosocial organization of social and political institutions, and as such can be mapped as a triangular relationship between men and women, among whom flows the desire for possession, power, and authority.

In situating Burney's tragedies as feminist Gothic dramas, I am arguing that the representation of the entrapped and suffering female can be used to depict and question the role gender plays in the active and insidious subjugation of women as daughters and wives, sexual and political objects.[23] Visual, aural, spatial, and narrative cues in tragedies can be interpreted as political statements about gender. These cues include, but are not limited to: (1) representations of suffering that are primarily specific to gender rather than other factors of social interaction, including, for example, female figures who endure conflict because of their status as wives, mothers, or daughters; (2) representations of action that show agency to be circumscribed by gender-defined ideas about behavior, or show passivity, manipulation, or punishment to result from a normative view of appropriate feminine behavior; (3) representations of conflict, character, and action that can be considered part of a general critique of institutionally entrenched differences between men and women and the relative power they exercise in the world depicted on the stage and, by implication, in the world of the audience. The prominence of these elements in any tragedy will vary, of course, and with it the thoroughness or exclusivity with which a tragedy might be said to deal with gender issues from a feminist perspective. While the primary conflict depicted in a play may not be immediately discernible as arising from questions of gender, the secondary or tertiary result of such conflict may indeed involve figures for reasons that are related to gender.

The critique of gender-specific oppression that pervades Burney's tragedies is dominated by her sustained analysis of the physical manipulation of female bodies by those in pursuit of political power. Punishment falls on female shoulders and authority is gained by the literal and figurative possession of women who are vulnerable because of their sex and their subordinate role in marriage and in father-daughter relationships. Burney's tragedies accomplish what Michelle Gellrich describes as "the troublesome culture-questioning areas of tragedy: its doubts about the viability and stability of social and moral order, its persistent way of alienating us from the simple extremes of benevolence and aloofness, its refusal to accommodate the traditional categories we would impose on characters and actions to make them safe and familiar."[24] By representing the bodily suffering of women as part of tragic action, Burney invites her audience to question the gendered hierarchies that permit such physical and emotional use and abuse by those seeking social and political authority. The worlds represented in Burney's tragedies are *not* safe and are relevant beyond the immediate historical events they describe.

I have divided my discussion of Burney's four tragedies into two chapters, based on thematic similarities between the works. While this disrupts the chronology of composition, it allows for comparisons to be made more easily between the tragedies concerned with wives and mothers, and those featuring father-daughter pairs. The male-female relationships of husbands and fathers to wives and daughters, and of mothers to children, are interrelated, of course. In *Edwy and Elgiva* and *Elberta*, the bond of marriage places the female figures in each play in jeopardy. For Elgiva, this is because she is the desired but forbidden object that distracts Edwy from his public role as king. For Elberta, the demands of marriage come into direct conflict with the demands of maternity.

Edwy and Elgiva is the only play of Burney's to be staged during her lifetime. *Hubert De Vere* and *Love and Fashion* were submitted to theaters but later withdrawn and though *The Witlings* was sought by Sheridan, it was never produced. Nearly all accounts (including Burney's own) suggest that the performance of *Edwy and Elgiva* (Drury Lane, 21 March 1795) failed due to her inability to make revisions to the script before the performance, bad acting, and poorly conceived dramatic devices and speeches. The production of *Edwy and Elgiva* was, in fact, a substitute for Burney's original plan to have *Hubert De Vere* produced. She withdrew the latter before production in favor of *Edwy and Elgiva*, which was accepted by Kemble in December 1794. This was a time of upheaval with the birth of her only child, Alex, in the same month. This event, and Burney's poor health following it, seems to have kept her from revising the play to her satisfaction.

The production was in rehearsal by March 1795 (although Sabor suggests it was underrehearsed compared to other contemporary plays) and featured the leading tragic actors of the day: John Philip Kemble was cast as Edwy, James Aickin as Odo, John Palmer as Aldhelm, and Sarah Siddons as Elgiva.[25] Contemporary reviews of the play, including Burney's own, suggest that the production was far from smooth, with Palmer forgetting most of his lines. Siddons is supposed to have remarked that "there never was so wretched a thing as Mrs. D'arblaye's Tragedy"; Hester Thrale wrote that it was "hooted off the stage."[26] In a letter to Georgiana Waddington, Burney recounts her response to the performance: "[t]he Piece was represented to the utmost disadvantage, save only Mrs. Siddons & Mr. Kemble,—for it was not written with any idea of the stage, & my illness & weakness & constant *absorbment* in the time of its preparation, occasioned it to appear with so many *undramatic* [ef]fects, from my inexperience of Theatrical requisites & demands, that when I saw it, I perceived myself a thousand things I wished to *change* The Performers, too, were cruelly imperfect, & made blunders I blush to have pass for mine" (*JL*, 3:99-100). As Sabor and Hemlow note, the reviews of *Edwy and Elgiva* were mostly negative. Many referred to the fact that the prompter could be heard throughout the performance; the *Morning Post* "complained that the play was 'one continued monotonous scene of whining between the two lovers, occasionally interrupted by the insolent Dunstan.'"[27] Others, however, admired the play. In the *European Magazine*, the reviewer observed that "The construction of the Play was entitled to applause, and the language was beautiful and poeti-cal." In the *Morning Chronicle*, the reviewer allowed that the play was Burney's "first essay" in dramatic composition and wrote that "The whole of the third act, and many passages of the rest, were worthy of the pen from which the Tragedy came, and were warmly applauded."[28] Burney was not to approach the public as a dramatist again, though Richard Cumberland offered to lend a hand to the revisions of her play (see *JL* 3:105-10). However, the three comedies Burney wrote after this event and her attempts to have *Love and Fashion* staged suggest that she did not view the eclipse of *Edwy and Elgiva* as an indication of her failure as a dramatist.

The "failure" of *Edwy and Elgiva* and Burney's response to it tells us much about the theater world at the end of the eighteenth century. Donkin, in *Getting into the Act*, contextualizes the process that led to the production of *Edwy and Elgiva*. She notes, for example, that as a woman playwright, Burney did not have as ready access to the business of theater production as her male counterparts. She did not attend rehearsals and did not watch over the production in a fashion that might have permitted her to make revisions to the play before it was offered to the public for approval. The play may have failed because of the combination of aesthetic weaknesses and theatrical infighting: "[i]n fact, the failure was not all hers. It was occasioned by gross theatrical mismanagement, Burney's illness during the pre-production period, and her failure to engage fully the production and rehearsal process."[29] Donkin notes that the actors' lamentable neglect of their lines, something pointed out in the reviews of the piece, was possibly as much their own attack on the manager of Drury Lane, Richard Brinsley Sheridan, as anything else, because of Sheridan's financial mismanagement of the theater.

Three manuscripts of *Edwy and Elgiva* survive. The Berg manuscript, with neither prologue nor epilogue, is in Burney's hand, boxed with her final revisions and supplementary notes in the hand of Burney's husband, Alexandre d'Arblay; of Burney; and of another. It bears signs of Burney's revisions following the production. A version also survives in the Larpent Collection of the Huntington Library at the University of California at Los Angeles. The Larpent manuscript is close to the performed version of the play, and contains the prologue and an epilogue by Burney.[30] The Cambridge manuscript (in the Emmanuel College Library) was a gift from Emmanuel's librarian, Evelyn Shirley Shuckburgh, in the 1880s; this version was edited by Benkovitz (1957). This copy was made by d'Arblay at the request of Burney's brother, Charles Jr., in January 1795, and it includes Charles Jr.'s prologue. D'Arblay's suggested revisions are written on the manuscript or on separate sheets.[31] Revisions to the Cambridge manuscript were probably made following the play's only production and Sabor suggests that the alterations in d'Arblay's hand, separated according to character, "could thus be incorporated in the actors' individual copies."[32] The changes to the text include both substantial and slight alterations to the verse and content. Some of the more substantial alterations include the change of "legal union" to "impious union" (I.ii.12) and "noble Aldhelm" to "pious Aldhelm" (I.ix.3), both of which emphasize religious ideals as the basis for moral evaluations of character. The scene depicting the seizure of Elgiva by Dunstan's ruffians (II.xi) has also been lengthened.

The fragmentary notes boxed with the Berg manuscript, along with d'Arblay's much neater annotation, include some interesting stages in the writing of *Edwy and Elgiva*. There are, for example, several scraps of nondramatic verse which tell the tale of Edwy and Elgiva and other scraps of drama in rhymed rather than blank verse. One scrap indicates a possible revision for the opening of act 2: "might begin with a Banquet scene— drums & trumpets. Edwy & the court entering as from the coronation. After taking their seats, a speech of welcome from the King. During the banquet, something sarcastic between Dunstan and the King or his friends, might create altercation and afterwards sullenness. which wd. make Edwy's retiring the more natural." This variant of act 2 is more attentive to theatricality and spectacle, indicating, as it does, the use of "drums & trumpets." The many versions of this tragedy suggest that Burney did intend to make revisions to the play before the production, or perhaps following it, with designs on publication.

The increased attention to Elgiva in the revised version, as Sabor notes, was something d'Arblay encouraged Burney to develop even further, by adding a plan for Elgiva's sacrifice of herself to save Edwy.[33] Burney's concern with Elgiva and, requisitely, with Siddons, is also reflected in a letter from d'Arblay to Charles Burney Jr., which Donkin does not note. D'Arblay indicates that Burney expressed to her brother an interest in having a more direct participation in the rehearsal process: she was, as Sabor reports, "eager to know of any criticisms of the play made by Charles, its 'principal *reader*' in the initial, pre-rehearsal reading, and by Siddons, the 'principal *hearer*.' She would thus be able to give the play 'a more theatrical *perfection*.'"[34] In considering Siddons her principal reader, in her efforts to increase the visibility of Elgiva, and in her postperformance observation that Siddons and Kemble were the only players to be admired, Burney demonstrates a practical sense of how to improve her play. Strengthening the female role, complicating the plot with the device of self-sacrifice, and emphasizing bodily suffering are logical improvements, especially given the rage for Siddons's performances of tragic roles.[35]

The story of Edwy and Elgiva (ca. 955) is found in eighteenth-century histories such as those by Robert Henry (*The History of Great Britain* [1771-93]), Tobias Smollett (*A Complete History of England* [1757-58]), Thomas Carte (*A General History of England* [1747-55]), M. (Paul) Rapin de Thoyras (*The History of England* [1724, trans. 1725-31]), and David Hume (*The History of England* [1754-63]). The story generally follows these lines: Edred, the brother of Edmund, ascended the throne upon Edmund's death, Edmund's sons being under age. During Edmund's reign, an Abbot, Dunstan, had gained increasing powers over the king and the allotment of funds to monasteries, subsequently crushing the secular clergy (those priests who were permitted to marry) and creating antagonism with them. On Edred's death, Edmund's son Edwy took the throne, and because of his hatred for Dunstan, began restoring power to the secular clergy and demanding from Dunstan an explanation of his unscrupulous use of the country's finances. Some historians write that Edwy fell in love with a woman named Elgiva, his kinswoman, and this apparently impious act, along with his accusations of Dunstan, led to the animosity between the king and the non-secular clergy. Dunstan left the country, but his popularity and the help of Edwy's younger brother, Edgar, allowed him to return. He eventually had Edwy excommunicated and replaced by Edgar.

During her time in court, Burney read Henry's *The History of Great Britain* (*DL,* 4:408). He mentions a "violent passion" which "Edwi" contracted for his cousin, and writes that their ensuing marriage was considered "a most horrid and unpardonable crime." In Henry's account, Elgiva "excited" Edwy to vengeance, which led to the banishment of Dunstan. Elgiva is referred to as "Queen" by Henry, who writes of her being branded and exiled. Returning later to England, Elgiva was "put to death, with circumstances of peculiar cruelty" and Edwy died of a broken heart.[36] Smollett, read by Burney in 1770, does not suggest that Edwy and "Athelgiva" are kin, but writes that Dunstan upbraided Edwy for his "effeminacy" rather than for his religious transgression. While Smollett does indicate that Edwy and Elgiva were divorced and that Elgiva was "branded in the face, and then exiled to Ireland," he does not suggest, as do other sources, that she returned to England. Edwy is said to have yielded to the "the torrent of misfortune" and he later withdrew "into a deep melancholy, which conducted him to the grave" two years later. In Smollett's account, Dunstan voluntarily exiles himself after he is accused and Edwy's main challenge is from his brother, "an ambitious prince, of very insinuating qualifications."[37]

Carte's history adds to Smollett's story the suggestion that without a papal dispensation for illegal marriages, "the husband passed for a wencher, as the wife did for a concubine or harlot." Burney uses each of these labels in her depiction of the accusations against Edwy and Elgiva. Carte quotes Malmesbury's note that Edwy was discovered by Dunstan "playing at ramps with his wife and her mother." In this version, the queen's face was disfigured with a hot iron, she was exiled, returned with a healed face, and was then hamstrung and put to death. Edwy and Elgiva are said to have been divorced in 958, after which Edwy died of natural causes "or treachery."[38]

De Thoyras's history is most intriguing. The initial story is unclear about the reason for Edwy and Dunstan's animosity, and suggests that Dunstan's voluntary exile and accusation of Edwy's impiety led to Edwy's death from "an excess of Melancholy." De Thoyras quotes possibly disreputable "*Monkish* writers" who say that Edwy "kept the Wife of one of his *Courtiers* for his *Mistress*." De Thoyras writes that "the King and his Mistress were so incensed against [Dunstan], that they would have proceeded to the taking away his Life, had he not prevented their wicked Design by voluntary Exile." The increasing perversity of the accusations against Edwy (the particulars about Elgiva) are relegated to footnotes, where de Thoyras writes in a gossipy tone: "[s]ome, to make the matter worse, say, he kept not only the Daughter, . . . but the Mother too, and that he was on the Bed between them both when *Dunstan* came to fetch him." A redemptive footnote, "[s]ome say she was his Wife," follows later, and added to it is a note that Elgiva was "branded" and "banished" by Odo, and upon returning, "Ham-string'd." Edwy's soul is said to be rescued from hell by Dunstan's prayers. De Thoyras closes the story of Edwy by pointing out that historians have variously elevated or condemned his actions.[39]

Hemlow proposes that Burney followed Hume's account of this story, but also found material for her tragedies "in the histories of Robert Henry and others."[40] Certainly Hume's history (which Burney refers to in her journal for 1768) makes the most explicit reference to the necessary connection between unacceptable female sexuality and religious power, going into some detail about the struggle between the secular and monastic clergy. In Hume's version, female sexuality and marriage are shown to be condemned in order to elevate the "grandeur" of the monastic order by contrast, which in turn elevated its control over the secular clergy and its monies: "a total abstinence from all commerce with the sex was deemed such a meritorious pennance, as was sufficient to atone for the greatest enormities. The consequence seemed natural, that those at least who officiated at the altar should be clear of this pollution. . . . Every instance of libertinism in any individual of [the secular clergy] was represented as a general corruption: And where other topics of defamation were wanting, their marriage became a sure subject of invective, and their wives received the name of *concubine*, or other more opprobrious appellation." Hume places Edwy's public marriage to Elgiva in this atmosphere of implied connections between economics, sexuality, and spirituality. Hume writes that Edwy was at war with the clergy before his coronation, when the incident in question provided an excuse for outright condemnation of him. Edwy, "attracted by softer pleasures," was in the queen's apartment, giving "reins to his fondness towards his wife, which was only moderately checked by the presence of her mother." They were discovered by Dunstan and Odo,

Edwy was upbraided for "lasciviousness," and Dunstan "probably bestowed on the queen the most opprobrious epithet that can be applied to her sex." Dunstan was then banished by Edwy, but his sway over the populace allowed Odo to have Elgiva seized and branded "in order to destroy that *fatal* beauty, which had *seduced* Edwy" (emphasis added). Thus, Hume does not forbear accusing Elgiva of responsibility for Edwy's impropriety. She is said to have returned, at which point she was "hamstringed; and expired a few days after at Glocester in the most acute torments." "[U]nhappy Edwy was excommunicated, and pursued with unrelenting vengeance" to his death.[41]

In Burney's play, Edwy and Elgiva are secretly married by the time of the action and Edwy resolves to make his marriage public as soon as his advisor, Aldhelm, speaks on his behalf to the clergy and gets its consent after the fact. Perhaps Burney chose to focus on a married couple in order to avoid the illicit sexual relationship of an unmarried pair, as is sometimes depicted in the histories. Aldhelm attempts to promote the idea of Edwy's marrying, but is dismissed. The clergy wishes only to discuss an impending reform of the convents, which will give it more power. The couple is discovered in Elgiva's chamber (with Eltruda, her attendant) and is accused of impiety. Edwy attempts to get the papal edict against their consanguinity revoked, while the monks, led by Dunstan, attempt to discredit the marriage. Edwy is told he must give up Elgiva, an act he agrees to at least until he can get their marriage sanctified. Elgiva is seized, injured, and exiled by Dunstan. He forms his plan of putting Edgar on the throne, but is himself exiled by Edwy for his misuse of state funds. Elgiva returns, they are threatened with excommunication, and she is again seized. Dunstan returns, supported by the populace, and civil war is declared. Edwy is torn between the war and his continued pursuit of Elgiva. The queen makes one last return, this time severely wounded, and is reunited with Edwy in an extended death scene. Upon her death, Edwy rushes into the fight, is wounded, and dies. Dunstan repents at last, and Aldhelm pronounces a final benediction on the couple.

While most of the histories noted above mention Elgiva, her role seems to be little more than incidental either narratologically or typographically, appearing as it often does in footnotes. When she is mentioned, it is consistently within the context of forbidden female sexuality, whether this taboo is due to consanguinity, sexual perversion, adultery, or her own desire for power. And while the queen is said to be punished in each account, the severity of the punishment also varies. *Edwy and Elgiva*, as the title suggests, is not exclusively about the queen, but comments on different forms of male power and authority, the conflict between church and state, the right use of reason by a ruler, and the relationship between a ruler and his people. I focus my reading here on Burney's representation of the way Elgiva is constructed as the antirational, licentious alternative to reason, good government, and moderate counsel. As such, she is a touchstone for every issue that confronts the king and his right to rule. Burney illuminates a lost side of history, exploring the effects of coercion on a female figure rather than depicting her only as a "by-the-way" figure to be accused of wrongdoing.

In *Edwy and Elgiva*, the relationship between Edwy and Dunstan is dominated by how each man views Elgiva, which influences in turn his view of his opponent. The possession or loss of the female body and the public image of this body are used or appealed to alternately by Edwy and Dunstan in order to achieve dominance over the other. For Edwy, Elgiva represents not only the object of sexual desire, but the threat of transgression, excommunication, and political impotence. Dunstan translates Edwy's physical, sexual association with Elgiva into his own political control over Edwy, based on a rhetorical construction of Elgiva as sexually dangerous. Dunstan's control of Edwy and Elgiva is not merely rhetorical, but enacts itself in physical domination that has sexual overtones. Elgiva is thus positioned physically and conceptually between husband and celibate; both see her in terms of her sexuality and associate this sexuality with political and religious control. Dunstan's desire to maintain Edwy in an exclusively male community, away from Elgiva, is also not without its strong homosocial dynamic.

Whether she is dominated by Edwy or Dunstan, Elgiva is uniformly overridden by male controlling figures. Her complete submission to Edwy is part of Burney's interrogation of sexual and political hierarchies and the points at which such hierarchies intersect, for it is precisely in Elgiva's submission to her husband—proper wifely duty—that she is most useful as a tool against him. As she says, "I have no fear, my Lord, if you have none; / I have no dread, if you are free from doubt. / My Honour rests on your's; my Happiness / My Faith, my Trust, all own no other Guardian" (I.v.46-49). In representing Elgiva as subordinate to and reliant on Edwy, Burney emphasizes Elgiva's complete lack of self-determination, and the vulnerability that institutions such as marriage and the domestic sphere demand of women. Elgiva is a political subject and a wife; her relative lack of power in both positions renders her unable to defend herself against external forces of coercion.

Elgiva's significance to Edwy as a devoted wife is rivaled by her importance to Dunstan as a demonized female threat, the fear of which he can use to his advantage politically. Dunstan publicizes an image of Elgiva that constructs her as sexually deviant and politically dangerous. In fact, his fascination with discussing Elgiva's sexuality rivals the obsession of which he accuses Edwy. Her provocative but tainted body is represented by verbal labels that serve as the prominent vehicles for accusations against Edwy, in the same fashion as her body is co-opted physically by Dunstan and Edwy. Alternately chaste wife or "courtesan" and "concubine," she becomes for Dunstan part of a public discussion of Edwy's piety, his ability to govern, and the security of his kingdom. When Dunstan initially reveals to Odo the alliance between Edwy and Elgiva, the latter is said to represent "black ruin through seduction's wiles, / Shameless" as she "allures" the king to "lawless vows, / Of impious love" (I.ii.8-11). The connection between spiritual, sexual, and political acceptability is the point on which the condemnation of Edwy rests. The main strategy of Edwy's accusers is to make explicit comparisons between the king's governance and his illegal and impious marriage to Elgiva, "[e]ntranc'd" as he is in "one absorbing passion" (I.ix.22). This is achieved by figuring the marriage as bordering "on blasphemy" (I.xi.107) and the wife as corrupt. If the union is not dissolved, in Dunstan's words, "Ruin on ruin falls upon our Heads.— / The papal power arraign'd—its justice scoff'd— / A Courtezan upheld—" (III.v.95-97). Dunstan's goals—the removal of Edwy from the throne, the reestablishment of the clergy's power—require a specific view of Elgiva's destructive potential and her removal from the political sphere.

The oral, public sexualization and condemnation of Elgiva are effectively represented in Burney's use of dialogue, because for Dunstan Elgiva ceases to have any individual identity beyond her sexuality and she becomes synonymous with abstract, feminized concepts that take the place of her name. He sees her allegorically, holding "England's King in base seduction's arms!" (II.iii.4), a "blot" on the "reign / A stain indelible" (II.iii.7-9). With repeated condemnations and the suggestion that Elgiva will "madden [Edwy] to ruin" (III.v.121), Dunstan connects Edwy's passion for his wife with political downfall that the country should not tolerate. Dunstan portrays himself as his country's spiritual and political savior, a status he achieves through his condemnation of Elgiva as both "Courtezan" and "Pernicious Concubine" (II.x.15, 18). The progress of the misconstrual extends from Elgiva's sexual threat (her "seduction's wiles"), to Edwy's impiety, the loss of religious integrity, and the collapse, by implication, of the state he should protect.

Dunstan enacts his power over Edwy through his condemnation of Elgiva to the point that Edwy himself is suspicious of his wife. While Elgiva's sexual guilt as the seductress is unchallenged, Edwy is given a way to avoid transgression, to be spared from the taint of base female sexuality. Dunstan thus tells Edwy, "Thou art safe. She's—lost" (II.v.48), and that he must "Remove her from [his] Sight; / 'Twere impious, henceforth, but to look at her" (II.v.52-53). The accusation, "She is undone. Take heed for her Undoer!" (II.v.59), makes Elgiva the partner exclusively condemned for the marriage. To this end, Edwy himself becomes doubtful of his right to marry Elgiva. Edwy first distances himself from her mentally, having become consumed by "Repentant horrour" (II.vi.11), and then vows physical separation as well: "—O Elgiv! I will fly thy *dangerous* Sight, / Nor listen to thy voice, nor speak to thee / Till I obtain the sanction of a Synod / To ratify our Union—" (II.vi.12-15, emphasis added). Reflecting on Dunstan's words, Edwy voices the accusations against her but cannot help but turn to her: "Impious to look at her!— / O fair— dread Object of my condemnation! / How look at ought beside!—Ah! fly Me, Elgiv!—" (II.vii.13-15). This interpretation of Elgiva forces her to take action (remove herself from him) and effectively denies her Edwy's protection and makes her vulnerable to Dunstan's control. Linguistic labels are shown to have clear effects on female physical autonomy and safety, as surely as they create a confined and condemned verbal space for the female figure.

Elgiva's image is manipulated verbally by Dunstan through his constructions of her sexuality as dangerous, religiously transgressive, and politically disruptive. Burney also uses the stage in *Edwy and Elgiva* in order to represent in visual, spatial terms Elgiva's physical position between men in conflict. Although the character of Elgiva appears in only a small number of scenes (fourteen of seventy-three), her presence or absence, the settings she enters, and under whose control she is are central facets of all of the dramatic action. The private space in which Edwy may indulge his desire for Elgiva is presented in opposition to the public space in which he might deny or defend this desire. By contrast, Elgiva is *forced* into the public eye through Dunstan's speeches of condemnation and then is physically removed from her seclusion, a movement that reverses more typical uses of confinement in Gothic drama. Kate Ferguson Ellis writes that ". . . the terror of the Gothic heroine is simply that of being confined and then abandoned, and beyond that, of being, in an unspecified yet absolute way, completely surrounded by superior male power."[42] Elgiva does not move consistently from freedom to confinement, but rather has forms of confinement exchanged without her consultation. Elgiva is Burney's least self-determining female figure, a figure almost entirely at the mercy of others' language and action. Pfister's distinction between story, where figures have control over the action, and event, where they do not, is relevant and in this case, gender-specific: Elgiva's experiences may be seen exclusively as events, for she is a "human subject . . . incapable of making a deliberate choice."[43] She participates in almost no desire or action except those which originate from others.

From the opening scene, the possession of Elgiva is allied with male participation in either the private, domestic sphere (equated with the female and the unacceptable), or the public, male sphere of government. The opening scene's "*Magnificent gothic Chamber*" contains two entrances: a private, hidden door which leads to Elgiva's apartment, and a public, state door. That Edwy guards the access to the "secret door" to Elgiva's "chambers" is undeniably sexual in overtone and represents physically the mutually exclusive alternatives for Edwy: the sexual and marital possession of the queen, or public duty. Our first glimpse of Elgiva shows her in a public space, but she is there secretly and fears discovery. After this, she never occupies public space except as the wounded victim of Dunstan's machinations, which further underscores the co-optation of her body by political agenda. She does not attend Edwy's coronation (which would be a sign of the legitimacy of their marriage), and accusations against her occur when representatives of the state burst into her apartment in act 2.

The female sphere, represented on stage by Elgiva's private chambers, is seen by Dunstan as a realm of the effeminate that threatens the ruler's very masculinity. Dunstan's misogyny leads him to define state government as something that cannot permit dalliance with a woman. He thus condemns both Elgiva and marriage in general by elevating over them the male, public arena of the clerical and the celibate, in a manner that is clearly homosocial. To Edwy's advisor, Aldhelm, who defends the marriage, Dunstan replies, "Whom should he seek, on whom bestow his friendship / If not on those with holy rites invested? / Here, in the priesthood, let him find his solace" (III.iv.31-33). Dunstan's ostensible fear is that Edwy will inadvisably entrust state secrets to his wife, and again, significantly, his language reflects an emphasis on the sexualized and fragmented female body: "Wouldst thou have Edwy trust a female Breast / With state transactions? / . . . / Trifles like those a monarch should disdain" (III.iv.45-50). Aldhelm, because of his defense of Edwy, is similarly suspected of an approval of women, which for Dunstan is incomprehensible. He forces Aldhelm to defend himself: "Heard I aright? speaks Aldhelm thus of marriage? / Of Women?—Nobles! . . . / Beseech the holy Bishop to explain / Lest on your mind's remain some strange suspicion" (III.iv.54-57). Heterosexual desire is uniformly suspected as a "threaten'd mischief" (III.iv.66), against which these "guardians of the Land" must "Assert [them]selves" (III.iv.67). As the object of this desire, Elgiva is the center of all attention and fear.

The rhetorical conceptualization of the female and male spheres, associated as they are with forms of sexual desire, has its corollary in the movement of figures on the stage and the level of access they have to stage settings. Except for a few instances, Elgiva is also not depicted as entering or exiting scenes independently, but, rather, the denial of her autonomous physical movements illustrates her figurative position as a political pawn. She is initially led by the treacherous Leofric to the state chambers. Later, in what should be sequestered chambers, she endures the accusations of Dunstan and is led out, fainting, between Edwy and her serving woman, Eltruda. When Dunstan seizes her again, she is gagged and *"force[d] . . . off"* by his ruffians (II.x). While Dunstan's position as celibate monk and announced misogynist is articulated clearly, he nonetheless maintains a threat of sexual violation that ensures Elgiva's submission to him, though it is never carried out. During Dunstan's initial seizure of Elgiva, her main fear is that her honor remain "untainted" (II.x.12), which might be considered a statement of her fear of what Ellis describes as the "omnipresent sense of impending rape" in the Gothic.[44] The threat of sexual violation that accompanies the first "rape" or seizure of Elgiva underscores the emphasis on the physicality of the female figure depicted on the stage, whether or not this violation takes place.

After Elgiva is seized, her body, mangled and pushed toward madness, reappears repeatedly and in increasingly severe forms of deterioration that symbolize male potency and the usefulness of the figure of the suffering woman to a display of male authority.[45] As Scarry notes, the *visibility* of torture is essential to a successful communication of an authoritative body's or individual's ability to punish.[46] Elgiva's first return, "Spent and exhausted" (III.viii.38), is accompanied by her fright at the imagined pursuing footsteps of her torturers, after which the figure is again led off the stage. We learn by the next scene that Elgiva has been publicly declared Edwy's queen, but, significantly, Burney at no time depicts her in this role in our sight; rather, another figure announces that she has again been "Torn from her home and husband," with cries that "rent the Heavens" (IV.i.28). This time Dunstan's ruffians are instructed to kill her, and they assert that her "blood gush'd out" at the attack (V.i.3). Elgiva is the sacrificial victim that reminds Edwy of his submission to Dunstan and that testifies to Dunstan's treachery.

With Dunstan's final seizure of Elgiva, her body is explicitly used as capital that is exchanged between men competing for religious and political authority. Edwy can either give up Elgiva as his queen in exchange for their absolution, or see Dunstan, the "Idol" of the people, take control of the kingdom (IV.vii.14). Forced as he is either to "lose her, or [himself] condemn her" (IV.vii.56), Edwy's alternatives between the monarchy and his marriage are narrowed considerably and his refusal to listen to his counselors' reasoned urgings leaves him only with the civil war in which he is killed.

Elgiva's final return, *"with a Bandage tied across her Breast, tottering, and leaning upon ELTRUDA,"* shows the progress of her madness as she reenacts the horror of her torture (V.iii).[47] This final reunion with

Edwy is perhaps the most notable change Burney makes to her sources, some of which mention a second torture, but none of which recalls any reunion with the king. Burney thus rewrites her historical sources to include a final confrontation between the object of desire and torture, her accuser, and her politically impotent lover. In de Lauretis's analysis, narrative is traditionally masculinist, focused on the male subject as "hero" who seeks out some form of self-definition (see chapter 1). Here, Elgiva's repeated circling back to Edwy disrupts momentarily the narrative of the king's rise and tragic fall by calling attention instead to her victimization by the political circumstances. Elgiva's suffering and punishment are not only physically embodied onstage (something that, as reviewers acknowledged, was unfortunately diffused in the production of the play, which had Siddons reclining on a couch), but are emphasized by her bandages and reenacted in her startled movements and speeches to now absent torturers.[48] She pleads, "O come not near me! / Murder me not!" (V.iii.25-26), and resolves to see Edwy one last time. She returns, "pale, pale and bloodless!" (V.xi.11) and dies, murdered by Dunstan so that he might control Edwy and, through his pawn, Edgar, the kingdom.

The presence of the dead, mangled female body signifies two things for Dunstan: his authoritative ability to punish and his guilt. Elgiva's body may also be read as a sign dual in nature for other on- and offstage viewers, because it is symbolic both of pleasure, in its distance from the spectator (which "implies the safe position of a spectator"[49]), and fear, in the threat to physical and sexual identity that the body represents. Joanna Baillie comments on the usefulness to tragedy of viewing suffering in the "Introductory Discourse" to A Series of Plays (1798): "In examining others we know ourselves. With limbs untorn, with head unsmitten, with senses unimpaired by despair, we know what we ourselves might have been on the rack, on the scaffold, and in the most afflicting circumstances of distress."[50] In Burney's play, the corpse remains onstage throughout the final scenes while a search is undertaken for peasants who will move from "this public Path" (V.xv.4) the body that has been used both physically and metaphorically as a path between men and between a king and his people.[51] It is the sight of the corpse that moves Dunstan to remorse:

> Her lifeless frame—that deed is surely done.
> True, as the Villain said, her look is innocent—
> Would I had not encounter'd it!—a sickness
> Deadly, unfelt before, benumbs, confounds me—
> Where may she be?—Who sent her hence?—Was't I?—
> By what authority?—Hush! Enquiry!—Hah!—[V.xviii.8-13]

Dunstan's only desire is to be "innocent of the blood of Elgiv, / The crying wrongs of Edwy!" (V.xx.10-11). Elgiva's corpse, one last time, evokes connections between the spiritual and the political, the control of one body over another, the body's physical presence, and its spiritual residence. Any potential erotocism is downplayed by Dunstan's references to Elgiva's innocence and his own culpability.

In the last two acts of the play, the conflict between Edwy and Dunstan and their individual pursuits for power becomes increasingly focused on the female body, its presence, its substance as wife and queen, and its susceptibility to physical violence. Elgiva's value as a woman and as the monarch's wife lies entirely in her body, in which is entwined her sexual identity, virtue, and religious purity. The play's final scene, of "slaughter'd innocence" and "mangled bodies" (V.xxiii.26), portrays the last use to which the state and the church puts Elgiva, as a symbol, along with Edwy, of "Virtue oppress'd" (V.xxiii.27) and of heaven's reward in the afterlife.

Burney shows throughout *Edwy and Elgiva* the incorporation of the female body, female virtue, and female sexuality in political struggles; the connections between Elgiva's sexuality, Edwy's piety and right to govern, and the state's protection are made repeatedly. When Elgiva is physically present on the stage, she is accused, frightened, wounded, and forced into madness and death. In her physical absence, she is verbally present as the object of scorn and is used to hold Edwy hostage to an enemy's political and religious authority. Her value to the state exists in its ability to define her sexual and moral identity and exists only in tandem with her relationships to men. In Burney's other tragedies, *Hubert De Vere, The Siege of Pevensey*, and *Elberta*, female bodies are also of the utmost importance, and again, these bodies are shuffled between men, held hostage, manipulated, and forced to die, all as pawns in male games, all in the interest of political power and the maintenance or subversion of hierarchies.

The married, childless woman is a threat to state authority if she distracts a political figure from his job. Once a woman becomes a mother, the potential for her to interfere with politics is increased dramatically because she has produced children who might challenge a ruler, or worse, who might be illegitimate. Many serious dramas of the end of the century feature a solitary, married female figure who is often linked with her father and who *is* a mother herself, but who seldom *has* a mother, as in *The Siege of Sinope*, by Frances Brooke (1781), and *The Fate of Sparta,* by Hannah Cowley (1788). These mother figures generally nurture sons, which prompts a consideration of the social position of women as biological links between generations and families. Elberta is just such a link, important as a biological resource that must be carefully regulated because her children pose a legitimate challenge to a usurper's political ambitions.

Burney's last tragedy also considers the events of a political struggle, this time in the distant past of postconquest England. The use of the historical past was common in late-eighteenth-century tragedies. One practical advantage this practice gave writers was the ability to refashion contemporary events in terms of a time past, in order to avoid the censorship that might have come with direct depictions of political upheaval or controversy. Herbert Lindenberger suggests that an added attraction of this transference was that it flattered the audience. He argues that "writers could seek out periods in which an older, reactionary view of life was colliding with some newer, more attractive dispensation: by identifying with the proponents of the new, the audience not only would feel it was experiencing the force of historical continuity, but it could flatter itself for being on the side of progress."[52] Given Burney's position in the king's court and her comparison of events there to tragedies, her experiences of female confinement and torture might in psychological terms have been easier to contemplate in this historically displaced form. Her use of the antique, though, could invite her audience not so much to feel superior to the barbarities of its ancestors as to observe the continuity of history where female oppression is concerned.[53] In comedies, where the effects of a patriarchal regulation of the female are less obviously (hence more insidiously) destructive, temporal alterations may be less immediately necessary to writers; few comic writers tended to place their plays in the past, by contrast to the writers of tragedy.

Elberta resembles Burney's other three tragedies in that it depicts the suffering of a solitary female figure, in this case the titular heroine, who is a political pawn. What makes the character of Elberta and the trials she endures different from those in Burney's other tragedies is the fact that she is a mother. Her drive to protect her family makes her Burney's most self-directing tragic heroine. Elberta's social status is complicated by the fact that her marriage and motherhood are generally unknown. She is thus treated as unmarried, a trait her opponent, Offa, wishes to exploit, thinking that marriage to her would bring fortune and status. Elberta is defined initially as a political and marital commodity (as a daughter of an important man), then as a wife who must endure her husband's reprobation and sacrifice of himself to the competing demands of war and family, and finally as a mother who suffers the starvation and kidnapping of her children. *Elberta* encompasses in one play the range of female experience that appears in Burney's tragedies.

While critics have tended to label *Elberta* as fragmentary, this term is somewhat misleading. The narrative of the play is completely conceived, but the rendering of it in a finished form is not. The play and notes for its composition survive on over three hundred fragments of paper that are preserved in no particular order (though the pieces have been numbered

by a modern hand) in the Berg Collection. Stewart J. Cooke's organization of these scraps into a coherent narrative suggests, as Sabor notes,
that *Elberta* "is much closer to completion than had previously been believed . . . [and] can now be read as a whole and fruitfully compared to
Burney's three previous tragedies."[54] The manuscript fragments for
Elberta resemble the manuscripts of Burney's other plays in their indication of ongoing composition and refinement over a long period of time.
She began writing the tragedy in the summer of 1791, shortly before she
left the queen's service. Sabor notes an unpublished journal entry in
which Burney contrasts *The Siege of Pevensey* with *Elberta*: the former
"was not dismal enough" and she returned to this new work of "deepest
Tragedy, which first had occurred to [her] in the worst part of [her] illness in January."[55] Burney worked on the play well into the 1800s. One
general plot outline, for example, is on paper with a watermark of 1815.
Other fragments are on notebooks, old letters, and envelopes dated between December 1785 and January 1811 and on calendars from August,
September, and October 1814.[56]

There are comparisons to be made between *Elberta* and *The
Wanderer* (1814), which Burney worked on during the same period. With
a presumed identity that varies as situations and environments change,
Elberta strongly resembles Juliet in *The Wanderer*. Although Juliet is not
defined by maternal obligations, she is forced to fend off the attentions of
the men around her because her married status is not publicly known. But
while Juliet seems destined to be "the wanderer," seeking in numerous
places and employments some security from want and aimlessness, Elberta
is not distracted by others' interpretations of her, though she cannot avoid
them. She wanders only to return to her family, seeking her children's welfare with a singleness of mind and ambition. While Juliet's and Elberta's
stories open at similar points, featuring metaphorical confinements of
choice demanded by secrecy or the literal restriction of bodily freedom en-
tailed by political struggle, they progress differently. Elberta's maternal re-
sponsibilities emerge as the forces that direct all of her actions, and she
seeks familial integrity in the face of political incursions.

Though many details of the plot of *Elberta* are missing, a general story
is evident. Elberta is the daughter of the late Ethelbert, who was a protec-
tor of Edgar Atheling. Her tormentor is her father's murderer, Offa,
Commander of Mercia. Before the time of the action, Elberta was captured
by Offa's men and taken to (or somehow meets) his heir, Arnulph. She and
Arnulph fell in love and were secretly married. Elberta was hidden in a cottage for five years, giving birth to two children during this time. The play
opens when a general amnesty has been granted by William of Normandy
to those loyal to Edgar Atheling. Elberta has again been imprisoned by

Offa in her father's castle, and he wants to marry her to gain her right to her father's status. She is entrusted to the care of Ceolric (a friend of her father's), is briefly visited by Arnulph, and then escapes to her children, heirs to both Mercia and East Anglia, who have been moved to a cottage nearby. To prevent this familial line from gaining power, Offa seeks to have the children killed. The family moves to a cave, and there suffers near starvation. Arnulph exchanges a casket (perhaps Elberta's) for food, though he had promised to deliver this casket, on Ceolric's behalf, to Offa. This compromises his honor as a public citizen and a soldier. The children are kidnapped by one of Offa's agents but are rescued by Elberta's servants. Arnulph dies after being wounded in a fight with Offa's soldiers, leaving Elberta in charge of the children, with a calm resolve against grieving.[57]

There is a strong element of Gothicism in *Elberta*. The heroine is confined by her opponent in a seized castle and later seeks refuge in a cave. As Sabor notes, these settings could have been spectacularly and elaborately staged.[58] Elberta's situation is particularly Gothic in the sense that Sedgwick describes: she is persistently shut off from that which defines her most completely, her family. She continually attempts to reunify the family, but it is repeatedly under siege, initially when the mother is separated from her children and later when the father threatens to leave and finally does. In some respects, the family in this play functions as a conventional tragic figure that is ruptured by divided loyalties and aims. On one side is Elberta's main concern: the welfare of the children and the distinct possibility that they might starve. Nourishment—or the lack of it—becomes her focus as she calls repeatedly for food and describes her children's deteriorating health. On the other side of the family is Arnulph, who is divided against himself. Elsewhere, Burney questions the way maternal identity is constructed (in *The Woman-Hater,* especially), but in *Elberta* the heroine's maternal imperative legitimates her activity and permits her, unlike Burney's other dramatic heroines, to be almost entirely self-directing.

Burney's dramatic depictions of motherhood can be read as participating in the general redescription of motherhood that was ongoing over the course of the eighteenth century. The gradual shift in attitudes towards motherhood that took place at this time has been much discussed.[59] Critics contend that the combined forces of imperial expansion, sentimentalism, and economics prompted a domestication and idealization of maternity that saw middle-class women encouraged (or forced) to turn their attentions from material to biological productivity in the interest of producing citizens who might contribute to British imperial projects as consumers and explorers. This newly emergent ideal of domestic, middle-class maternity was accompanied by changes to medical practices and to attitudes toward breastfeeding and a stratification that increasingly differentiated between women of different classes and races on the basis of their activities as mothers.[60] An ideology of maternity as ideally nurturing and devoted to the interests of society and family, yet passive, is described by Felicity Nussbaum, who writes, "[n]ew attention to the management of children, and to the affectionate bond between mothers and children, idealized women's socializing and educational role over their children while recruiting those women to a domesticity associated with the national destiny. New ideologies of maternal affection and sentiment between mothers and children, conflicting with the nascent doctrine of feminist individualism, encouraged women to adjust to a domestic life compatible with the pursuit of empire."[61] Mary Wollstonecraft advocated women's education as a means of strengthening "the progress of knowledge and virtue" and made just the equation between motherhood and nation building that Nussbaum describes. Wollstonecraft argues in *A Vindication of the Rights of Woman* (1792) that, "[i]f children are to be educated to understand the true principle of patriotism, their mother must be a patriot; and the love of mankind, from which an orderly train of virtues spring, can only be produced by considering the moral and civil interest of mankind; but the education and situation of woman, at present, shuts her out from such investigations."[62]

As the maternal impulse was refined and granted central importance as a female duty, deviations from it were likewise rendered increasingly as suspect and subject to regulation and punishment. Lower-class and racially "Othered" mothers were often dismissed or demonized as monstrous and were seldom allowed to identify with the same maternal ideal that motivated their middle-class counterparts. The failure of the middle-class mother was also feared: "the domestic woman gained power to shape the public realm, particularly the nation, through procreation and education of her children. If the 'natural' instinct for motherhood is somehow absent or twisted, the 'unnatural mother' refuses these duties and is instead capable of heinous acts that threaten lineage and even civilization itself."[63] Marilyn Francus suggests that the increased emphasis on the ideal mother created a new form of maternal monstrosity as its counterpart after the midcentury: "[t]he refusal to mother is the only active monstrosity available to the domesticated mother. . . . As female integrity becomes determined by maternal service to her children, female power is displaced onto her children, her spouse, and society, all of whom assess her success or failure. Yet because active mothering ultimately requires the good mother to be recessive, she is akin to her absent counterpart. Accordingly, both the angel in the house and the absent mother lead to a remarginalization of the mother as a literary subject in eighteenth-century literature."[64] Burney's representations of motherhood provide interesting literary illustrations of these attitudes toward mothering: she depicts both the ideal mother and women accused of maternal deviance. Unfortunately, these portrayals of motherhood have been almost entirely overlooked by critics of her work in favor of a concentration on Burney's relationship with her father, that Doody describes as a "religion." Doody argues by contrast that Burney perpetually suffered abandonment by mother figures, beginning with the death of her own mother.[65] Certainly, mothers are conspicuous in their absence from the novels. Only Camilla has a living mother, but even Mrs. Tyrold's maternal influence is limited by her long departure from the location of most of the novel's action. The mothers of all of Burney's other novelistic heroines are dead, their influence passed on to a father or guardian.

Elberta and The Woman-Hater (see chapter 6) contain complex representations of mother figures and portray in detail the various ramifications that an ideology of domesticated maternity could have for women. (A mother figure appears in A Busy Day as well, but in this play Burney critiques parenting more than mothering specifically.) Burney shows the role of mother to be one regulated by male figures who seek to use female reproductivity as a tool to substantiate their own desire for political and familial authority. Requisitely, these male figures punish women whose mothering transgresses the bounds of married, middle-class maternity. Burney's mother figures move between the demanding poles of striving to be good mothers, on the one hand, while suffering regulation and punishment, on the other, when the nurturing of children has the undesired effect of throwing marriages, class distinctions, male reputations, and governments into upheaval. Burney is attentive as well to how the maternal ideal varies with social class. Her conclusion seems to be that the strict regulation of maternal impulses makes active motherhood a role that cannot be fulfilled without serious suffering or punishment, or at least the debilitating fear of punishment. Burney shows the process that demonizes the "absent mother" and the lower-class mother in The Woman-Hater, while the maternal impulse to nurture and protect is shown in Elberta to run counter to the interests of male heroism and male political superiority and therefore to have negative physical effects on the female protagonist. While Elberta is not a middle-class mother, the ideals that are shown to underlie attitudes toward her do conform to those outlined above: she is supposed to be passive and nurturing. Her refusal of this passive role allows her to bridge the gap between maternal self-sacrifice and self-direction, but also exposes her to her husband's criticisms.

Burney's depictions of motherhood shed some light on her view of dramatic narrative and generic fluidity as well. Male figures in Elberta and The Woman-Hater fear the maternal body because its reproductivity is potentially disruptive of social orders and hierarchies; legitimate or illegitimate heirs can challenge a male figure's political or familial authority. In *The Woman-Hater*, the unregulated female body jeopardizes familial legitimacy, opens the door to lower-class usurpation, and fragments the patriarchal family. *Elberta* focuses on a noble mother of a regal heir and male figures who believe that political authority thus necessitates the control of Elberta and her ability to reproduce. This patriarchal perception of woman as a reproductive vessel that must be regulated has its narratological counterpart, as I discuss in chapter 1. De Lauretis writes that narrativity "specifies and even produces the masculine position as that of mythical subject, and the feminine position as mythical obstacle or, simply, the space in which that movement occurs." Narrative reconstructs the world as a "two-character drama in which the human person creates and recreates *himself* out of an abstract or purely symbolic other—the womb, the earth, the grave, the woman."[66] If narrative conventionally envisions women as spaces, a narrative that includes mother figures potentially intensifies this dynamic because the creative female space is both literal and figurative, both an element of the story's subject matter and its plot pattern. In *Elberta*, such a spatialized dismissal of the female is resisted. Burney shows how male figures envision Elberta as both reproductive space and obstacle, but she disrupts the male pursuit of authority in a counternarrative that focuses on maternal impulses. The mother figure challenges the male figures' efforts to create themselves in the image of political triumph, paternal authority, or martial heroism. Burney even goes so far as to announce that the heroic is misguided and self-destructive; female resolve survives male heroism.

Despite superficial differences between *Elberta* and *The Woman-Hater*, the two plays share a number of similarities that suggest a connection between Burney's view of maternity, her use of generic conventions, and her disruptions of social, gender, and genre hierarchies. *The Woman-Hater* is generically extremely fluid. It is sentimentally comic in its ending, but is very much a narrowly averted tragedy. Its themes—female licentiousness, its threat to male social status, and the abandonment of feminine responsibility—are familiar to late-eighteenth-century tragedies.[67] Burney imaginatively cast Sarah Siddons and John Philip Kemble in the roles of Eleonora and Wilmot in *The Woman-Hater*; the fame of these players' performances of tragic roles was widespread and their appearance in a comedy could only substantiate the tragic undertones of the story. The trials of mothers are thus not only relegated to Burney's drama, but are found more specifically in a tragedy and a comedy with serious tragic undertones. These plays might imply that female experience has more potential for being "tragic"—either in generic or more general, experiential terms—when motherhood is involved, because a woman's body and her sexuality are then more intensely connected with patriarchal lineage and, in the case of *Elberta*, with the security of the nation itself. Given the contemporary connection between national identity and maternal reponsibility, transgression against the maternal invites the destruction and purgation so familiar to tragedy. Further, because tragedy is conventionally focused on the masculine, a tragic narrative about maternal self-reliance and survival, in the case of Burney's plays, is that much more challenging to gendered generic expectations. While the reunion of the Wilmot family at the end of *The Woman-Hater* is comic in providing reintegration, reunion, and reevaluation, it serves to reestablish male authority with a tragic undertone that lingers beyond the play's close. In *Elberta*, the catharsis of extreme emotion is as much that of the female character, who survives to observe her husband's and her persecutor's destruction, as it is our own.

The Woman-Hater concentrates on the coercive potential of an ideology of maternal self-sacrifice. *Elberta* emphasizes the strength that such an ideal might give women when all female action is motivated by an adherence to just such an ideal and all other social roles (of wife, particularly) are subordinated to the role of mother. While the maternal role in *The Woman-Hater* leaves both Eleonora and the nurse reined in by others' evaluations of them, Elberta achieves a degree of independence and agency because of this same role, though she is no less vulnerable because of it. These plays share the view that maternity is circumscribed by male authority, for each mother figure is chastised for elevating the maternal over the wifely and over male authority and honor.

In the first section of the tragedy, Elberta resembles Burney's other heroines because she is perceived to be a marriageable virgin. Her opponent has already seized her father's property and possessed his castle, which he fears refunding to her in the event that she marries another man and has children. Offa thus seeks to use Elberta in a variety of ways, all to secure himself financially and politically. Offa seems to be the male heir named in Elberta's father's will, so he considers three options: accusing her of treason and confining her as a "Prisoner of State" (I.viii.25) so that he may keep "the Inheritance . . . still [his] own" (I.ii.8), blackmailing her with treasonous papers of her father's (I.vii.4-5), or marrying her himself and sending "Saxred to prepare her for an abrupt courtship" (variants I.iv.11-12, El. 63), which he determines to do. The effort to rush the marriage is of paramount importance because an envoy bringing amnesty to Elberta arrives and asks Offa to hand over this prisoner, who is newly given "refuge" by "conquering William" (I.i.11, 13).

The offer of marriage comes to Elberta when she is most vulnerable. She is isolated and tells her guard, Ceolric, about her sense of solitariness in terms reminiscent of *The Wanderer*: "Sever'd from every tie of human fondness, / . . . / Alien and orphan in her native land / . . . / Sever'd from . . . all! all! all!—" (I.x.7-15, third ellipsis in the original). Ceolric comments to Elberta about Offa's proposal in a statement that constitutes the most explicit criticism of coerced marriages to be found in Burney's drama (a similar comment appears in *Love and Fashion*): "The common race of men view youth and beauty / As sole ingredients for the nuptial knot; / Their own choice satisfied, they ask no more" (I.x.36-38). Elberta's response to this statement reflects her present turmoil: "ill [men] scan / The delicate female Heart, and ill conceive / It's secret agony, its latent horrour, / It's bitter pangs, from exquisite disgust—" (I.x.45-48). Despite Elberta's status as a married woman, which should make her invulnerable to Offa's proposals, she must suffer nonetheless because she cannot avow her marriage without implicating her husband as a traitor. In this respect, she resembles Elgiva, Geralda (*Hubert De Vere*), and Adela (*The Siege of Pevensey*), whose "choices" are presented to them as influencing male security as well as their own safety.

Despite Offa's threats, Elberta is shown in numerous fragments to be a character of strong convictions. She is "firm in innocence—and . . . disdainful—" (El. 28; Sabor, 235), even when faced by imprisonment and accusations of treason. The captive Elberta is introduced to us as a figure who is certainly distraught, but not defeated. In her self-possession, she is unique among Burney's tragic heroines. She meets secretly with Arnulph and, while he appears doubtful about her eagerness to see her children, she doubts not that she acts rightly: "No!—think of the joy! / . . . / O but to hold them to my Breast once more! / Think of the bliss to see them once again / . . . / And view the opening smile of dawning memory / That cries Ah! is that you, my mother?" (I.xii.27-36). When Offa interrupts this secret meeting, Elberta declares,

> All that is female in me now of fears
> Confusion, terror, and timidity
> I banish, to give place to firmer virtues.
> Slander calls forth a courage new to me,
> A vigour that disdains to shield itself
> . . . .
> Our sexe's modesty becomes a traitor
> To honour, liberal worth, and noble feelings
> . . . .
> Far from the praise retir'd of female modesty
> Be the mute silence that submits to slander
> Her fair unspotted chastity of fame. [I.xiii.1-14]

Burney represents Elberta's strength, which she derives from her concerns for husband and children, as something summoned by downplaying the stereotypical feminine virtues of modesty and silence.

Unlike the other tragic heroines, who suffer extreme physical and mental degradation and decay, Elberta does not become increasingly controlled by another; she turns her energies toward her children's security, rather than seek the preservation of male figures and their political aims.[68] She privileges her children's welfare over the possibility that her guard, Ceolric, might be punished; she demands that others seek food for her children; she assertively rejects the public in favor of the private. Elberta actively fights the trespass of the political onto the domestic rather than lamenting its threat or being overcome by it. Ceolric is supposed to deliver a casket to Offa, but she persuades him instead to go to her children in their cottage. Arnulph cannot guard the children because he is about to return to his post (variants II.v). He does, however, offer to deliver the casket. Again, Elberta summons up a picture of her children in order to persuade Ceolric to help her:

> There they may wait, and wander, and expire—
> O were they here! . . .
> Their little Hands, uplifted, should implore—
> Should
> With eloquence that distances all words—
> The very picture distances all words—
> O pity! pity! generous Ceolric! [II.v.11-17, ellipsis in original]

This character is perhaps Burney's most complex rendering of a woman in a tragic plight. The strongly gendered tendencies toward caregiving and familial preservation are linked with an equally strong sense of individual assertiveness that resists the demands of the public sphere on the private.

Familial and political allegiances alter greatly once Elberta is reunited with her family and from here on the figure's maternity is increasingly emphasized. She flees her captivity, fearing the illness of one of her children. Arnulph, who is also at the cottage, represents her action as a hasty, foolish, and dishonorable political mistake. He asks how, from a mind like hers, "So little spoken by its sexe's weaknesses / So open, noble, / Could [he] expect this? Frivolous impatience / Should have no weight in Honour's scale" (III.vii.21-24). When she defends herself and asks what tie is "superior to [the] paternal," he replies that honor is "the first tie of manly responsibility" (III.vii.35, 36). Elberta feels, by contrast, that "Honour is indeed most noble / But there something is of yet higher Cast—/ Innocence!" (III.vii.37-39). It is clear that Elberta has her own vision of obligation that is primarily personal and maternal rather than social. Caught between emotional ties and political action, an opposition enforced by enemies, allies, captors, and husbands alike, Elberta's maternal role triumphs over all other demands placed on her. Later, when Informo surprises the family in a cottage and threatens to reveal its whereabouts, Arnulph asks why they should "reward such baseness," and Elberta's clear answer is that the "little ones" cannot be betrayed (III.vii.56, 57). Arnulph and Elberta are shown to be at odds over the relative claims of honor and familial preservation.

Arnulph's turmoil is derived not primarily from his children's suffering, which does deeply affect him, but from what this forces him to do. He must choose between his sense of public and private duty when he exchanges Ceolric's casket for food for his family. At this crucial point, Arnulph announces his torn loyalties:

> Ah Heaven!—well—take it hence—buy—purchase—sell—
> Do what thou canst—save but their precious lives—
> And only pray—for me, good Wilfrid—pray
> Madness or Death relieve me!—
> . . . .
> Honor?
> Avaunt, thou phantom!—Nature take me wholly!— [IV.v.2-11]

When Ceolric is seized because he cannot produce the casket for Offa, Arnulph's choice between personal ties and political honor are put to the test. He ultimately elects to sacrifice himself in order to clear Ceolric's name and he thus permits the public to alter in fundamental and dangerous ways the security of the family.

The rupture between parents and the events leading to Arnulph's departure turn on the very question of sustaining and nourishing the children. Arnulph feels that the demands of fatherhood are subordinate to the demands of government. He repeatedly asks if there are *any* duties, familial or otherwise, which might reasonably challenge a high-minded sense of honor. Although he might try to reconcile his apparently dishonorable actions with heaven, the idea of his own stealth overpowers him: "death and torture! / Destruction—Infamy!—a Robber!—oh!—" (IV.vii. 4-5). His wife and children will live, but "never more sweet peace / Shall visit this torn Heart!" (IV.vii.8-9), for his mind "wages internal war" against itself (IV.xvi.55). It is telling that Arnulph's metaphor for his mind is a political one. If Elberta's continuous exhortation is for food, Arnulph's is for the restoration of his honor. Elberta's turmoil seems motivated by a sense of failed familial duty, Arnulph's by the sacrifice of his public obligations. Although he turns himself in so that he might spare his children some infamy (IV.xv.15), it is clear that he is obsessed with the state of his own mind. Arnulph believes that "duty, just though hard, demands each sacrifice / Each strict observance—In / The Public Good, that cement of society" (IV.iv.19-21). Honor is that "Unbidden monitor of human claims / As conscience of divine! thou noblest spur / To generous efforts" (IV.xvi.37-39).

These debates over the quality of honor culminate in Arnulph's leave-taking at the opening of act 5, when he makes the choice between family and honor. Burney reconsidered this scene several times, something indicated by the numerous surviving reworkings of it. It is thus particularly useful to have the alternative textual considerations of the event available. In one version, Arnulph ". . . looks tenderly at the Cave—he hesitates whether to take leave or not—at length resolves to bless himself with one last embrace—but not to let them know tis final but leave his sad tale with Envoy for their vindication and refuge" (variants V.i; El. 191). The verse version also contains two scenes in which Arnulph initially debates whether to "seek—or shun a last adieu" (V.i.11) and then tells Elberta that they "sure shall meet again" (V.ii.1). The latter version implies that Elberta knows little of Arnulph's reasons for departure, for she asks him to "Live! for thy Children Live—if me thou hatest!" (V.ii.5). In one fragment, "He tears himself away from her—unexplained—but most tenderly—blessing her and her Children—charging her not to follow" (variants V.ii; El. 187) and in yet another, "arms himself with fortitude for death after unconscious leave-taking of his Wife and Children" (variants V.iv; El. 182). Still another variation suggests that Arnulph leaves without any explanation, instead depicting Elberta arriving to find Arnulph gone (variants V.v; El. 177). The combination of all of these accounts of one pivotal scene reveals the writer's changing sense of character (the strength of Arnulph's familial ties are in question), of the conflict between central figures (whether or not Arnulph confides in Elberta), and of sentimentality (the pathos of representing an emotional leave-taking or describing it instead).

Elberta, once left alone, becomes increasingly involved with the welfare of her children. Elberta's initial physical confinement typifies the visceral suffering of Burney's tragic heroines, but her more extreme suffering is found in her mental response to her children's status: their abandonment, sickness, starvation, and kidnapping. Power over this female figure is achieved indirectly by those who seize her children or force the confinement that starves them of the nourishment mothers are supposed to provide. In this fourth tragedy, Burney shifted her focus from the physical to the psychological complexities of coercion. The existence of numerous similar fragments shows Burney's repeated efforts to rework different aspects of the play, those that might have been particularly problematic or especially important to the action and characterization. Elberta's repeated calls for food for her children is one such motif, appearing in at least nine fragments. The recurrence of this theme announces it as an important evidencing of Elberta's search for her family's sustenance, in contrast to Arnulph's desire to preserve honor. In one scene, she defends the cave entrance against soldiers, drawing strength from her maternal "instincts." In another, Informo steals her children, and this leaves Elberta completely alone, "alarmed and dismayed," lamenting the loss of both husband and children (variants V.v.16-24; El. 177). It is at this point that Elberta becomes a wanderer, most resembling Cerulia of *Hubert De Vere*. She enters *"wildly"* and cries,

> Where are my Children?
> . . . .
> . . . I see them—
> They mount the upper regions of the air
> Ah See!—they beckon me!—
> . . . .
> Arnulph?—O where is Arnulph?
> Can you not tell me?
> Is yonder his pale corse?— [Variants V.xii; El. 167]

Her speech approaches raving and her emotional state suggests near madness.

The necessity of reading this play's prose *and* verse segments is strongly apparent in the last act, because of the numerous scenes for which there is no dialogue, but only prose summaries. This lack of dialogue may imply that Burney worked to flesh out the narrative with dialogue in a sequential fashion. The closing act of the play contains Arnulph's death and Elberta's resolution to survive her husband and protect her children rather than consider her own demise. Elberta vows, because of a promise to Arnulph, to live for his sake and to uphold his memory (variants V.xiii; El. 154). The verse version ends with Elberta's last speech to her children:

> Weep not for him—he's gone—'tis true—but
> He's gone to sweet forgiveness—O my Children
> For me, for me your tender tears let fall
> He's gone where penitence is lost in [deleted word]
> To pardon most benign—and tenderest mercy.
> . . . .

Yes! I will live!—to Heaven's high will resign'd—
I'm wondrous glad he's dead—for now I'm calm—
'Tis marvellous how I'm changed! I grieve at nothing. [V.xiii.9-18]

This ending poses the possibility that it is female survival that is the central theme of the play, not "female dereliction."[69] The closing scene includes plans for a "Moral on Strict Conduct Through all temptation and Trial of adversity" (variants V.xiii; El. 154). This ending is ambiguous, for it is unclear whose "Strict Conduct" we are to admire: Elberta's, for adhering to her sense of familial duty, or Arnulph's, for attempting to maintain strict personal honor, though he leaves his family fatherless. The conventional values that close a classical tragic drama, with a community purged by the hero's rise and fall, are questioned by a play that contemplates how the hero's adherence to public honor exposes his family to tribulation. This play manages to combine a tribute to the maternal actions so stereotypically valued in women—self-sacrifice, devotion, nurturing—with a simultaneous critique of marital bonds that are antagonistic to family unity (a critique the play shares with *The Woman-Hater*), and with a critique of conventional tragic narratives. Elberta survives, having asserted her own priorities against the typically masculinist ideals of heroism, honor, and community.

A manuscript that reveals different stages of composition is a particularly interesting document for investigating the workings of the dramatist's mind, as Morrison notes.[70] A narrative of composition can be contemplated alongside the story in the play itself. The combination of prose and verse fragments in this text is strongly suggestive of the distinction between plot and story in that it shows how, out of a larger narrative, a specific series of events has been selected by Burney for dramatic representation. For example, information about Elberta's history exists in summarizing fragments but not in verse, which suggests that at some point they may have entered into the dialogue only as expository material in the early scenes, had she continued working on the play. The information contained in one of Burney's prose fragments fills in the action that precedes Elberta's initial appearance in the play and creates a sense of a fictional existence that transcends the textual one: "Arnulph, son of the potent Baron, in the wars meets [Elberta and her father, Ethelbert], falls enamoured of Elberta, his Daughter, privately marries her, and keeps her in retreat five years, with two Children, visiting her in secret. Her person unknown, and all around too much loving her to betray suspicions" (El. 292; Sabor, 235). We also find details about Elberta's initial capture here: "accidentally wandering alone, she is encountered by Informo. . . . He knows, and seizes her—and carries her to Offa" (El. 292; Sabor, 235). The delineation between represented and narrated action can be traced in Burney's work, because the play fragments show the decisions about what would be visual, aural, and verbal, and what would be left to speculation for the audience.

There are several fragments that offer further indications of Burney's view of the figures and story she constructs. Numerous scraps tell of the initial arrival of Arnulph to meet the imprisoned Elberta (variants I.v; El. 58, 62, 63). Burney's notes imply a creation of individuals from stock or formal elements. One such stock component that she works with is the romance plot, which she incorporates into the political conflict. Arnulph is described as a "high spirited young officer whom [Offa] hates for romance and chivalric character" (variants I.v; El. 62). In the verse, Offa speaks alone, saying, "I trust not hot Romance—/ Sooner I'd trust / Fire with my Parchments, Water with [words missing] / Than Prudence to the hot romance of Youth" (I.vi.3-6). Arnulph's romantic chivalry marks him as the play's hero and provides in him the qualities that lead to one of the main conflicts, the divisive demands of familial obligation and a sense of civic-mindedness. The characterization of the hero is hinted at in another fragment, which provides for readers at the same time a rare sense of eavesdropping on the consciousness that produced *Elberta*: "Offa particularly desires to avoid Elberta's meeting Arnulph—a captive Beauty is just the thing to instigate interest and chivalry in a young Hero—and a young Hero is just the thing to catch—soften—the heart of a Captive Beauty—Such liaison though trite since the beginning of the World, will be current to its end" (variants I.vi; El. 36). Burney's description of her characters as generic types—the captive Beauty and young Hero—not only pokes momentary fun at the plot of an otherwise moving tragedy, but also suggests Burney's fundamental awareness of drama as a series of formal elements that, varied individually, compose a dramatic action.

Some prose summaries suggest a very hasty jotting of narrative components as ideas became scenes and were fleshed out into the action and dialogue demanded by drama. For example, one scene leading up to Arnulph's leave-taking (which seems to have taken no decisive final form) is sketched as follows: "Arnulph, perceiving Cottager and his wife, retreats. She says she must take breath, he answers they may be too late, . . . speak of the grand Trial, of pity great folks should be thus rapacious—never satisfied—however splendidly superior—name dishonour and a General—They are going—" (variants IV.xix; El. 202; ellipsis in original). The minor figures Arnulph is said to overhear are not developed with dialogue, but instead serve as the plot device that reveals to him the punishment of another man for his own actions, which intensifies his sense of having violated a trust. This fragment implies not only the blocking of the scene (Arnulph eavesdrops, retreats, and hides), but also a sense of haste and suspense, and a commentary on a common theme of tragedy: the flaws of "great folks." These examples, along with numerous others, reveal that Burney was not casually putting a story on the stage, but was intimately acquainted with the specific elements of drama that distinguish it from fiction. The indications in *Elberta* for blocking, for instance, suggest a conceptualization of the story *as* represented rather than narrated.

While some scraps provide details that substantiate character qualities, others introduce alternative versions of similar scenes, the discrepancies between which are interesting in and of themselves. They range from minor changes in names to substantial shifts in characterization that potentially alter the focus of the play, especially where the relationship between the two main figures is concerned. I have already mentioned Burney's experiments with Arnulph's departure from the cave. The controversy between husband and wife is evident in a reading of both verse and prose fragments, but they also suggest that Burney's sense of the severity of this marital division may have increased or faded away at different points in the composition process. In one variant scene (it is unclear why the verse was not added to the full version) of an early discussion between Elberta and Ceolric, Elberta announces her distaste for Arnulph's high-minded sense of duty:

He's not the man I thought him—I detest not
He who emprizes what is termed imprudent,
'Tis mostly generosity and nobleness—
But he who follows wild his wish of youth
His fervour of romance, and risk of ruin—
And, once engaged, fails and becomes faint hearted
Involving others—and himself retreating—[.] [variants I.x.40-48;
El. 21]

It is possible that Arnulph's "compulsion—to defend his Country—" was what originally took him away from his family and into battle. A military commission is what later prevents his protection of the family, what prompts Ceolric to surrender the fateful casket, and what leads eventually to Arnulph's death. This additional scrap provides a hint of discord that alternately appears and disappears from the action and dialogue.

Elberta draws together numerous threads found in Burney's other tragedies. Like Elgiva, Elberta is a political threat because she is married (but also because of her children). At the same time, she is at least momentarily like Adela (*The Siege of Pevensey*) or Geralda and Cerulia (*Hubert De Vere*). All are seen as valuable political resources because they are thought to be marriageable women. All of the tragic heroines discover to some extent that the ties that should bind them to husbands and fathers only make them vulnerable, and Elberta is no different. She faces opposition from her husband for acting to reunite herself with her children, and she challenges his self-sacrifice because he values his public reputation and obligation above personal responsibility. This play depicts the agony associated with the choices to be made by a female figure who is challenged by all of the roles women are asked to fill, and to fill properly, as daughters, wives, and mothers. She is a heroine with a great deal of self-control and direction, yet her emotions dominate her actions and her speech, and she is not immune from suffering when political ideals impinge on the personal and domestic spheres she wishes to preserve.

Burney herself was an enthusiastic mother and her letters following the birth of her son, Alex (December 1794), are filled with admiration for him and delight at his very existence. That her literary depictions of mothering are so few, and that they show the intense trials of mothers, is somewhat surprising. The question of why Burney relegated her depiction of mothers to her drama is also intriguing and one for which suggestions rather than answers are possible. Motherhood, as Nussbaum and others suggest, is intimately tied up with the status of the female body and its connection with sexuality. Dramatic genres and their conventions provide strong possibilities for powerful representations of motherhood and the ideological constructions that influence it because they offer us the body *as body* on the stage. Straub's work on the bodies and sexualities of actors and actresses (in *Sexual Suspects*) reminds us that the stage was inevitably linked with notions of the public significance of bodies. The maternal body's participation in the making of families, communities, and nations is thus quite appropriately the stuff of drama. As Veronica Kelly and Dorothea E. von Mücke note in discussing Elaine Scarry's notion of the significance of physical bodies to the exercise of authority, "the fundamental cultural activity of making a world, of creating artifacts and fictions, takes its genesis in the body's capacity to suffer."[71]

Burney, through her drama, can *show* symbolic family unity or the negative gaze of masculine disapproval; she can emphasize the mother's desperate search for food by dialogue that persistently calls attention to a child's suffering and a mother's fears. Burney sought out a highly politicized, potentially public artistic space in which to play out the complex and shifting attitudes towards mothers in British society, a space distinguished from the conduct book, pamphlet, or novel by the physical nature of its displayed ideas, its embodiments of stereotypes, and its potential for exhibiting women who flout these stereotypes and idealizations with varying degrees of success. She could play out the problems of motherhood by varying the familiar dramatic conventions of comic and tragic resolutions or of the characterization of heroes and heroines. Her desire to place images of motherhood on the stage may attest to the significance granted to this role by English society at the end of the eighteenth century. It also attests to Burney's strong sense of how a maternal ideal may serve the interests of society as a whole, but may also subject the women who undertake the role of mother to ridicule, imprisonment, or threats of violence. At the same time, she shows us that the ideal grants women a nurturing role that could focus their energies and direct their actions.

4

The Daughter's Tragedy
Hubert De Vere and The Siege of Pevensey

Daughterhood has always been heavily circumscribed by ideals for appropriate behavior, many of which resemble those that define what it means to be a wife or mother. Richard Payne Knight writes in *An Analytical Inquiry into the Principles of Taste* (1808) that a man's love of his wife "partakes of the nature of parental affection; as that of the woman for the man does of filial; whence the terms of endearment would naturally be transferred from the one to the other: that yielding delicacy too, which constitutes the principal charm of the female character, as it is nearly allied to comparative weakness, so is it, in some degree, allied to comparative littleness of person; which may therefore be considered as an ingredient of feminine attractions, though it has nothing whatever to do with abstract beauty of form. . . ."[1] Knight's conflation of filial and marital affection provides a telling commentary on the defining, socially sanctioned relationships a woman might have with men at the turn of the century. As wife, mother, or daughter, a woman's behavior was circumscribed by obedience and deference. In *Hubert De Vere* and *The Siege of Pevensey*, Burney explores in detail the demands made on daughters' "yielding delicacy."

While it was *Edwy and Elgiva* that eventually reached the stage, *Hubert De Vere* was the tragedy which Burney originally reworked for submission to theater manager John Philip Kemble, at Drury Lane.[2] Letters dating from July 1793 to February 1797 show that Burney was editing a play for the stage. In most letters, Burney is typically reticent regarding her dramatic efforts; she is hesitant to name the piece she is working on or to indulge in details about it. Burney's first mention of the "little Secret transaction" comes in letters written between 16 and 21 July 1794, when she writes to her sister Charlotte of a "*business answer*" received from her intermediary, Charles Jr., for which he was to be thanked "*in confidence*"

(*JL*, 3:69). Another inquiry about "*a business like manner*" is repeated in a second letter from this batch of correspondence (*JL*, 3:71). Hemlow speculates that Burney sent the manuscript of *Hubert De Vere* (or perhaps *Edwy and Elgiva)* to Charles Jr. in September or October.[3] Sabor suggests, however, that Kemble saw her play earlier than this and that Burney's efforts to have it produced were noted in the press.[4] Burney appears to have continued to get outside assurances from her father, family friend William Locke, and others. On 10 August 1794 she wrote to her father that she had given Lock her "historic dismality" and that he was "sanguine about it beyond my most darling hopes, & equally to those of my far more intrepid Companion [d'Arblay]. He has made but one critique, & that upon a point indifferent to me, & which I shall yield *without a pang*. He pronounces peremtorily upon its success—however, I am prepared for its failure, knowing the extreme uncertainty of all public acts. I have heard no word from Charles & indeed—he and Mr. K[emble] have not yet had the *Doloric*" (*JL*, 3:74). In this letter, Burney reflects momentarily upon the problems surrounding professional playwriting and her perpetual fear of public disapproval.

Edwy and Elgiva was the play that reached the stage. This did not, however, mean that Burney lost interest in her "dismality." Having survived what can at best be described as a disappointment in the production of *Edwy and Elgiva* in 1795, she began to revise *Hubert De Vere*, as she tells her father on 26 January 1797:

I took it into my mind to look at a certain melancholy ditty of 9 acts, which I had once an idea of bringing forth upon the stage, & which you may remember Kemble had accepted, but which I with drew before he had time to shew it to Sheridan, from preferring to make trial of Edwy & Elgiva, because it was more dramatic—but which I must always aver, NEVER WAS ACTED. This other piece you have seen—& it lost you, you told me, a night's rest— which, in the spirit of the black men in the funeral, made *me* all the gayer!—however, upon this re-perusal, after near 3 years interment, I feel fixed never to essay it for representation. I shall therefore restore it to its first form, that of a Tale in Dialogue, & only revive, & endeavour to make it readable for a fire-side. And this will be my immediate occupation in my Episodical moments. [*JL*, 3:258]

Her attention to concerns of genre is apparent, as she notes the failure of some productions to fulfill all the expectations of dramatization and performance. Although she seems to regard *Hubert De Vere* as a closet drama, the existing manuscript could be staged and she goes on here to write about production possibilities.

It is possible that Burney returned to *Hubert De Vere* in 1797 out of a desire to make money. A section that was later edited out of this same letter suggests that some financial transactions between an "abominable Mr. Lewis" and her father led her to ponder her own financial situation and question her "original intent of *lying fallow* for some years to come. And therefore I shall prepare my Dramatic Tale as well as I can, & then ponder & consult upon its production probabilities" (*JL*, 3:258). The Lewis in question could be Matthew Gregory Lewis (1775-1818), whose name on its own could have encouraged Burney to dream of dramatic success, given his triumphs as a Gothic dramatist and novelist. Burney was still working on the play in February 1797: "[w]hat I can command of time from my little seducer [child Alex] goes still to the Tale in Dialogue" (*JL*, 3:280). *Hubert De Vere* fades from further reference in the journals and letters, however, and the next play she mentions is *Love and Fashion* (15 January 1798; *JL*, 4:65), which, like *The Witlings*, was to endure a particularly troubled voyage into public light, a course cut short once more by family troubles and protestations.

Hubert De Vere exists in two manuscripts, both in the Berg Collection. One (which I designate as Version A) is a foul copy, with the edited subtitle "A Dramatic Tale, in five parts." The other (Version B) has the subtitle "A Pastoral Tragedy" (this is Sabor's text). Both copies are heavily altered by overwriting and glued or pinned overlaying paper. The "Dramatic Tale" has corrections on pieces of paper bearing the postmark of 1814, the other version on paper with postmarks of 1824, 1830, and 1835. This indicates that Burney returned to *Hubert De Vere* very late in life. Hemlow writes that Burney timed the acts (totaling 2 hours, 26 minutes) around 1836.[5] Scraps pertaining to *Hubert De Vere* can also be found in the set of folders labeled "Miscellaneous Pieces of Manuscript, 1772-1828," which contains two fragments on the play, as well as the following observation, written when Burney was timing it: "33 minutes Altogether excellence greatly rising wants chiefly poeticality but very touching very elevating very saddening & worth rectifying De Mowbray too much of crime unless earlier marked to repentance & remorse & only called off for safety. make that change & all his soliloquys will be extra good & new Devere admirable Geralda exemplory Cerulia a little modified & her disapperance more [obscure word] & marked Great interest awakened" (*BC*, IVa). These notes—like those for her other plays—indicate that Burney maintained an interest in her tragedies despite the failure of the one production. The timing implies a mind still attentive to exigencies of production.

Like the other tragedies, *Hubert De Vere* is set in the past, during the reign of King John (1199-1216).[6] De Vere has been accused of treason and exiled by John to the Isle of Wight, where the action takes place. De Vere's love, Geralda, has married another man, Glanville, and her uncle, Baron De Mowbray, has continued to plague De Vere for reasons unknown, stationing officers to "watch [for], or fabricate, some crime" (I.3) that will be De Vere's final downfall. De Vere is aloof, lamenting what appears to be Geralda's love of Glanville's money rather than himself. De Mowbray has his vassals urge a village maiden, Cerulia, to fall in love with De Vere, and after much pursuit De Vere finally relents. De Mowbray helps this effort by appearing to Cerulia as an astrologer who predicts her union with a man whose name begins with "H." The sudden arrival of Geralda, now widowed, forces De Vere to choose between these women, and the abandoned Cerulia becomes a mad wanderer. Geralda informs De Vere that Glanville had blackmailed her into marrying him by threatening exposure of her uncle, whose treasonous papers Glanville had in his possession. De Vere's exile was originally the fault of De Mowbray, who substituted De Vere's name for his own on these same papers. De Mowbray's treachery is uncovered, along with the fact that he is Cerulia's father. King John pardons De Vere but they cannot prevent Cerulia's death. She returns to De Vere, raving about churchyard specters beckoning her to dig her own grave. She dies of a broken heart and of the madness that has possessed her with ideas about her own demise. De Vere and Geralda are left weeping over her "untimely bier" (V.443), praising her "spotless Innocence" (V.448), and finding solace in the thought that her innocence brings her immortality.

As in the other tragedies, in *Hubert De Vere* female behavior is regulated by male-directed marriages and manipulated romantic desire. Burney returns repeatedly to the relatively powerless position enforced on women by the denial of marital choice. Both female figures in *Hubert De Vere* are pushed into relationships with male figures in the interests of political intrigue. Geralda is blackmailed into a loveless marriage at the price of her reputation and De Vere's honor, which remains tainted while he is in exile. She becomes an object of public infamy. De Mowbray's vassals describe her as a "frail, futile Woman" who "Merits no more regret, but haughtiest scorn" (I.26, 29). De Vere shares in this demonization of Geralda, whom he perceives to have been easily led by a fickle desire for wealth. In an apostrophe, he goes so far as to warn his enemy, Glanville, about Geralda: "Fair as it seems, 'tis hollow; all within / Of soul, or mental faculty, is wanting; / All nobler splendour of essential worth, / Founded on Honour, Faith, and God-like Truth" (I.88-91). Geralda is a "barbarous hypocrite" filled with black duplicity, whose "ravenous Hate demands [De Vere's]

Fame!" (I.98, 106). Her escape to the island prompts from him scathing references to her moral inferiority, though he discovers later that her actions were coerced.

The characterization of Cerulia is a significant feature of *Hubert De Vere*. She most thoroughly fits a model of a completely submissive, innocent virgin. Cerulia's innocence—suggestive both of guiltlessness and gullibility—draws attention to the forces that damage her because she is so entirely unsuspecting and pure. As a married woman, Elgiva is perhaps more easily construed as predatorily, sexually aware. Elberta's marriage and maternity mark her also as mature and chaste, if not virginal. In this respect, *Hubert De Vere* can be categorized as what Robert Bechtold Heilman labels a "Drama of Disaster": a portrayal of "all the injuries and unhappiness that can or are believed to come from without, that are not invited by us but imposed upon us, that make victims of us, and that let us feel guiltless."[7] He qualifies victims in terms of the source of their victimization: nature, society, political forces, evil individuals, or themselves. Victims—unlike tragic heroes—reach no point of realization, achieve no reordering of self, and possess no great wisdom.[8] A conventional tragic hero or heroine is marked by superior understanding. Heilman's analysis offers a distinction that is useful for a feminist interpretation of tragedy, for it considers the presence of forces that are imposed upon figures, in this case because of gendered notions of the exhortations to which a woman might be susceptible. While none of Burney's heroines invites upon herself her own suffering, Cerulia seems, more than any other figure, unaware of the larger context of her trials.

In *Hubert De Vere*, tragedy strikes kings and vassals, but victimization plagues only women, because their relative personal and sociopolitical weakness incorporates them easily into political struggles. If one plots the figures of this play on intersecting scales of personal gain and situational control, the female figures, Geralda and Cerulia, have the least to gain in terms of political power, finance, or status, but suffer the most due to an inability to exercise control over their movements and desires. Cerulia stands to gain the least, even less than Geralda, from any of the intrigues and manipulations that take place over the course of the play. Geralda, the victim of De Mowbray's treachery, also comes to a realization about her plight that Cerulia is denied. Cerulia must endure the most devastating effects of coercion, not only mentally and emotionally, but also physically. Like that of Elgiva and Elberta, Cerulia's suffering is finally felt on the level of her physical being. Unlike her counterparts, however, her suffering turns her mind and body toward self-inflicted torture. She is a passive, preyed-upon female dramatic figure. Her tragedy is entirely personal, though the causes of it are uniformly political. Burney suggests that qualities highly valued in women—their innocence and obedience—are those which most expose them to punishment.

Burney depicts in *Hubert De Vere* the male figures' apparently simple division of women into two categories: the innocent virgin and the fallen woman. While Geralda is evaluated against deeply moral standards of behavior and is found wanting, Cerulia's innocence is admired and preyed upon so that she will perform to De Mowbray's satisfaction. She is repeatedly described as a paragon of virginal virtue: uncultivated, artless, and sexually naive.[9] (Her name is evocative of springtime.) Beauchamp, De Mowbray's vassal, describes her as having "young, unresisting softness" with which "The artless Virgin gives [De Vere] all her soul" (I.75, 76). She is "unpractic'd" (II.54), caught in De Vere's "snares of pity" by her "artless nature" (II.55, 57), and remains "all unconscious of each subtler aim" that leads her to De Vere (II.76). In her innocence, she is susceptible to Gifford's control as he urges her to desire De Vere: "lighter to allure, her [heart's] enslav'd" (I.79). Cerulia's desire is ideal because it is dictated to her. She is placed in the awkward position of being encouraged to want an uninterested man, to simultaneously be aware enough to experience longing yet innocent enough to maintain her purity.

The preservation of female purity is used initially in a cynical manner by De Mowbray, because he acknowledges that the consummation of Cerulia's desire for De Vere would remove both parties from his control. De Mowbray is thus eager that she be preserved "Strict to the path of honour" (II.58). It is unclear whether or not De Mowbray knows Cerulia is his daughter from the outset or whether the sight of her once he reaches the island reveals their relationship to him because of her resemblance to her mother. His awareness that she is his daughter makes his desire for her preservation more understandable, though he does not deviate from his path of using her for his schemes. He enacts the same coercion that other parent figures do in Burney's drama. In the guise of the astrologer, he speaks paternally and appeals to Cerulia's sense of duty.[10] He tells her "Resistance were a crime" (II.208): "Hear me, young Damsel, hear! / Prepare thee to be courteous, kind, and docile / To him thy planet fates thee for thy husband" (II.210-12). Cerulia is even encouraged to accept illtreatment. She is told to "Heed not [De Vere's] roughness" (II.220) and she replies that her obedience is complete. This is a tale of the insistence that a woman do as she is told, at any cost to herself. Obedience (that is, in fact, filial) is so naturalized for Cerulia that she never questions the forces that push her toward De Vere.

Cerulia serves a dual purpose for De Mowbray: she is used to punish De Vere by denying him Geralda and also by threatening his status, which makes the manipulation of her an issue of class as well as gender. Believed by the islanders to be an orphaned shepherdess, Cerulia is considered beneath De Vere. A union with a "maid unknown, unportion'd, / An humble rustic Orphan" will "taint the high born Hubert's lineage" (I.53-55). In terms of class and propriety, Cerulia is willing to denigrate herself before De Vere, inserting herself at the bottom of hierarchies which she describes with pastoral images of birds: "What though the Dove may fascinate the Swallow, / No Dove will hail the Swallow's humble greeting!" (I.126-27). She admires De Vere's "Nobleness and high desert; / A grander, loftier,— not a prouder Nature" (I.137-38), and she says that "All I love—shine high, like Stars, above me!" (II.206). Only De Vere can elevate her socially and morally, because she, "through his blessings, become[s] bless'd [her]self!—" (I.172). Like Burney's other tragic heroines, Cerulia is well socialized, submissive, and generous in her acceptance of her own worthlessness.

Cerulia's extreme malleability is indicated in Burney's stage directions and dialogue, which specify how figures are to enter and move about the stage more clearly than those in her other tragedies. The blocking for this figure in the stage directions and the descriptions of her movement emphasize on the one hand Cerulia's unsuspecting nature, and on the other how this innocence is played upon. She is frequently described as subject to persuasion: she is "urg'd with Hope, with Flattery foster'd" in her "fond, unwearied chace of the stern Exile" (I.68, 69); "how oft has Gifford urg'd [her]" (I.149); she is "prompt[ed] . . . on, with fresh persuasion" (I.151); De Mowbray will "exhort her to pursue De Vere" (II.164). The figure's physical movements on the stage show her either urged to take action or reluctant to do so without permission. She frequently enters or exits accompanied by other figures, mostly Gifford, who leads her around the stage, to "guide [her] to [Hubert's] presence" (I.185). When Cerulia enters the stage, she enters *"gently"* and *"stands aloof"* (I.117), *"appears at a distance"* (II.135), and *"drops at [De Vere's] feet"* (II.303). At other times, she is reluctant to leave the scene, or is told to do so, and she questions if she may return: "Shall I return?" (III.101), "May I come?" (IV.103).

The scenes that explore the triangular relationship between De Vere, Geralda, and Cerulia all involve implied blocking that emphasizes De Vere's control over Cerulia and thereby her subordination to both Geralda and him. Significantly, the so-called "conquest" of De Vere by Cerulia is merely reported (III.1-47); the difficulty of reconciling such a conquest with Cerulia's extreme passivity may have prompted this decision on Burney's part. De Vere's interactions with Geralda, by contrast, are dramatized, which strengthens visually our understanding of his desire for her and his avoidance of Cerulia both physically and psychologically. Once the reunion of De Vere and Geralda is achieved, Cerulia is relegated to the status of trespasser on their space. She receives no explanation for this, and each time De Vere tries to explain, he is interrupted by Geralda: the control of dialogue, too, is therefore symbolic. This is the tragic counterpart of the comic interruptions Burney explores in *The Witlings* and *A Busy Day*. After Geralda's initial rediscovery of De Vere, she controls the represented space. It is De Vere who must enter and depart, depending on his emotional strength and curiosity (he leaves and returns twice in act 3). Geralda is also able to infiltrate De Vere's domestic space and, physically supported by him, asks him to "conceal" and "Enclose [her]" in his cottage (III.386, 389). This leads De Vere to lament over "lost Cerulia!" (III.390), and he flees upon Cerulia's next appearance. The virgin's painfully intense desire to please him keeps her from following. Her madness is initiated by De Vere's demand that she leave Geralda and him. She explains, "I know not where I am!—my senses wander—" (IV.166), and she later *"runs wildly off"* (IV.288). After De Vere commands her to return to her own cottage, his failure to join her denies her any further access to him, and he is allied with Geralda from this point forward.

In the final act, a Gothic supernatural emerges, to which Cerulia submits in a manner that parallels her submission to all forms of male direction. She returns to her community, raving about a midnight vision in a moldering churchyard, where she obeys "Three hideous Spectres" that call upon her to dig her own grave (V.93). Death is a tangible presence for Cerulia, a presence only she can see and feel. At this point in the play, she is completely incapable physically, and enters and leaves the stage supported by others, driven by her death wish. She describes vividly the details of her night in the churchyard:

> . . . spent, o'erpower'd, motionless I fell,
> Calling on Death!
> . . . .
> I shriekt—I knelt—I prayed!—
> Till, faint the dew of Death crept, clammy, o'er me
> And Icicled my Heart. [V.80-81, 130-32]

Cerulia's mind produces phantasms that substantiate the message she receives from the male figures in the play: she deserves death, she is at the beck and call of forces stronger than herself, and she cannot seem to control her fate. If it is appropriate that Elberta's mental turmoil leads her to see the specters of her beckoning children, Cerulia's visions of these three punishing ghosts is equally significant. Sabor suggests that Burney's use of the Gothic is "hypothetical" because Burney "chooses not to enact but to envisage" Cerulia's visions.[11] Another alternative to this reading is possible. The specters may be described rather than represented so that this Gothicism remains exclusively connected with the heroine and stands solely for her psychological disturbance, rather than serving as a more general generic indicator. Cerulia alone experiences the Gothic supernatural, while she suffers in isolation. More than a Gothic play about a woman, this is a play that features the female mind's construction of its own Gothic atmosphere.

Cerulia's final appearance in social space is as a madwoman who reports her solitary anguish, "*pale and faint, her head bound with wreaths of Cypress; her Hair disshevelled and flowing*" (V.33). Although she has had no effect on the course of events, she interprets her downfall as that of a typical tragic protagonist: a "sad reverse of fate" because "Hubert is false!—" (V.42, 54). All the images she uses to describe herself are pastoral (all is "thorny, miry, rugged" [V.50]) and gendered. She is

> Like some poor fragile Weed
> By rude or wanton hand unkindly sever'd
> From the tall prop that seem'd to give it strength,
> Yet but sustain'd its weakness, Hubert lost
> Gone is my hold on life: faint, faded, drooping,
> I shake—I fall!— [V.61-66]

Cerula's raving stumbles upon an important commentary about male-female relationships: male support actually maintains female incapability and reliance rather than offering strength. In effect, Cerulia has looked into her grave and she calls on death. Like Elgiva, she circles back to the scene of the crimes and demands a momentary pause in the hero's quest for political absolution. Her disintegrated body is the initiator of this pause, calling attention to an abusive body politic and to the different ways in which political subjects experience powerlessness.

Female madness in *Hubert De Vere* is combined with torture, hallucination, self-denigration, and the "unspeakable horror" familiar to Gothic drama. The element of self-torture makes Cerulia's a tragedy of disaster and victimization and suggests a feminist interpretation. Doody argues that the injunction to Cerulia to dig her own grave is allegorical,[12] but this exhortation functions more powerfully on a literal level. As Epstein notes, "Burney does not merely report or mirror institutions of oppression; she posits and dramatizes violence as an effect—the inevitable effect—of oppression."[13] Patriarchal, paternal coercion, the artificial construction of desire, and the final denial of it all result in a woman's annihilation of self. Cutting-Gray writes about the narrative gaps in Burney's novels that appear because the heroines "must resort to sickness, madness, or fits of hysteria in order to be heard, that is, to become nameable. Crises occur for the heroine because the world requires of her innocence, selflessness, and silence while simultaneously requiring that she respond decisively to concrete situations."[14] While I disagree with the implication that sickness or madness are forms of last-resort agency, this statement could easily be applied to Cerulia as well. This innocent figure's madness occurs because of the hidden De Mowbray name that is hers, but of which she remains unaware. The same figure that holds the power to name and save her, her father, is, of course, the figure responsible for her silence and her death.

I return again to Sedgwick, who writes of the resolution to Gothic tales:

> It can be said that when an individual fictional "self" is the subject of one of these [Gothic] conventions, that self is spatialized in the following way. It is the position of the self to be massively blocked off from something to which it ought normally to have access. This something can be its own past, the details of its family history; it can be the free air, when the self has been literally buried alive; it can be a lover; it can be just all the circumambient life, when the self is pinned in a death-like sleep. . . . [O]nly violence or magic, and both of a singularly threatening kind, can ever succeed in joining them again.[15]

The depiction of Cerulia's final demise reveals a violent combination of divided entities: the figure exists in the liminal space between life and death, raving and silence, and while she rejoins her community, the joining is one of extreme suffering and is a prelude to her death.

Cerulia's approaching death leads to a final, physical challenge between men, to see whose "blood . . . must bathe this Victim's Tomb" (V.379). It is only at the play's close that De Vere is informed of the true source of Cerulia's desire for him, and he perceives her as the "hapless victim at Misfortune's shrine!" (V.438). Although he laments Cerulia's tragic end, his trials have been resolved, and he praises the restored Geralda: ". . . Matchless Geralda! / With what noble pity thy Eye beams lustrous! / . . . / Oh! weep with me o'er this untimely bier!" (V.440-43). While De Vere discovers that his honor was tainted unjustly and his exile was undeserved, his more immediate trial is to be torn between two lovers, one he believed false and the other thrust upon him unsought. While Cerulia's innocence leads to her complete destruction, De Vere's virtue and Cerulia's death permit him to escape from the situation.

The changes Burney made to both existing manuscripts of *Hubert De Vere* suggest, among other things, that she was attempting to focus attention on Cerulia and her suffering, particularly in this final scene. That Burney entitled the manuscript found in d'Arblay's personal effects following his death *Cerulia, A Tragedy* is not as mistaken as it may appear. Burney deleted from Version A a long speech by De Vere that treats the death of Cerulia as only part of a greater political tragedy. In this speech, he calls for a future time when power will be better exercised and justice will reign:

> But O to this blest Land arrive the period
> When Power uncurb'd no more may give the reins
> To arbitrary vengeance, or Caprice.
> When Britain's King shall call his dearest blessing,
> Next to the still small voice of self-approvance,
> His grateful people's well-earn't love: & hail
> In general chorus with his happy subjects
> Fair Justice as his Kingdom's Guardian Angel. [V, Version A]

A suicide attempt by De Mowbray is similarly cut. Geralda's speech about the sweet appearance of Cerulia in death once ended this version but is marked for deletion: "Sweet Shade! oh see! how gentle still its look, / . . . / There Peace indeed Companion is to death—" (V). This speech draws attention to some modicum of moral compensation achieved by Cerulia in death and was perhaps deleted because Burney wished to maintain a focus on Cerulia's suffering rather than her salvation. Version A, so revised, ends with De Vere calling for tears to be shed over Cerulia's "untimely bier." Burney adds to Version B a similar, though truncated, speech by Geralda regarding Cerulia's innocence in death but also adds a closing stage direction: "*They bend over* CERULIA *on Each side; the Village Maids group, weeping, around: and the curtain drops to the sound of the Church Death Bell*" (V.453). This ending, more theatrical than the other, calls attention audibly and spatially to the corpse, suggesting this is the main focus of the tragedy. Cerulia is the object of the gaze of on- and offstage spectators, and the act of looking itself is brought to the level of conscious engagement by the dialogue. The conclusion, like that of *Edwy and Elgiva*, again implies the simultaneous safety and vulnerability of the spectator.

In its depiction of Cerulia's transition from innocent to haunted and ultimately suicidal woman, *Hubert De Vere* is one of Burney's most compelling works. The Gothic terrors and the radical transformation of Cerulia from gullible innocence to raving madness would have been an excellent vehicle for a tragic actress. Haunted by phantasms of her own mind, Cerulia performs an act that is ultimately the most submissive possible: she dies, having completely fulfilled the ideals that compose feminine virtue, as advocated by the male figures. This is not so much proactive suicide as it is a movement toward her only real alternative. It is especially the case in *Hubert De Vere* that "[a]s social subjects [Gothic heroines] are positioned, motivated, constrained within (subject to) social networks and cultural codes that exceed their comprehension or control."[16] As I suggested in chapter 3, this depiction of containment can be seen as effective social commentary. Doody's insistence that the play is "an allegory of Frances Burney's feelings about her father" limits the power of representing a female subject who is tried by circumstance and pushed beyond recuperation because of her innocent and submissive nature.[17]

In ending *Hubert De Vere* with the death of Cerulia, Burney substitutes for the suffering of the wronged hero the single death of an innocent woman. De Vere is a typical tragic hero, whose virtue gains admiration even from his enemies, but his agony does not endure and he does very little to help himself. The political conflict is resolved, he regains his love, and he is restored to his king's favor. Geralda's trials are likewise attenuated at the play's close, though they have been perhaps more demanding than De Vere's (a forced marriage, the betrayal of her lover, capture, escape, and recapture). Thus, while the play is named the tragedy of Hubert De Vere, the full-blown effects of the tragic situation rest entirely on Cerulia in the form of both physical and mental torture. Cerulia's suffering because a lover is lost—a love first forced upon her and then denied due largely to her father's machinations—operates ultimately on the most basic physical level, chilling her to the bone and leading to hallucinations that bring on her death. Cerulia does not achieve a recognition of the true (public) nature of the tragedy she suffers (a recognition said to be typical of most tragic protagonists), a sense of redemption, or the realization that she suffers because of others' actions. She may demonstrate a "tragic flaw" in that she is manipulable, but this flaw is more an indication of systemic constructions of femininity than individual qualities. She suffers because she adheres completely to ideals of female behavior and does what she is told, wants what she is told to want. Such disproportionate punishment is depicted intensely in *Hubert De Vere*, for Cerulia's suffering is incommensurate with her innocence and with the pastoral setting. Perhaps Burney is being most ironic in this play, in the title and the setting, which seem incongruous with the depth of Cerulia's suffering.

In *Hubert De Vere*, *Edwy and Elgiva*, and *Elberta*, the mad wandering and return of the female figure is the main dramatic vehicle for a sort of momentary female voice. The source and strength of this voice is ambiguous. I suggest that these heroines do not rebel as much as they serve as accusing signs of treachery. The distinction I am making is a fine one. The dramatist may use the female body for political commentary, although an explicit acknowledgment of this function of the body may not manifest itself in terms of the play's internal world. Cixous and Clément comment on wandering and the fear of the madness that they view as an element of female energy. In their description of a madwoman lies a distinction between docility and threat, the one which may become the other because the woman

> doesn't hold still, she overflows. An outpouring that can be agonizing, since she may fear, and make the other fear, endless aberration and madness in her release. . . .
>
> This power to be errant is strength; it is also what makes her vulnerable to those who champion the Selfsame, acknowledgment, and attribution. No matter how submissive and docile she may be in relation to the masculine order, she still remains the threatening possibility of savagery, the unknown quantity in the household whole.[18]

Female experience is represented almost exclusively in Burney's tragedies via an emphasis on the body that sustains exile and punishment and that calls attention to treachery. A form of dramatic *écriture féminine* takes over, as the body itself—tortured and near death—speaks for the woman whose language is distorted by madness or silenced by death. It is this female body that makes "visible," in Elin Diamond's words, a text of patriarchal control.[19] In *The Siege of Pevensey*, another female figure appears, whose movements and voice are similarly dictated to her. Her docility and her yielding delicacy, however, do not result in her death and the patriarchal control in the play is made visible by other forms of submission and obedience.

In *Edwy and Elgiva* and *Hubert De Vere*, the central female figure is defined by her position as a wife and as a daughter, respectively. In Burney's final tragedies, *The Siege of Pevensey* and *Elberta*, the trials of the female figures are complicated because multiple layers of patriarchally defined social roles are superimposed on these figures. Elberta is simultaneously a daughter (and therefore an heiress), a wife, and a mother of future heirs. In *The Siege of Pevensey*, the only female figure, Adela, is alternately defined by her roles as daughter and as marriageable woman. These roles, considered together, prompt a consideration of the male authorities between whom women are transferred: fathers and suitors. Adela is used by the state to coerce her father and her suitors because of her strong sense of filial duty and the price she fetches as a bride. The emphasis on father-daughter relations in *The Siege of Pevensey* places it more firmly within the usual compass of Burney's novels. The filial relationship of victim to aggressor—Cerulia to De Mowbray—remains secret for the most part, after all, in *Hubert De Vere*. Doody suggests that the father-daughter bond was not only personally resonant for Burney, but was a contemporary cultural obsession: "there was a large cultural investment in insisting on the beautiful purity of father-daughter relations, the daughter becoming a kind of emotional resort for flagging male authority. Filial duty from the female offers reassurance in a blissful uncontaminated relationship that does not remind the father of his brute physicality but vindicates his authority under the guise of tenderness."[20] More than Elgiva, Elberta, or Cerulia, Adela fluctuates between being an active subject in the use of her person and a passive commodity whose movements and allegiances are determined for her. Her main trial is to negotiate successfully the intense conflict between filial duty, self-preservation, and the acknowledgement of personal desire.

One fair copy of the play survives in the Berg Collection. With few deletions and revisions, the manuscript of *The Siege of Pevensey* is the least difficult to decipher of the four tragedies. D'Arblay has appended a note to act 3 indicating his puzzlement over the appellation of "tragedy," but he acknowledges that he is unfamiliar with the history on which Burney bases her play: "Il me semble qu'on ne peut appeler *tragedie* une Piece dans la quelle il n'y a pas une goutte de sang versée." (The formal tone of the note "à Miss Burney" suggests that it was written before their marriage.) Hemlow writes that Burney timed the piece in 1836, the acts totaling about 2 hours.[21] Save the reference quoted in chapter 3, when Burney refers to *The Siege of Pevensey* and *Elberta*, there is no specific mention of this play in Burney's journals and letters, nor any indication that she attempted to have it published or performed.

The Siege of Pevensey is about a historically distanced civil war.[22] King William II ("Rufus the Red," 1056-1100), England's second ruler after the Battle of Hastings in 1066, is at war with his brother Robert, Duke of Normandy, over the English throne. Pevensey Castle, controlled by the Earls Mortaign (uncle to William and Robert and head of Robert's forces) and Arundel, is now under siege by William's forces. Adela is the daughter of the Earl of Chester, commander of William's troops. She has been held in Pevensey as a hostage for three months, after being seized by Robert De Belesme, Arundel's son. The main movement of the plot consists of the repeated transfer of Adela between the king's forces and the castle's. She is exchanged for another prisoner, ransomed for money, and ransomed so she might be granted to a suitor. De Warrenne, the king's Chief Justiciary, wants her (and her dowry) ransomed so that they can marry. De Belesme (who has grown to love her) returns her unransomed to her father, for which he is imprisoned by his own superiors when he returns to them. The fact that Chester permits De Belesme to return to the castle casts a treacherous light on his own motives, and his love for Adela is then used to ensure that he does not betray his king. Adela offers herself up as a prisoner, passing back into De Belesme's hands to save him the shame of apparent treason, and he proposes marriage to her in order to save her from De Warrenne. Her greatest fear is that she would be unable to procure her father's consent for the nuptials, and she is about to tell Chester of their intentions when Chester, De Belesme, and she are captured by William. In the final act, Adela believes that she must marry De Warrenne in order to save her father's life. She bargains instead for life in a convent, giving up her dowry to the king, and is about to be led off when a truce is announced. Chester grants Adela to De Belesme, who pledges allegiance to William.

As this plot outline suggests, *The Siege of Pevensey* deals simultaneously with two types of hierarchy, the familial and the political. The family is represented as a microcosmic form of the body politic, ruled by a father-king.[23] The mouthpiece for this view, significantly, is Chester. He advocates that rulers be regarded as virtuous fathers and he urges William to respect his subjects as he might his children, who he should not overpower by terror (II.ii.85). Chester urges that "the all-pervading influence / Of Home-experience" (II.ii.112-13) be used as a model for political rule, a domestic version of the loyalty that flows from constituents to their head: "Each loyal voice, with one consent, repeat[ing] / Long Live Our King, The Father Of His People!" (II.ii.142-43). Leaders must "Leave far behind all arbitrary force, / And work through every fissure of the soul / To prompt allegiance by impulsive tenderness" (II.ii.128-30). In short, the king should not abandon the principles of virtuous governance because a civil war is being waged, and this state of chaos should not permit rebellion from the ruled.

Because of his belief in a gentle but firm public and private hierarchy, Chester laments civil war's subversion of the usual alliances that underwrite social and familial order: "Each bond dissolv'd, each genial tie o'erleapt, / Order revers'd, and Nature violated" (I.i.41-42). Eager to decry the power of war (importantly, between two branches of a family) to disrupt "natural" human civility for the ignoble benefit of controlling people, Chester vows to act decently toward others despite "The arts of war [that] admit such sophystry / As in the times of peace would make men shudder" (I.vii.8-9). He persistently urges his king to rule benevolently, by encouraging his subjects to feel an "equality of soul," "the birthright of humanity!" (II.ii.98, 99).

Chester's idealistic view of government extends to his sense of himself as a parent. He speaks repeatedly of his refusal to compel Adela's actions or thoughts, so that Adela, at the outset, appears to have been blessed by an unusually liberal father. He rejects the ransom of his daughter to the hand of De Warrenne, whose interest is said to be more financial than emotional. Such a politically motivated exchange would replace, in Chester's view, one form of imprisonment for "an harder, longer bondage . . . / A life's captivity" because of Adela's aversion to De Warrenne (I.i.63-64). In Chester's eyes, mental liberty does not compensate for being limited to "the mere name of freedom to her person" (I.i.66). The first explicit offer of money for Adela comes from De Warrenne, but Chester reminds him that money alone will not secure marriage to a woman whose "filial duty merits not compulsion" (I.iii.31), though he admits that her gratitude may be solicited and her mental freedom may make her "open to each generous propensity" (I.iii.34). The strategic starvation of the castle means that "She, useless, will the first be left unnourish'd,— / She, Captive, will the soonest be abus'd!—" (I.iii.14-15), but this does not move Chester to grant his daughter to a man against her will. As I suggest below, however, Chester's ideal of the benevolent parent includes a sense of the unquestioned authority of the ruler/parent. He *is* willing to enact a form of mental captivity on Adela when she seems to transgress his will.

Although Chester uses the family as a symbol for political order, he subordinates his role as father to his patriotism:

My guide is Honour, though my Heart is Adela's.
And [William] shall see I hold my country's cause,
Howe'er less dear, more sacred than my own.
Thus am I driven to double Vigilance,
Fiercer hostility and inhumanity,
Lest—what alone I prize above my Child—
I fail in Duty to my King and Country! [I.i.73-79]

Because his daughter is a political prisoner, Chester's love for her makes him appear unreliable and he must prove to his king and his daughter that their interests do not compete. As the exposition shows, Chester has chosen to emphasize civic over parental sympathies and Adela has remained a prisoner for three months.

Adela's physical location is of paramount importance because it reflects which male political and personal constituencies hold her in their sway. The action of *Edwy and Elgiva* turns largely on Elgiva's absence, which increases her value by heightening Edwy's interest in the forbidden object of desire and thereby distracting him from monarchical duties. In *The Siege of Pevensey*, Adela is the most visible figure, shown alternately in the "home" and "enemy" camps, as she is traded between them.[24] She is shunted literally between men eight times during the play's action and is frequently discussed in terms of her exchange value many more. Each exchange expresses, in turn, a literal or figurative price for this woman who has no value in and of herself, except perhaps to De Belesme, who only accepts for payment the joy of reuniting father and daughter (I.ix.46-47). The main point of these exchanges of Adela is to determine the price of a stolen woman, and just what she signifies to her various possessors. As Mortaign suggests, during civil war "State exigence annuls all private property" (III.i.31). Human beings cease to be private citizens. Adela is thus bought and exchanged strategically. Her king wants her for De Warrenne, so he might ensure both De Warrenne's and Chester's loyalty ("'Tis through his Daughter he must be secur'd" [II.iii.6]). De Warrenne wants her dowry and Chester wants what he calls his "Treasure" back with him (I.i.71). As commodity rather than consumer, and dominated as she is by her sense of daughterly duty, Adela has little power in these transactions. The only exchanges that Adela prompts herself are her voluntary return to the castle to protect De Belesme's honor and her exchange of her dowry for convent life.

An actantial model of character usefully illustrates the functions of some of the figures in this tragedy (it can certainly be applied to the others as well).[25] According to the structure outlined by Aston and Savona, a "Sender" (a force or being) acts on a "Subject," initiating a quest for an "Object" in the interest of the "Receiver," while being "helped" or "opposed." Adela is the Object of several different Subjects' quests, including De Belesme and De Warrenne, and in a different context, Chester and the king. Adela as Subject (figure 2) has only one Object in mind: the security of her father. To this end, she is aided only by De Belesme, and is opposed by almost all other figures. The Sender for Adela's quest (or the force that acts on her) is her sense of duty and the Receiver is Chester, or, what amounts to a corollary, Adela's sense of having acted properly. A telling, related model is that in which De Belesme is the Subject in a lover's quest (figure 3). With Adela as his Object, his motivations are love and honor, but the beneficiary of the pursuit of Adela is not immediately himself, as is typical of romantic quests, but rather is Chester, who is reinstated as the prominent male figure in Adela's life. The fulfillment of De Belesme's pursuit can only come after Chester, in his paternal and patriarchal role, grants Adela to him. That the play's primary subject is political intrigue rather than romance is clear in the collection of all the other main figures, including Chester, under the label of Opponent.

Figure 2. Actantial Model of *The Siege of Pevensey* with Adela as Subject

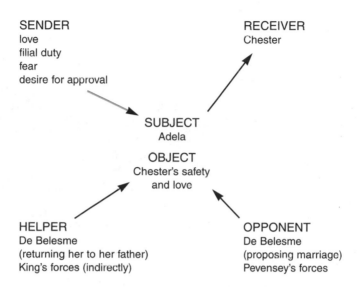

A triangular representation of Adela's position between numerous male figure-pairs (William and De Warrenne, De Warrenne and De Belesme, Chester and William, Chester and De Belesme) and the different motivations for their use of her (romantic love, filial duty, political control, blackmail) provides another way of interpreting the figures in *The Siege of Pevensey* (figure 4). The ties between these figures are all different but interdependent. Such a geometric illustration outlines the position of the female figure in this play: she is central, but central because she exists in a position between so many male figures who control her movements and dictate her desires.

Hubert De Vere and *The Siege of Pevensey* share in common a critique of the dangers faced by well-socialized women who adhere to norms of feminine behavior. Neither Cerulia nor Adela is faced by what Heilman describes, in reference to a male hero, as the tragic protagonist's "choice between counterimperatives of such authority [so] that one has to act faultily and yet cannot feel that he could act more wisely."[26] Adela, in having to choose between father and suitor, always feels that she could have (and should have) acted more wisely, that is, by being more loyal to Chester. While this play, like Burney's other tragedies, is what Heilman labels a "drama of disaster," the result here is not, as he asserts, that the protagonist is allowed to "feel guiltless."[27] This tragedy invites feminist

Figure 3. Actantial Model of *The Siege of Pevensey* with De Belesme as Subject

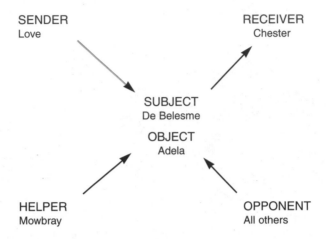

analysis because the heroine is punished by her own guilt about *appearing* to make choices that she does not actually make because this atmosphere, laden as it is with patriarchal and filial ideology, severely curtails her alternatives. The ideology of filial duty proves its coercive power the more strongly because it so successfully disguises itself to Adela as "normal" and thus unquestionable.

Adela is faced with the choice between an affectionate, if secretive marriage to De Belesme, and the sacrifice of her romantic desire to secure her father's honor. Her sense of filial duty is remarkably strong, for it prompts her to evaluate and commodify herself in a fashion that resembles the male figures' evaluations of her. Although Burney may indeed be creating a female figure to be admired for her sense of duty, the sense of obligation brings on intense psychological conflict for Adela, so we also perceive a critique of uniform obedience and the forces that demand it. As Hope M. Leith suggests of Voltaire's heroines,

> In the face of a complex system of strict but overlapping and conflicting duties to various male authority figures, these female characters inevitably fail. They take blame, they are tormented by guilt, and they are punished. . . .
> Guilt, like blame, is internal rather than external, but it stems from conscious violation of one's duties.[28]

Figure 4. Triangular Representation of Adela's Position in *The Siege of Pevensey*

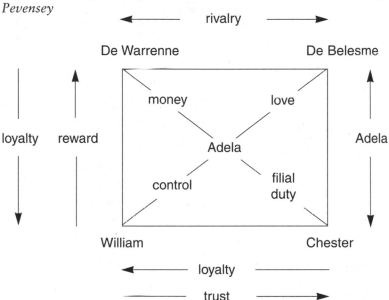

Burney emphasizes the turmoil that plagues Adela because she cannot conceive of a romantic relationship that has not been approved by her father. Adela clearly loves and respects De Belesme, but this love is constructed by Chester as competitive with her love for her father. While Adela is no more fallen in her actions or desires than Elgiva, Elberta, or Cerulia (that is, not at all), she preemptively responds to the accusation of misbehavior and is punished both mentally and emotionally.

While Chester claims the utmost respect for his daughter, Burney clearly displays the power of his near-mythical view of father-daughter harmony to delineate all Adela's choices and movements, to the point where the daughter's greatest mental and emotional anguish emerges when he feels she is ignoring his decrees. Adela demonstrates what Leith identifies as a "struggle to reconcile two male systems of authority, paternal and marital."[29] The coercive side of Adela's relationship with her father is glimpsed in the intense language Adela uses to envision her role in the larger political sphere. All of Adela's actions respond to her sense of her father's desire, which is a palpable presence throughout the play. Even when Adela offers to be reimprisoned to protect De Belesme's honor, her motivations are directed simultaneously toward suitor and father. She suggests that "the loss of [her] preserver" is more dire than "Ten thousand

Deaths" (II.xiv.3-4); however, she also fears wounding "Chester's honour" (II.xiv.9). Adela represents her self-sacrifice, "for Ransom,—or for Death!" (II.xiv.34), as her "just doom" as "Earl Chester's Daughter!" (III.iii.1-2). Doing what is bid by her father's "life's tenour" and her childhood teachings (III.iii.16), Adela's offer of herself to save De Belesme is ultimately a filial act, an offering to her father's honor, a desire for approval, and at least partly a fear of failing him (see figure 1). If we recall Knight's comparison between a woman's regard for her father and for her husband, it is not surprising that Burney represents a female figure in this position as acting simultaneously for father and lover, to the point where she might even feel confused about the forces that motivate her.

When De Belesme proposes marriage, Adela's trepidation is increased not by her self-imposed imprisonment, nor by the alternative of marriage to an undesirable man, but by her fear of marrying without her father's approval. De Belesme's argument is that if Adela remains single and refuses De Warrenne, her refusal could jeopardize her "Father's safety" (III.xii.35-36). If she marries De Belesme, this sort of coercion is denied to the man who controls Chester, namely, his king. She can be convinced only by assurances that her father would approve of the match and that the marriage does not make her any less a daughter.

Adela's situation is an impossible one: she may preserve her father by transgressing the first rule of her relationship to him, the "first great Law of life, filial obedience" (IV.i.2). The idea of marrying without parental consent plunges her into doubt and self-chastisement:

> O dreaded act!—Will Heaven such nuptials bless?—
> The first great Law of life, filial obedience,
> Broken—revers'd!—How will he bear to hear it?—
> His Child—his age's promise—Thus unsanction'd
> To change parental for connubial bonds!—
> And with an Enemy?—O De Belesme
> Why do I mix thy kindred simpathies
> With enmities of state? Were but the times
> Propitious to thy virtue, the wide universe
> Holds not a son so fitted to De Chester;
> So like in Honour, so complete in courage,
> Of spirit so lofty, yet of Heart so gentle! [IV.i.1-12]

Her sense of ignoring the proper authority in her life—her father—sets her on a path toward complete self-denigration, which Burney represents by Adela's imitation of her father's voice in place of her own: "O that my generous Father knew my conflict! / Would he not say Take De Belesme—and end it!" (IV.iv.4-5).[30]

The meeting between Adela and her father following Adela's promise to De Belesme is remarkable, as Doody notes.[31] When alone, Adela requests approval from an absent father, imagining what she wants him to say. Chester's actual response to the mere suggestion that she has acted without his permission preempts all of her explanations about her motivations. Father and daughter both attribute to the other what they wish to hear, but Chester never listens to Adela's hopes, and Adela is completely absorbed by Chester's moral devaluation of her. Although she is appraised by all the men who control her passage between enemy camps or between father and suitor, by far the most emotionally troubling assessment is her father's. The same disjunction that exists between philosophical ideals of government and the actual submission that governing figures demand is replicated in the relationship between Chester and Adela. Despite Chester's lengthy claims of liberality and female freedom, Adela must submit to her father's will. He achieves this not through physical compulsion but with rhetorical demands for emotional loyalty. Adela, in Sedgwick's terms about the Gothic, is "massively blocked off from something to which [she] ought normally to have access."[32] Simply put, she cannot have a sympathetic husband because of an unreasonable father. This is admittedly a harsh criticism of Chester, who speaks liberally of his daughter's freedom to be self-determining in her marriage choice. But he does fulfill the same function as the Gothic enemy castle, providing in his own way an atmosphere of confinement that puts Adela at the mercy of forces outside of her.

The father-daughter meeting is heavily laden emotionally and rhetorically. Burney displays Adela's upheaval by showing her nearly incapable of speech, while her father speaks for her, either by ventriloquizing the sentiments he feels she should be expressing, by discussing public opinion about her disobedience, or by implying that some deeply deplorable act is the cause for her silence. This scene—the silent, agitated woman interrogated by a father who demands her complete obedience—would have made for powerful theater. Chester is passive-aggressive, in popular psychological terms, for he achieves Adela's obedience without ever actually commanding her to obey. There is a telling disjunction between the locutionary and perlocutionary elements of Chester's speech. The message he desires to communicate is not immediately identifiable in the words he utters; he frames his discussion in terms of Adela's well-being, but demands instead a recommitment to the ideals of filial submission. Every statement he makes about her actions forces her to a point where she can only "choose" to obey him.

Chester's immediate strategy is to make connections between Adela's silence (the cause of which he does not yet know) and inevitable moral degeneration:

Nay, tell the whole at once.
Concealment is in youth the nurse of danger;
'Tis Art's first step, simplicity's first fall:
Where early practic'd, 'tis at virtue's peril;
Candour is sullied; Innocence foregoes
That delicate, yet dauntless openness
Which rather does not know, than shuns disguise. [IV.v.33-39]

He both proclaims her innocence but suspects her of "some deep purpose" (IV.v.43), but he fails to perceive that his suspicions suggest he
himself is dissembling when he claims that she "shalt not find [him]
rigid" (IV.v.49). The next step in Chester's interrogation of Adela is to
make a direct link between her actions and his own integrity. Clearly,
while he claims to "aim not at compulsion" (IV.v.61), this is entirely what
he seeks, and he makes her responsible for the honor of their house,
adding that any happiness she might be seeking is illusory. His final triumph is to tell her, "I know thou dost not mean to lose thy Father!"
(IV.v.90). He assures her in highly coercive ways that he will not abandon
her, by announcing that his faithfulness to her is what makes her liable to
their enemies' manipulations:

Those who would win thee to unfilial deeds
May plead thy pow'r o'er my parental feelings
To ensure forgiveness; and conscious favour
May whisper in thy Ear thy Father's fondness
Could not behold thee suppliant and in anguish
Yet fiercely turn away inexorable.
Be this presum'd: I seek not to disclaim it.
Yet hear me, thou poor Adela!— [IV.v.91-98]

Threatened by this loss of "virtue's rapture" (IV.v.104) and overcome by the
religiously laden idea that she has her "Father's Love" because she has
"ne'er offended him" (IV.v.107-108), Adela must do all she can to preserve
her father's "aching Heart" (IV.v.120). The restoration to complete and unquestioned daughterhood is finally achieved when Chester laments Adela's
loss of moral and sexual purity, if she pushes him "Beyond the term that
sees thee all unsullied, / All angel-white!—all blessing—where thou art
blest— / The anxious parent who now folds thee fast / To his supporting
Bosom!—" (IV.v.121-24). She has, however, *already* capitulated: "O cease!
o cease! / O my lov'd Father! rend not thus my Heart!" (IV.v.110-11). De
Belesme can only leave her now to her father's protection.

There are two climaxes in *The Siege of Pevensey*. The first is this
reconciliation of Adela and Chester, and the second comes with the

choice she is given by William when she is captured along with Chester and De Belesme. William determines that she will "find a Tamer in the Lord De Warrenne" (V.i.12), who desires her because "she is fair, and rich" (V.iv.13). The lives of both Chester and De Belesme are represented to Adela as being in her control, for William and Flambard will "Give her to think 'tis her's to kill, or save [Chester]" (V.x.31). What William does not tell Adela or Chester is that Chester is in no danger at all, because his troops have threatened to rebel against the king if Chester is harmed. Adela thus believes that her public acceptance of a man she hates will save her father's life. When Chester sees Adela's real distress over this "choice," he offers his own life for her freedom; she refuses. What follows is clearly not what Morrison labels as an easy escape by Adela from a dilemma "by means of prayer."[33] A "compromise" is reached when Adela recognizes that all William really wants is her dowry, which she will forfeit to him in exchange for his pardon of her father and his permission that she can live out her days in a convent: "For life confin'd, I wave these nuptial rites, / And leave to thy arbitrament my portion,— / While yet my Father lives— . . ." (V.xii.65-67). This last exchange is deemed satisfactory by all concerned: the exchange of a woman's physical for her mental freedom so that she might bless her father and save his life. Chester frames this "decision" as virtuous and praiseworthy: "my spotless Child, / Cherish thy filial joy!—Thou savst thy Father!—" (V.xii.74-75). The last-minute arrival of Arundel with a message of peace from Mortaign and the duke saves De Belesme's life, grants the throne to William, and saves Adela from the cloister. Her first response to this is a thrilled exclamation about the "unlook'd for" mercy that reunites her with her father (V.xvi.2). Her reward is her bestowal on De Belesme, who finally receives the homage he is due.

While *The Siege of Pevensey* is happily concluded—that is, a marriage will take place, a war is ended—the steps taken throughout the play to reach this point are truly tragic from a woman-conscious point of view. Adela must prove her worth repeatedly to suitor, father, and country. What lingers beyond the "happy" ending are questions about the acceptability of such coercion and the possibility that coercion is continual for women, even in "happy" situations like marriage or familial reunions.

Burney's tragedies examine the pressures that civil war and conflict place on individuals, marriages, and families, for both men and women. These pressures are shown to be particularly acute and personal for female figures who suffer emotional and physical anguish as they are sought out, manipulated, confined, and tortured by male figures who want authority over them and, by extension, dominance in a political arena. This is not to overlook the fact that male figures are also depicted as suffering and dying, but they tend to be shown in the process of exacting revenge or recuperating honor or morality (this is certainly the case for Edwy, Arnulph, Hubert, De Belesme, and Chester). The female figures, by contrast, are guiltless subjects caught up in conflicts between men, useful to them because of qualities that are particularly attributable to their gender: filial duty, marital potential, sexual virtue, or maternal obligation.

While Doody wishes to attribute both the flaws and the virtues of these plays to Burney's need to express herself and her psyche,[34] the tragedies have merit not only as a stage in the development of a writer, nor purely as psychological documents, but also as stageable plays. They depict in powerful ways the extent to which women are made to suffer, even die, because they are subject to the control of others, control that is based on socially determined views about feminine behavior, duty, obligation, commitment, and sacrifice. What is most obvious about each of the tragic heroines is that she is persistently caught between competing ideals about how she should behave, or has her actions circumscribed by desires that conflict with each other. Most often, the personal is pitted against the political, the familial, or the marital. To some extent, Burney implies that the female, which she links to the private and personal, is permitted no place in public negotiations except as a commodity that is bartered, imprisoned, or ransomed.

These plays urge a reconsideration of the ways in which institutions like the family, religion, marriage, and government interpellate subjects by appealing to their ideologically informed sense of action and duty. As Burney suggests, women are particularly vulnerable to this process. Her tragedies provide a feminist example of the shift in tragedy described by Lindenberger, who writes of the suffering of the "mute and ineloquent" in martyr plays: "[w]ith the democratization of tragedy since the late eighteenth century, the tragic figure comes to have increasingly less awareness of the nature and meaning of his fate. The progressive stages of growth which accompanied the martyrdom of earlier heroes are obviously impossible for those who can at most display a sense of shock at what has been done to them."[35] Burney emphasizes the inaccessibility of the concept of personal growth for her female figures.

Edwy and Elgiva appeared onstage in 1795, as the Terror in France dashed revolutionary ideals and displayed a corruption of leadership that was deeply and publicly troubling. The final decade of the century saw a number of tragedies that examined an enduring subject, the use and abuse of authority, in a manner resonant with political activities contemporary to them.[36] They include the conservative *The Siege of Meaux* (1794), by Henry James Pye, in which revolution is averted and an aristocratic family is saved; Jephson's *The Conspiracy* (1796), which also shows the triumph of benevolent rule over usurpation; and Sheridan's immensely popular *Pizarro* (1799), with its foiled Napoleonic figure. William Henry Ireland's hoax *Vortigern* (1796) depicts a corrupt quest for power at the same time as it plays havoc with ideas of literary authority and abused artistic power. Burney's tragedies show the exercise of authority as it relates most clearly to the control of a woman by powerful social institutions: government, religion, marriage. Her female figures can be placed in a context of revolutionary upheaval, when shock prevails over understanding in the face of aggressive events. Tragedy at the end of the eighteenth century was a fluid genre that included challenging depictions of female subordination and martyrdom along with more general representations of the victims of political upheaval, victims who may speak only through their damaged bodies. In her late comedies, Burney also considers the power of the family, marriage, and finance to mold and direct female behavior and to confine female choice, but she does so without the intense concentration on physical confinement and torture. The power of institutions, however, is depicted as no less successful, if it is less violent. Confinement occurs in different forms and coercion is shown to have both overt and subtle manifestations.

5

~

"Choice" and Evaluation
Love and Fashion

Burney's tragedies expose and question the limited control women have over their physical occupation of space in a male-dominated world. The bodies of Elgiva, Elberta, Cerulia, and Adela are the literal sites on which overt and implicit forms of oppression are enacted. The comedies, varied as they are in content and characterization, do not exclude the evaluation of women as particularly physical bodies that are tyrannized by patriarchal hierarchies and institutions. Courtship, marriage, and membership in a family all have their physical, bodily components. This being said, the female figures of Burney's comedies are oppressed less by physical coercion and torture than by socially sanctioned practices. Such practices—marriage, in particular—disguise physical exchange under ideological layers of emotion, duty, and desire, all of which influence the position of women in relation to the men who court them and the families they will leave and subsequently join once they are married. This is not to suggest that physical coercion and torture are not similarly informed by ideology, but rather to emphasize that the power enacted over the female figures in the comedies is perhaps less overt, and possibly more insidious, than physical manipulation. The power of male prerogative that is present in courtship, marriage, familial organization, and moral judgment are all the more effective *because* they do not usually leave extreme physical evidence in their wake. With no corpses to be buried, structures of oppression are more easily perpetuated and less overtly questioned.

Three of Burney's four comedies (*The Witlings, Love and Fashion,* and *A Busy Day*) explore the practice of equating social and personal desirability with financial advantages when marriages are being considered. Cecilia faces social ostracism and the end of her betrothal when her money evaporates; she is reincorporated into Lady Smatter's fold once her monetary value is reestablished. As I discuss in chapter 6, Eliza Watts (in

A Busy Day) faces a similar evaluation when her money speaks more loudly to her fiancé's family than do her personal qualities. Both Cecilia and Eliza discover that their ideals about marrying for love rather than ledgers are scoffed at by others. In Love and Fashion, Burney creates a heroine, Hilaria Dalton, who is genuinely attracted to the idea of marrying for money and the material advantages it offers. This decidedly self-interested fantasy is counteracted by her romantic attachment to her beloved, the fittingly named Valentine. Hilaria's dilemma would seem at the outset to be a matter of personal choice, but Burney shows how complicated the idea of female choice is by showing Hilaria's desires alternately for "Love" and "Fashion" to be manipulated by male figures who help create her desire in the first place, and who evaluate her vociferously when she strays from their dictates. Love and Fashion incorporates several of the issues raised in Burney's other plays: the subjection of women to male standards of morality and feminine behavior, the omnipresent shadow of finance looming over marital transaction, and the sense that female choice is ultimately illusory.

Cecilia in The Witlings seems to be largely lacking in personality. Apart from her romantic ideals and the departure from Lady Smatter's house, she says and does very little. Her problems are solved by others and she seems to return to the same social and romantic situation in which she is introduced to us. The heroines of the late comedies—Hilaria, Eliza, and Joyce (Sophia is a different story)—are no more free to do as they please than is Cecilia. However, the heroines' responses to the competing forces of finance, the family, and class are more psychologically complex in the late comedies than in The Witlings. This is not surprising, given Burney's development as a novelist in the intervening years. Eliza finds her desire to reunite with her family and marry Cleveland countered by shame about her family's manners, fear that her relatives will inadvertently convince Cleveland and his family to reject her, and a variety of presumptions that others make about her financial worth and her social status. Joyce (in The Woman-Hater) is forced to reconcile her father's oppressive demands for silence and obedience with her own wish to be physically active, noisy, and argumentative. Eleonora (in The Woman-Hater) must somehow reconcile her husband's history of erratic behavior with her need to protect her child and fend for herself. Hilaria is caught between Lord Ardville, Sir Archy Fineer, and young Valentine. Each man readily evaluates Hilaria's actions according to what he wants from her. For Ardville, she should fit the portrait of a pretty, unopinionated, young wife. Valentine wants a morally upstanding, pretty, young wife, and Sir Archy needs her money.

Love and Fashion is the first of the three late comedies Burney wrote at the close of the century, following the success of Camilla (1796) and during the initial stages of composition of *The Wanderer*. This same short period (delimited by Burney's departure for France in 1802) also saw the composition of *A Busy Day* and *The Woman-Hater*.[1] *Love and Fashion* was offered by Burney, through Charles Jr., to Thomas Harris, manager of Covent Garden Theatre, in October 1799. Covent Garden was known for producing comedies, and Harris had a reputation for willingly taking on new mainpieces.[2] It was to be produced in March 1800, Burney was offered £400 for it, and advertisements were made.[3] The death of Burney's dearest sister, Susanna, just returned from marital misery in Ireland but not reunited with her family, was the reason for the withdrawal of the play, but this was perhaps more of an issue for Dr. Burney than it was for Burney herself, and was as much linked to his sense of female propriety as to family sorrow. In any case, the play was withdrawn in February 1800, after Burney had received comments from Harris about the production and had notes for revisions. Burney, too, was deeply affected by her sister's death. She wrote to Esther Burney on 11 February 1800 that "the idea of bringing out a Comedy at this period—though its whole materials & business had been all arranged so long before it, was always dreadful to me. The aid it is *possible* it might have brought to other matters I relinquish without murmuring, to be spared so jarring a shake to all within" (*JL*, 4:397).

Harris's comments were reported to Burney in letters from Charles Jr. in the final months of 1799. They uniformly suggest that the play would be a great success. The table to which Charles refers is *Love and Fashion*: "Mr. H. admires the Table—& will bring it into use in the month of March! . . . [W]ith Hilaria He is in love;—& thinks it the first female character on the English stage:—quite drawn from nature:—no Book, German, French, nor English, consulted: all from nature" (*BC*, Scrapbook, "Fanny Burney and family. 1653-1890"). Charles finishes the letter by adding that "H. . . . is surprised, that you never turned your thoughts to this kind of writing before; as you appear to have really a genius for it!" Harris suggested revisions that included reducing the roles of the servants, Dawson, Innis, and Davis; altering the quick redemption of Mordaunt's sensibility at the end; and, if Joseph Munden were to play the part, altering the role of Davis to a valet "of the old School" (*BC*, Scrapbook, "Fanny Burney and family. 1653-1890"). Another letter from Charles Jr. to Burney (8 November 1799) recounts his meeting with Harris, who was eager to meet Burney as well.

In addition to these as yet unpublished letters, there is an unusually large number of references to the play preserved in Burney's published letters. The process of composition and the possibility of production passed over the same terrain of personal and parental fears about writing for the theater that Burney experienced in the late 1770s. Like *The Witlings*, *Love and Fashion* was written in relative secrecy and is referred to in a family code, foreign phrases, and eventually with the distress that was entwined with Burney's often turbulent relationship with her father. Beginning in January 1798, Burney refers to a "scribbling business" (*JL*, 4:65) in covert tones, and writes "*Entre nous*" (*JL*, 4:126) to her correspondent, Charles Jr., in March 1798. As if secrecy might also permit a necessary distance, Burney identifies herself in the third person when she writes to Susanna: "[a] *particular* friend of mine has something just now in project that she had given me leave to confide in you, with oaths of secresy, upon your arrival—but I dare not trust the secret to the post. If you can guess the person, do: though I must not *name* her, I may assent or dissent to your conjecture. Cherchez aux coins de la Lettre" (*JL*, 4:171-72). Susanna joins in the conspiracy by asking Burney to explain the "enigma" by writing "between hooks" (*JL*, 4:172, n. 10). In another letter, Burney writes, "I know you will be curious about *some*thing—so I will not omit to mention that *noth*ing whatsoever is yet done, & we are come to no determination whether *any* thing ever *will* be done" (*JL*, 4:328). Pronouns suffice as Burney tests the ground for her work, simultaneously referring to and effacing her efforts, avowing and disallowing her originality.

In other letters, the play is represented not by abstracts, but through metaphor, as a material good to be marketed and exchanged as Charles Jr. and Burney saw fit. It is important to remember that despite her lack of public recognition as a playwright, Burney was familiar with the artistic and commercial world of theatrical production. Burney's metaphors reflect the commercial realities of the theater business. It is thus in a letter to Charles Jr. that the play is referred to again as a "table," similar to others that might be "advertised," but not yet to be sent to a "Broker." She writes that the broker "will never take it for this year's sale so late, full as I see him of such articles: & it is better not to remain in *his* garret till another, but in that of the carpenter himself. However, you are left to your own ultimate discretion" (*JL*, 4:270). In a letter to Esther Burney, Burney dramatizes a business transaction, just as her brother had done for her with his own meeting with Harris. Burney again relies on the metaphor of furniture. The description of a theater manager as a tradesperson, an upholsterer, is apt:

Scene St. James's Street
Enter Agent & Upholsterer, *meeting*.
. . . .
AG. I want to speak to you upon a little business. A Lady—a relation of Mine—has written a play—Will you act it?

UP. A Lady?—Is it your sister?—

AG. Suppose it is—Will you Act it?

UP. If I see nothing that seems positively against its succeeding, certainly. But — —You must let me have it.

AG. When you please.

. . . .

AG. All she urges is secrecy. She is bent upon making the attempt unknown.

UP. And why?—A *good* play *will* succeed,—& sometimes a bad one—but if there be a circumstance, as here, that will strongly prepare the public in its favour,—why should we lose that circumstance?

AG. I will speak to her about that: but be very secret meanwhile, especially if you decline it, as it is then her intention to try the other house,—& it *must* not be blown upon. [*JL*, 4:361-62][4]

Burney and Charles continue to employ this material metaphor in other letters. She refers to her trips to London to see the "Upholsterer" and to gain news of the "Table" (*JL*, 4:377). These commercial discussions are remarkably different from the emotional view Burney had of her tragedies. It is clear that Harris acknowledged Burney's considerable reputation and she was astute enough to threaten playing off one theater against the other, as Inchbald did. She had recently experienced great financial success with *Camilla*, the proceeds of which she transformed with d'Arblay into a home. The references to the materiality of *Love and Fashion* might reflect this sense of the exchange of literary objects for financial gain.

Dr. Burney begins to figure prominently in Burney's discussions of *Love and Fashion* after the death of Susanna in January 1800. One letter refers to his pleasure not only in the secrecy of her authorship but in the public denial of it (*JL*, 4:392). Perhaps the most revealing letter, however, is that addressed by Burney to her father on 11 February 1800 following the withdrawal of what she calls her "poor ill fated" project (*JL*, 4:394-95). In this letter Burney directly addresses her father's involvement in her career, an involvement which she identifies not only as meddlesome and hypocritical, but as explicitly preventing success. Burney announces clearly that her and her father's views of her authorship are contradictory: his displeasure in her playwriting is to her "unaccountable" and his interference regarding *Love and Fashion* seems especially grave considering her "panics & disturbance" over her sister's death. The language Burney uses here establishes her troubled relationship with her father as a dichotomous one of inherited talent, which she feels should be acknowledged, and subservience to the power he has to punish her, as her father. She refers to his "ample punishment" but avows she has committed no "crime" in wanting what she has "all [her] life been urged to, & all [her] life intended, writing a Comedy." Dr. Burney's "trepidation" has doomed his daughter to "*certain* failure." The language is also sexualized, the play described in her father's words as a "wanton risk." Burney avows that her authorship is an act provoking only perhaps "*DISGRACE*" or "*disappointment*" but not "shame" and "blush[es]."

In this letter Burney describes not only her own sense of her profession, but the attitude toward it that she would like to solicit from her father. She claims that her creativity is something "not at [her] own controll." Her method of seeking her father's approval is heavily disguised: she ventriloquizes him, challenges his authority (by making him responsible for her apparently indiscreet venture because of her literary inheritance), flatters Dr. Burney's own creative attempts, and deflates him with suggestions of his underlying envy of her. Writing of her own sense of confinement in the paddock of fiction, she implores him to "cease to nourish such terrors & disgust" and say,

> "After all—'tis but *like Father like Child*—for to what walk do I confine myself?—She took my example in writing—She takes it in ranging—Why, then, after all, should I lock her up in one paddock, well as she has fed there, if she says she finds nothing more to nibble—while *I* find all the Earth unequal to my ambition. . . . Come on then, poor Fan—The World has acknowledged you my offspring—& I will *disencourage* you no more. Leap the pales of your paddock—let us pursue our career. . . .["]
>
> I am sure, my dear Father, will not infer, from this appeal, I mean to parallel our Works—no one more truly measures their own inferiority, which with respect to yours has always been my pride;—I only mean to shew, that if my Muse loves a little variety—She has an hereditary claim to try it. [*JL*, 4:395]

The transferences are curious: not only does Burney suggest that it is the world, rather than her father, that acknowledges their tie of blood, but she also substitutes for her own active imagination a Muse who has inherited Dr. Burney's ambition, and a joint "our" career for her own. She asks less for his approval than that he cease at least to disapprove, to "*disen-courage*." This request, by the most successful novelist of the end of the century, confirms both the serious regard Burney had for her play-writing and the extent to which this activity was highly questionable where family politics were concerned.

When Burney later refers to her final, failed entrance into the world of theater, she is once more restrained: "My Agent is *dead silent*, & my own wishes & desires about it are nearly in the same insensible state. . . . All I have myself interfered with, is a renewed insistance on *incog*, if any trial is made. For I am indeed inexpressibly earnest" (*JL,* 4:477-78). Burney's comedies thematize the numerous restrictions on the ways in which female figures can insert themselves into the public sphere, through their marriages and their family positions. The limitations on such public identities include those which Burney felt herself: the need for propriety, the restraint of ambition, and the subordination of personal to family concerns. Each of these confinements is evident in Burney's letters describing the fate of *Love and Fashion*, her last advertised attempt at writing for the stage.

While Burney gave up immediate plans for production, she did not entirely abandon her interest in this comedy. At least some of the revisions for *Love and Fashion* contemplated by Burney survive, boxed with the play text in the Berg Collection. There are two sets of notes: one written on an 1801 memoranda book of d'Arblay's; the other on unbound scraps of paper, including old envelopes. It is clear that she returned to the play periodically until very close to her death. The changes she considered include alterations to names and traits (a Lord Rigby replaces Lord Ardville in a cast list drawn up sometime after 1822, on an envelope of 4 September) and to the plot. As late as 1838 she observed that a "General Change" to Valentine would add "force, effect & nobless to his Opening" and that there is "Much too Much of Innis." As Sabor notes, she also timed the play.[5] All of these revisions suggest, as do the emendations to her other works, that she was ever loath to give up her drama.

The notes in d'Arblay's memoranda book are less involved than the unbound notes. In the former, Burney mentions only scraps of the plot for early scenes of the play: one note describes some letters received by Hilaria, and her comment that she has refused both her proposals. The use of letters as a device to further the plot is found in the latter set of revisions, proposed after 1818, when Burney moved to Bolton Street (as indicated by the envelopes). In one fragment, Hilaria enters holding two open letters and comments on these "Monuments of [her] triumph! Harolds of [her] Destiny!" Another scrap has her contrasting the letters, one from "Ld. Rigby" and the other from Valentine, one promising "Fashion enshrined in Title Coronet & Jewels," the other a sign of "Love insidious Love" that "will not suffer the poor Heart to live only by the Eyes." It would appear that the version of Hilaria who comments on the letters is more cruel than the heroine of the surviving manuscript of the play. She says, "O Lord Rigby! how happy you could make me if you would only be so very good and kind as to entail . . . your Estates to Valentine— . . . & die out of hand!—I should so love your money! so honour it with trophies & pomp & make up for you such a beautiful suit of mourning!— Alas! alas!" Burney seems in this scrap to have intended to preserve Hilaria's conflict between love and fashion, but perhaps also to intensify her moment of decision by having two letters from her suitors arrive simultaneously.

Burney's overall impression of the play is recorded in notes she made to each act when she timed all but act 5, perhaps in 1836 when she timed *Hubert De Vere*. These comments mix positive and negative responses and include further notes for changes that might be made. She wrote of act 1 that the "2 Lords" should be "designated more clearly," that Hilaria is "*Manqué*," Miss Exbury "mawkish," and that all should be "rewove & rewrote." Act 2 is "*Pretensious*," while Act 3 has the comment that it is "Long & unmeaning no interest but the momentary . . . The Ghost stale & Innis insufferably stupid." Act 4 fares better, being "long & wordy but highly comic in parts of Ghost & S. Archy & excellent in Hilaria alone . . . Sr. Archy Hilaria excellent." No timing is given for act 5 (the play would have totaled about 3 hours) and Burney's response to this act is condemnatory: "alltogether mawkish unfinished un-anything" (*BC, Love and Fashion* box). *Love and Fashion*, it would appear, sometimes maintained only negative interest.

Love and Fashion has a series of romantic and economic plots with conflicts that originate from the contact between two branches of one family. The combination of many disparate, if topical, trends of contemporary comedy (mysterious identities, ghosts, wayward sons, a marriage plot) may in fact be the primary error of the play, and we recall Harris's main objection that there was too much concentration on the servants. The play does lack the unity of action of the tragedies or the other late comedies, and in this respect it seems most closely to resemble *The Witlings*, with its two related but largely discrete plots. The proud and rich Lord Ardville, recently returned from India, wants to marry Hilaria Dalton, the ward of his visiting elder brother, Lord Exbury. Hilaria's affections are placed entirely in Exbury's son, Valentine, though she has been advised against him by her cousin, Sir Archy Fineer. Hilaria has thus recently refused both Valentine's and Lord Ardville's proposals, which has enraged Ardville to the point where he has ordered Exbury from the house. Valentine's brother, Mordaunt, has spent the family fortune on his debts, and Exbury is forced to reduce his household and retire to less expensive living, which further suggests to Hilaria that Valentine is not a good match. Sir Archy Fineer is, not coincidentally, the object of the

First page of the manuscript *Love and Fashion*. Courtesy of the Henry W. and Albert A. Berg Collection, New York Public Library, Astor, Lenox and Tilden Foundations glances of Valentine's sister, Miss Exbury, though to her frustration Sir Archy fails to declare himself. He is obsessed with assuring Hilaria that Lord Ardville is the only prudent (financially viable) choice to be made, and he serves as Lord Ardville's emissary. Hilaria is rushed by Sir Archy into accepting Lord Ardville, but she delays actually meeting him. Miss Exbury is not the only woman waiting for a gentleman's declaration. Innis, Hilaria's maid, is told by a mysterious fortuneteller that she will marry well, but she too is left unapproached. The attentions of Davis (Exbury's valet) and Dawson (Ardville's butler), however, are steady and competitive.

Hilaria's apparent wavering between love and fashion procures for her the economic-based reprobation of Sir Archy and the romantic, idealistic censure of Valentine. After the household has moved to a humbler dwelling, a bailiff arrests Valentine because he took on debts of his own in order to contribute money to help his brother and father with what is now a family debt. Mordaunt, the prodigal son, returns to his senses and is appropriately remorseful for the trials he has caused his father. Hilaria, in order to help Valentine, offers herself to Lord Ardville at last if he will aid the family financially, but then proposes instead to return some jewels to him if she can stay with Valentine. In order to avoid appearing as if he has been refused by Hilaria, Lord Ardville gives the jewels to the young couple anyway, as a wedding present. He discharges Valentine's debt, awards him a settlement, and transfers his anger onto the toadying Mr. Litchburn, who hangs about the wealthy throughout the play. It would seem that true love and fashion are united at last for Hilaria.[6]

In *Love and Fashion*, Burney parodies the devices of Gothic theatrical spectacle that came into vogue over the last quarter of the eighteenth century. As Cox suggests, Gothic drama's use of the supernatural and the spectacular successfully wedded high and popular forms of dramatic art in a "new aesthetic of sensationalism."[7] In Burney's play, the parodic element is a ghost that is believed to inhabit the house into which the Exburys move. Fears of the supernatural and the occult contribute to the comedy of the play when concealed characters are mistaken for specters. Ghosts appeared on the stage in such plays as Matthew "Monk" Lewis's *The Castle Spectre* (1797), which Burney saw performed in February or March of 1798 (*JL,* 4:129). Cautionary humans dressed as ghosts appear in other comedies of the period as well. In Inchbald's *The Wise Man of the East* (1799), derived from Kotzebue, the "ghost" is Ava Thoanoa (really Claransforth Sr., believed to have died in a fire), who is able to restore the family fortune to the virtuous Metlands. This play also has a Mordaunt-like profligate son in the young Claransforth, and the ghost is used to encourage him to reform his ways. In *The Second Marriage,* by Baillie (published in 1802), a servant tries to "spook" a new stepmother into re-forming her ways by appearing as the dead first wife.

A further mystery to be cleared up in *Love and Fashion* is the identity of the "Strange Man," who is the disguised bailiff.[8] This stranger is taken for a fortuneteller and he does not disabuse anyone of this idea. He tells Innis that she is to marry above her station and he dupes the menservants into appearing foolish in front of her. In the case of both the specter and the mystery man, objects of superstition and fear terrify the lower-class characters but are proven to have rational causes when they are demysti-fied by the patriarch, Lord Exbury. The bailiff's emergence from the strange man's disguise is just one replacement of superstition by law and order. A romantic order is similarly reasserted when Hilaria sacrifices for-tune for love and the idealism of youth wins out over the curmudgeonly pride of age. The "haunting" of the country house is explained once Valentine is discovered to have hidden himself in it. This "ghost" may be seen as the superstitious and parodic corollary of the more serious haunt-ings that occur in the play. Valentine hides himself so that he might "haunt" Hilaria, who is consistently under the scrutiny of the men who wish to direct her choices. In this respect, the peripheral part Valentine oc-cupies in *Love and Fashion*, as noted by Doody,[9] may be considered an important element of his characterization as a judgmental "looker" rather than a "doer," in a fashion similar to the role played by Edgar in *Camilla*. Valentine is (like Censor, and like Wilmot in *The Woman-Hater*) the self-appointed moral authority of the play, who keeps Hilaria in his line of sight. She is plagued by his accusations of moral degeneration and immi-nent suffering. His dire warnings lead her to change her mind about her marriage and sacrifice herself for his well-being.

Burney's dramatic acumen is further apparent in the familiar theme dealt with in *Love and Fashion*: the dilemma between choosing a com-panionate marriage or one based on financial interests. While other drama of the period tends to feature this debate between lifestyles as a dilemma faced by young couples (as in Garrick and Colman, the Elder's 1766 *The Clandestine Marriage*), Burney centers the conflict between money and love exclusively in the heroine, who tries to take charge of the decisions that will directly affect her.[10] The issue of female choice is paramount here, and Hilaria's anguish in this regard, as she considers a life of financial re-straint or the sacrifice of herself for the good of the Exburys, is acute. While her "choice" between the two suitors is strongly influenced by the men around her (Valentine and Sir Archy), in the final act her offer of mar-riage to the man she dislikes in order to save the man she loves is genuine. Although the potential unhappiness this sacrifice raises is never realized, Hilaria does believe her future to be altered irrevocably. Even this moment of agency, however, is brief, and is subsumed in the fact that the old suitor is literally "bought off" so that he will give up his claims to Hilaria. In the apparent finality of Hilaria's act, *Love and Fashion* differs significantly from a play like Sheridan's *The Rivals* (1775), in which dramatic irony permits the audience to be aware that Lydia's love for the Ensign is not one that will actually sacrifice her social station. We have no comparable ease about Hilaria's initial act of self-sacrifice.

While Hilaria's final offer of herself in exchange for Valentine's family's security seems to emerge from within her (as a selfless act that has real consequences), her vacillations between a life of love and one of fashion emerge from the manipulations of others. The play does not show Hilaria as being compelled by the "choice" between Valentine (love) and Ardville (fashion), so much as it reveals the extent to which she lives in a world where female choices tend to be circumscribed by pre- and male-determined versions of femininity and attitudes toward marriage and finance. Hilaria is manipulated alternately by Sir Archy and Valentine. Each man bases his view of women on stereotypical notions about them: they are fickle, easily led, and purely money-conscious. In Valentine's mind, the ideal woman should be above petty concerns and devote herself to emulating the virtues of forbearance and sacrifice. Valentine and Archy view Hilaria's wavering between choosing "love" or "fashion" simplistically (in fact, not as a conflict at all), because they expect her to see the issue as a "typical" woman. Such a simplified, gender-based evaluation of a woman's deliberations further demonstrates the male figures' view that women can be easily deciphered in both moral and financial terms. Hilaria is misunderstood by the male figures around her, largely because of the idea that women can easily make "choices" they have little control over, even when their choices will affect them in long-term ways.

This woman's placement in *Love and Fashion* between two contradictory urgings about lifestyle choices, each represented by a male figure, is similar to the female physicality in Burney's tragedies. Burney suggests that much female turmoil is brought on by a conflict between male characters with competing views of female behavior and with competing agendas. The desire for a marriage of convenience is conceptualized by Valentine as inappropriate and immoral; the desire for love is viewed by Sir Archy as naive and fruitless. Hilaria, like the tragic heroines, is further led to believe that she cannot make a lifestyle "choice" without this choice having severe repercussions on others, so that the elevation of others' welfare over one's own (a stereotypically feminine virtue) is encouraged. Hilaria is led to believe that if she marries Ardville, she denies the Exburys their family money and will suffer Valentine's eternal condemnation. If she marries Valentine, she will deny Archy (and herself) a comfortable life. The only solution to this lose-lose situation is the literal exchange of woman for money.

Hilaria Dalton's position between two authoritative male figures is symptomatic of that of several Burney heroines who exist without family ties, though her relationship to Lord Exbury is patterned on a father-daughter connection. Hilaria is also placed between two families insofar as her marriageable state raises the possibility that she could leave Lord Exbury's guardianship to become Lord Ardville's wife, or remain in the family by marrying Valentine. Like Adela in *The Siege of Pevensey*, she moves between a series of men: Lord Exbury, Archy, and Valentine are her advisors, Valentine and Ardville are her suitors. Her refusal of both men's proposals leads to problems, not the least of which is Lord Exbury's forced removal from Ardville's house at a time when Mordaunt's debts have become very trying.

Straub's and Epstein's studies of Burney's fictional heroines provide useful counterparts to this analysis of Hilaria's dilemma. Straub's description of a dichotomy in *Evelina* resembles that I outline above: the opposition of two different social formulations of female destiny. She writes that "the ideology of romantic love as the raison d'être of female life is juxtaposed, in the novel, to another set of cultural expectations about the course of women's lives that is equally ideological, equally embedded in late eighteenth-century ways of thinking about female maturity."[11] She goes on to write about the troubling endings of so many turn-of-the-century novels (Austen's and Burney's come to mind), wherein the heroine's marriage ends the novel but leaves unresolved the potential conflicts that she will face as a married woman. Straub suggests that the problem with the "happy-ever-after" ending is an awareness of the "other" set of expectations, that "powerlessness and loss—not happiness—were the defining features of growing out of the conventional period of youth and sexual attractiveness."[12] This description of postcourtship relationships is relevant to *Love and Fashion*, for Hilaria's concerns about her marital "choice" stem not from fears about her immediate future, but about the years ahead, when beauty will fade. This fear is exploited by Sir Archy when he urges her to seek the financial security he would prey upon.

Epstein examines the violence and ruptures that characterize Burney's texts. She is not unlike Doody in her concentration on a psychological portrait of Burney as well as of her characters. Epstein writes that Burney's fictional heroines "share a problem that is also that of their creator's nonfictional surgical ordeal [her mastectomy]: how to remain a properly behaved, decorous eighteenth-century lady while burdened with legitimate, and terrorizing, anger at situations that limit her autonomy, and how to weight the risks of rebellion against the humiliations of submission."[13]

While Hilaria expresses annoyance more than rage at her dilemma, her response betrays a deep-seated fear about her future. It is clear that her autonomy is very much curtailed, for she senses that being "properly behaved" and "decorous" require her to be oblivious about her future security, and further, that any notion of material comfort should be beneath her consideration. Otherwise, she is subject to insulting accusations about her moral stature. The risks of rebellion in either case are not inconsequential. A coercive ideology of female conduct that leaves women the alternatives of moral naiveté or selfish materialism is compellingly dramatized in *Love and Fashion*.

When Hilaria first appears, she performs as her name suggests, with a light-hearted, eager anticipation of the next fête in "London—animated London!" (I.ii.61). Her love of fashion, her unstable situation as a ward, and the repercussions her choices have are reflected in the setting, a *"magnificent Drawing Room"* (I.ii). The room's attractive glitter must be left behind when the Exburys move, all because of Hilaria's refusal of Ardville. This threat cannot help but warn Hilaria of the difficulty of acting without acknowledging the financial exigencies of life and remind her that it is not her drawing room in the first place, but that it could be if she marries Ardville. Both Hilaria and Miss Exbury, who is in the room with her, have a taste for the high life. Hilaria, however, attempts to prove to Miss Exbury that she rejected Lord Ardville not because of her love for Valentine, but because he is ugly: "really, his countenance—his deportment—his eyes—Oh!—" (I.ii.33-34). Valentine's poor fortune is, conversely, unredeemed by his attractiveness, and Hilaria feels that with him she would be "poor and obscure, and, consequently, miserable" (I.ii.39-40). Miss Exbury asks Hilaria, "Will you never, then, marry, till you can unite Love with Fashion?" and Hilaria answers, "Never!" (I.ii.41-43). Hilaria is thus introduced as if she were shallow and interested only in money, in the company of a clearly self-absorbed young woman.

If it is apparent that Hilaria wants a financially advantageous match, it also becomes apparent that she has not been permitted to make such a decision on her own. Moral decisions and financial acumen have been juxtaposed in the persons of her advisors. We are told that Sir Archy has been "enraged" (I.ii.24) by Hilaria's refusal of Ardville because it was his idea that she should refuse only Valentine. Hilaria, however, cannot trust her own actions, for she admits when she is alone that she cannot get Valentine out of her thoughts (II.i.3-4). Although she announces her happiness that she resisted him (II.i.6), she has "never been happy since!" but has been "gay—so nobody has found it out" (II.i.6-7). Hilaria's actions and wishes seem dictated by two forces: familial pressure and the need to maintain public appearances. Female romantic desire that transgresses orders and social approval is a theme Burney frequently explores. As Burney's use of the figure alone onstage implies, genuine desire is counterproductive for and discouraged by Hilaria's small community, and so must remain private.

Not unlike Cerulia, Hilaria is repeatedly discussed by men or encounters men who tell her what her ideals not only *should be* but, in effect, *are*. The male authorities who construct versions of Hilaria to suit themselves include Lord Ardville, Sir Archy, and Valentine. Where Hilaria and Ardville are concerned, Burney makes effective use of the stage space. Lord Ardville constructs his view of Hilaria entirely in her absence, in his discussions with the sycophantic Litchburn, which suggests in and of itself Ardville's interest in hearing no opinions that compete with his own. That he and Hilaria have no direct contact with one another until the final scene tellingly communicates the relatively insignificant position she occupies in his mind. Ardville reveals to Litchburn that his concern is less with Hilaria's rejection than with his fear that the people around him may have heard about it and conclude that he has "been playing the part of an old fool" (II.ii.84). He fears and anticipates a cuckolding. His main challenge, in fact, is not to gain Hilaria, but to win the unstated competition against Valentine. Securing Hilaria will gain Ardville public admiration and, better yet, disappoint his brother's family. In fact, Hilaria is represented by Lord Ardville as a "little fool" who he senses has, in the community's view, inappropriate power over him (II.ii.120). Lord Ardville prides himself on the belief that he seldom makes an "error of judgement" (II.ii.178-79), and he is content to believe that Hilaria's rejection of him could not be because of her own inclinations. This refusal to grant her agency is not surprising.

The marriage of convenience as a family economic affair is aptly illustrated in Hilaria's relationship with cousin Archy, whose main aim is vicarious financial success, for which he is willing to exchange his relative. Sir Archy rivals Lord Ardville and Valentine in his implicit dismissal of Hilaria, which lurks under his disingenuous solicitations for her welfare. Sir Archy Fineer announces his self-interest in Hilaria's match: "If I make this match, the coterie of Hilaria,—her opera Box,—her purse, occasionally—and her Table habitually, must be mine. 'Twill be mighty convenient. Yes, I'll e'en tie the noose for her" (II.ii.134-37). The image of confinement expressed here—a knot that is at once the marriage tie and a mechanism for punishment—is ironically appropriate in its reflection of Hilaria's subordinate position and Archy's power where the marriage is concerned. To achieve the match, Sir Archy alternately preys on Hilaria's desire for luxury and ingratiates himself with Lord Ardville through flattery. To the latter, he strategically represents Hilaria as a woman of "Youthful inexperience" who "may sometimes stand in need of friendly counsel" (II.ii.172-73). His counsel consists of presenting Hilaria with the idea that marriage to Valentine means a tawdry, dull, and unfashionable life in the country. Archy is nearly successful, too, in persuading Hilaria to reject this life.

In Sir Archy's view, affection in marriage is superfluous to financial security, or is a laughable ideal. Emotional detachment, even physical revulsion, are small prices to pay for luxury: "who, of any fashion, live enough together to care whether their mate be hideous, or adorable?" (II.iii.17-18). Hilaria is told that Valentine actually loves fashion as much as she does, and because of this he may not wait for her "true love," but will find sexual satisfaction elsewhere. As Archy says, "Very possibly [Valentine] may have some business—some little engagement—in town" (II.iii.66-67). Sir Archy explains (and unwittingly exemplifies) that "all men are alike" in dissembling when there is something they want (II.iii.72). He then paints to Hilaria a picture of herself as a wealthy, fashionable widow. She is not permitted to speak in her defense. Archy's satisfaction at his manipulation of her is evident in his description of her as a "deer . . . fairly caught" (II.iii.123) and he patronizingly believes that he understands her "better than [she does her]self" (II.iii.118-19). What he does not admit is his own part in forcing her silence, and then speaking her consent to Lord Ardville. In keeping with the suggestion that much of the conflict in *Love and Fashion* is between competing men rather than between men and women, it is fitting that it is Sir Archy's consent to Lord Ardville, rather than Hilaria's, to which Valentine responds.

Valentine's view of love and marriage is idealistically based on a sense of moral superiority that in his eyes condemns Hilaria *almost* beyond his ability to redeem her. Her acceptance of Ardville renders her the soul of "sordid depravity" (III.ii.382). Her "choice so obviously mercenary renders her unworthy even of regret" (III.ii.423-24) and she is a vain "slave of Fashion—and [Valentine], a plain, but feeling man, [who is] happy to have escaped her" (III.ii.428-29). The scene in which Valentine voices his repulsion contrasts strongly with the drawn-out coercion of Hilaria by Sir Archy, which should reveal to the audience that Valentine's condemnations are melodramatic and unjustified. When it comes to Valentine's conflict with Lord Ardville and Sir Archy, Burney uses the figures' physicality and their occupation of the stage space to underline their romantic opposition. Valentine and Lord Ardville are present in an equal number of scenes, though it is Valentine who actually comes into contact with Hilaria.[14] At the same time as Valentine is romantically opposed to Lord Ardville, he is ideologically opposed to Sir Archy, so while he pontificates to Hilaria about marital values, he is implicitly arguing with Sir Archy, with whom his values clash. It is thus appropriate that it is Valentine and Sir Archy who battle each other unknowingly, leading to fears of the ghost.

In representing Hilaria's relationship to male figures, Burney manages the stage well. She reflects through speech and action Valentine's mistaken evaluations of Hilaria and the confinement of her desire. Hilaria is alone when she experiences an epiphany of sorts, one that renders country life attractive to her. She hopes that she does not repent her new-found appreciation for Nature and the "charm of rural Liberty" (III.ii.439). Valentine surprises her at this moment, but his desire for secrecy makes him retreat from the scene before he hears her virtuous resolution to give up fashion, and he leaves her open to the addresses of Sir Archy and Ardville. Hilaria is symbolically prevented from speaking by the entrances and exits of the male figures, who speak and move unrestrictedly. This is a terrific dramatization of a woman who is not permitted to speak her own mind. Valentine's retreat from the scene is accompanied by his own resolution to be Hilaria's savior: "And is such a creature made for so base a prostitution of all faith, all sincerity? ah! she wants thought more than heart! She is plunging into a gulph of which she sees not the depth. What if I try—though hopeless, alas, for myself!—to rescue her from such false vows? such worthless ambition? such contemptible motives of choice? . . . Yes! ere I see thee consigned to age, to avarice and to regret, I will probe thee, Hilaria, till I pierce thee to the soul!" (III.ii.479-87). The undeniably sexual imagery is disconcertingly joined with a tone of moral assurance and martyrdom.

Doody urges us to respond to Hilaria as a heroine who petitions for female choice, and indeed Hilaria's response to what seems to be an unpleasant, sealed fate indicates that she is far less naive than Valentine believes. Again, the juxtaposition of scenes works well in creating dramatic irony, for the audience is permitted to see both how much Hilaria is coerced by Sir Archy and how she regards her own situation, despite Valentine's blindness to these events. Hilaria does recognize that she has entered (or has always existed in) a market where her body (necessarily virginal) and her desire must be somehow regulated. For Archy, the regulatory ideal is money, while for Valentine, it is morality. This recognition is an intense moment of truth for Hilaria and her turmoil is considerable. She explicitly describes herself in economic terms, as having made a "wretched barter [of] . . . my whole self, my free existence, for wealth and vanity thus encumbered! . . . Alas! that I should scarcely suspect I had [a heart], till the instant of selling for-ever its dearest natural rights!" (III.ii.542-45). It is telling that Hilaria assumes the agency for her match with Lord Ardville, though the play testifies that Sir Archy has had a significant part in convincing Hilaria of what her attention to fashion and finance should be. This scene parallels scenes in *The Witlings* because Hilaria announces her observations to her servant, Innis, who responds to them quite matter-of-factly. For her, as for the milliners, such romantic notions are luxuries.

Hilaria's sense of having "sold out" to Sir Archy's pleadings is further heightened when she encounters a peasant couple whose "true love" compensates them for their material shortcomings. Her response to this couple, however, rather than illustrating her clear change of heart about Valentine, reveals that she is, in fact, not completely swayed by his unambiguous moral message. Upon retreating to a country vista, she admires healthy living and beauty, but reflects that "Happiness is so impossible without Wealth" (IV.iii.58-59). The sight of the young wood cutter and hay maker (they are unnamed in the "Persons of the Drama") gives her pause for thought, for she overhears them speak of their devotion to each other and their noble work. This set piece is so strongly pastoral, romantic, and sentimental that its moralizing message seems deliberately artificial at best and overwrought at worst. This is perhaps Burney's way of commenting on Valentine's own romantic idealism. Hilaria, who resolves to "fit up . . . [their] little cottage" and "furnish [their] wedding Garments" (IV.iii.119-20), undercuts the moral message of the scene by imposing charitable consumerism on the two.[15]

Hilaria's discussion with Sir Archy following her reverie confirms that she has not given up her love of luxury and wealth. She only regrets that it must be accompanied by Lord Ardville: "'Tis so shocking—so abominable, giving a man one's hand, when one hates him so cordially! . . . when I get into my carriage . . . to see Him at my Elbow!—when I enter my house to have no right to prevent Him from entering it also!—and, when I want to be alone—O Sir Archy!—to make a scruple of bidding the footman shut the door in his face! . . . Is it not provoking one can't marry a man's fortune, without marrying himself? that one can't take a fancy to his mansions, his parks, his establishment,—but one must have his odious society into the bargain?" (IV.iii.130-41). The artificiality of the ghost, the "Strange Man," and the pastoral couple provides a foil for Hilaria's superficially interpreted, but deeply felt fear of a "discordant" union of fashion with an unpleasant husband (IV.iii.152). With trepidation about being a "prisoner for life" (IV.iii.154), Hilaria is about to reject Ardville again, but is swayed by some beautiful jewels and even more convinced when Archy persuades her that in accepting Ardville's wealth, she might save Valentine and Lord Exbury from ruin. Burney plays on the exchange of one "jewel" (Hilaria's virginity) for another.

Unfortunately for Hilaria, she is discovered by Valentine when she is admiring her bejeweled reflection in a mirror. Although she has once more sought to delay her face-to-face meeting with Lord Ardville, at this point she appears to Valentine as an entity with no qualities save that she is Lord Ardville's young wife-to-be and as such she is morally reprehensible, according to Valentine. As Doody points out, Hilaria's self-sacrifice is misinterpreted by Valentine, who is eager to see her as "merely a Vassal, a cypher in the dominion of Fashion" (V.ii.47).[16] He encourages her to consider the nature of the man she will marry, rather than his financial status, as testimony of her own finer human nature. Valentine appeals to a "natural" view of both human desire and marital bliss when he assures Hilaria that Nature will ultimately rise up and assert its "claims" over her, and all other vanities will lose their charm. Just as easily as Sir Archy was willing to paint Hilaria a picture of her widowhood, Valentine talks of "Honour bartered for wealth . . . Domestic bliss sacrificed for luxury . . . and guilty, premeditated divorce!" (V.ii.104-8).

The height of Hilaria's debate over lifestyles comes when Valentine is finally threatened with imprisonment, which persuades her more forcefully than his moral upbraidings. Hilaria hides Valentine in a closet and flies to Lord Exbury to ask for his help, for she is "upon the brink of perjury and wretchedness, and [has] not fortitude to act for [her]self!" (V.iii.6-7). She gives herself to Ardville, if he will give the jewels to Valentine or take on his debts. This exchange is a comic rendering of Adela's offer of herself to save her father in *The Siege of Pevensey* (which again underscores the similar construction of filial and marital duties). While Valentine protests, Lord Exbury seems to view this exchange as a viable one that will maintain the family circle intact; in this respect, he is not unlike Chester. Valentine is not content to be saved, but continues his protestations as he further condemns Hilaria's "perjured vows" and her "boon" (V.iv.196). Hilaria finally makes a tentative suggestion about returning the jewels to Lord Ardville and marrying Valentine, uncoerced, having seen the light of conjugal bliss and the dread of a loveless marriage.

Hilaria's moral "coming around" is presented as the education of a wayward young woman: "it was Valentine who opened my Eyes to the error of my conduct" (V.iv.208-9). The choice between love and fashion has not really been made, however, for Hilaria and Valentine are permitted to have both. Like Pinchwife in Wycherley's *The Country Wife* (1675), Lord Ardville hates, more than anything, the fear that he has been cuckolded. He seeks now a way to save face, and he offers the jewels to the lovers, along with the discharge of Valentine's debt and a settlement. Lord Ardville turns his attention to Litchburn, blames him for his own rumored foolishness, and casts him from his household. Everyone present takes turns extolling the virtues that compensate for a lack of monetary reward, because everyone is seen to have acted generously. Lord Exbury patriotically asks what "Fortune or distinction [is] unattainable in Britain by

Talents, probity, and Courage?" (V.iv.292-93). Felicity and virtue will bless the union of Hilaria and Valentine, who will welcome working for each other. However, such assurances of moral rectitude are overblown, as they are at the close of all of Burney's comedies, for the satisfying resolution of the conflict has not arisen from talent, courage, or employment, but from a last-minute exchange of material goods for a woman's promise, and then the granting of permission to marry in return for the protection of a man's pride. Further, neither Valentine nor Hilaria seems likely to be devoted to much labor.

Love and fashion are not the only two values opposed in this comedy. Different male constituencies also represent different views of how wealth is acquired and maintained; this opposition is also explored in *A Busy Day*. In both plays, an older, established tradition of inherited wealth is contrasted with a newer form of financial acquisitiveness. Lord Exbury is the elder son of the family and his estate is only a "natural Estate, . . . being no more than what comes to him from Father to son" (I.35-36). He is "genteel-behaved, and agreeable!" and his servants adore him (I.37). By contrast, the younger Lord Ardville has acquired his income by "fortune-hunting" and by colonial projects in India, where he made his "great fortune" (I.32). True to his colonizing impulses, Lord Ardville is described as "*highty* and *imperial*!" and is generally disliked (I.38). Lord Ardville has undertaken not only colonial but marital fortune-hunting as well, which adds an ominous note to Sir Archy's view that Hilaria is a hunted "prey." Ardville married well in India and his first wife died (IV.161). The characteristics of the two lords imply that inherited wealth makes for better people. The play's analysis of types of wealth is complicated, however, by the fact that it is Exbury's son who squanders the family fortune, a fortune that would have passed "naturally" to him eventually. It is the younger son, Valentine, who tries to retrieve the fortune by seeking an honorable commission in the army (V.171). In the end, it is Lord Ardville's more commercial and dishonorable wealth that saves the Exburys from ruin and provides for the match between Hilaria and Valentine. The old ways of inheritance and gentility are admirable but fragile in *Love and Fashion*, and the new commercialism of the empire is reliable, if distasteful and dependent on selfishness. It is thus doubly ironic that Exbury praises the "Fortune or distinction" attainable in Britain (V.292), because he is saved by wealth acquired elsewhere through avaricious means.

The conflict between love and fashion is created and perpetuated by male figures who manipulate Hilaria into making what they consider to be the "right" choice (the choice that best satisfies them). Burney features throughout the play curiously untroubled male figures whose views of financial decisions and moral virtues are apparently unambiguous. Sir Archy is willing to urge Hilaria toward a marriage of convenience without qualms. That he is entirely mercenary is suggested by his also being Mordaunt's agent with his creditors. Valentine makes no effort to view Hilaria's situation as that of a woman whose security rests largely in her ability to make a good marriage. As Doody notes, Mordaunt is the quintessential disaffected man, untroubled either by celebration or downfall.[17] Certainly, many of the men provide foils for Hilaria's dilemma in that they are faced by a similar situation themselves, but respond in very different ways. Lord Exbury faces decamping and downsizing his luxurious dwellings: he is to let "Exbury Hall" and "Spring Lawn," will discharge most of his servants, and will remove to the country. He describes this event with the overblown moral terms used by his son, as an "evil which must now burst publicly upon [his] house": "I must renounce the world for the present myself, or know I shall leave my children to obscurity and distress" (II.i.25-30). Lord Exbury gives some weightiness to the necessity of living frugally, and he does acknowledge that it is unfair to ask Hilaria to do the same thing by marrying Valentine. By contrast, Hilaria's need to look out for herself financially is dismissed by Valentine as immoral rather than practical. Male figures are able to respond with a sober sense of the severity of financial distress; they for the most part do not grant Hilaria this same pragmatic view of money.

Love and Fashion represents the challenge of reconciling desire with practicality, a challenge that was familiar to women whose marital prospects were directed by economic concerns. This "choice" for Hilaria is further directed and manipulated by men with competing values. She can marry an indifferent man who she finds completely despicable, but be financially secure, or she can marry a man she loves, but who seems unable to provide a luxurious life. Valentine also brings into the match a rigid and condemning moral code that has already judged Hilaria negatively. The solution rests finally in the willing exchange of money and the marriageable woman and, while love and fashion seem finally to be united, male pride and inflexibility and female self-sacrifice provide for this solution. The ultimate aim of the resolution is not to make Hilaria happy, but to keep Valentine out of jail and firmly in his father's presence and to keep Lord Ardville from being an object of public ridicule.

Burney represents in *Love and Fashion* an aspect of female experience she would explore in other works, such as *The Wanderer*: how female "choice" in matters of money, marriage, and family is highly circumscribed, and how women who have few opportunities to direct their futures are nonetheless subject to public and private chastisement, no matter what their decisions may be. These are ideas familiar also to Evelina,

Cecilia, and Camilla. In *A Busy Day*, Eliza Watts's desire to choose her husband and to act independently is challenged by her and her fiancé's families. In *The Woman-Hater*, Joyce is heavily circumscribed by her relationship with her father, but experiences a range of freedom when she escapes from his purview. These two late comedies take issues raised in *Love and Fashion* and strengthen the context of the family, representing it as an institution that carries with it a specific view of the female submissiveness that serves to confine women's actions and determine their movements in all social spheres.

6

Family Matters
A *Busy Day* and *The Woman-Hater*

A Busy Day and *The Woman-Hater* were probably written, like *Love and Fashion*, before Burney departed for France to join d'Arblay in 1802. Burney may have started *A Busy Day* in December 1801, when she wrote to d'Arblay of some prospects for earning money (*JL*, 5:92). A manuscript of *A Busy Day*, a fair copy in d'Arblay's hand, survives in the Berg Collection. He may have transcribed it after Burney's arrival in France; it bears numerous revisions by both Burney and d'Arblay. *The Woman-Hater* exists in two versions, both in the Berg Collection. One is heavily corrected, the other more neatly revised. Burney drew up cast lists for *A Busy Day* and *The Woman-Hater*, which drew upon the leading players of Covent Garden and Drury Lane, respectively. The players she specified for *A Busy Day* include Thomas Knight as Lord John, Alexander Pope as Cleveland, William Thomas Lewis as Frank, Joseph Shepherd Munden as Mr. Watts, John Fawcett as Mr. Tibbs, Isabella Mattocks as Lady Wilhelmina, Mary Anne Davenport as Mrs. Watts, and Maria Ann Pope as Eliza. Other parts were not assigned. Burney cast in *The Woman-Hater* Thomas King as Sir Roderick, John Philip Kemble as Wilmot, John Quick as Old Waverley, John Bannister as Young Waverley, Jane Pope as Lady Smatter, Sarah Siddons as Eleonora, Dorothy Jordan as Miss Wilmot, and Maria Theresa De Camp as Sophia. The astute casting choices Burney made again remind us that she intended these manuscripts as scripts aimed at eventual performance.[1]

These late comedies focus primarily on the coercive potential the institution of the family has in confining female choice and evaluating daughterly and wifely behavior according to very strict notions of obligation, loyalty, and obedience. *A Busy Day* and *The Woman-Hater*, along with *Elberta*, contain Burney's only versions of the intact nuclear family (however temporary its existence may be).[2] The tensions Burney explores in these late comedies are familiar to her readers (class conflict, the financial contingencies of the marriage market, and the pursuit of named legitimacy as a guarantor of social status), but the concentration of conflict among those who are biologically related intensifies the disjunction between the wished-for affective tie and the reality of the hierarchies and inequalities found within families. Lynda E. Boose and Betty S. Flowers suggest that "[r]ather than a natural, essential, transhistorical entity, the family has been recharacterized [since the early 1970s] as a thoroughly cultural production, an entity whose capacity for biological reproduction has masked recognition of its monumental historical importance as a site for ideological reproduction."[3] One theme of these late comedies is aptly described by this view of the family, for Burney recognizes the ease with which the family as a "natural" and biologically based entity is invested with emotional power and a sense of necessity and desirability. However, families are shown to be simultaneously, and with quiet effectiveness, the source of numerous social rules and evaluative standards that are especially forceful and negative for wives and daughters.

I use the term "familial ideology" to refer to the many forces that encourage, implore, demand, or coerce family members to behave in specified ways.[4] Such forces often reduce female individuality to a state of unquestioned filial or wifely affection for and submission to patriarchal authority, whether the patriarch is husband or father. The family is thus an original source of gender definition. Again, the relationship between gender and other categories of social organization is clear, because the family is also an institution that helps maintain inheritance lines, paternal authority, misogyny, and distinctions between social classes. As Chris Weedon writes, women are particularly troubled by

> conflicting definitions of the true or desirable nature and function of the family and more specifically what it means to be a wife and mother. . . . In conservative discourse the family is the natural basic unit of the social order, meeting individual emotional, sexual and practical needs, and it is primarily responsible for the reproduction and socialization of children. Power relations in the family, in which men usually have more power than women and women more power than children, are seen as part of a God-given natural order which guarantees the sexual division of labour within the family. . . . The organization of society in family units guarantees the reproduction of social values and skills in differential class and gender terms.[5]

As an apparatus of a more general conventional (conservative), patriarchal ideology, the family serves two related functions in the maintenance of hierarchies of both class and gender. "Undesirable" members of society can be barred from families that are thus inoculated against usurpers who threaten biological and deportmental "breeding." The submission of wives and daughters to a patriarchal authority also, ideally, guarantees the legitimacy of children and the transmission of social class from parent to child.

The coercive potentialities and social exigencies of family life are, in Boose and Flowers's term, "masked" by an idealized view of its ability to provide its members with affection, approval, and protection. It is this idealization that Burney challenges. In *A Busy Day*, the family is exposed for its failure to provide emotional support for its members and for its blind prejudice against outsiders. In *The Woman-Hater*, daughterly and wifely obedience is enforced by paternal misogyny that cows women. In *A Busy Day*, the strength of intra- and interfamilial interaction successfully maintains class divisions and gender oppression, while in *The Woman-Hater*, "family values" (particularly of female submissiveness) cannot completely contain individual passion or ensure that illegitimacy and usurpation are uniformly punished. In *A Busy Day*, Eliza ultimately submits to traditional familial relationships; in *The Woman-Hater*, Joyce successfully establishes herself as an individual free of a patriarchal family unit.[6]

A Busy Day, as Doody notes, is a female Nabob story.[7] Eliza Watts is a young woman who has just returned to England from India, where she inherited a large sum of money from her guardian, Mr. Alderson.[8] Her fiancé, Cleveland, has also returned, summoned by his uncle, Sir Marmaduke Tylney, to what he thinks will be an announcement of his inheritance. Eliza discovers a merchant-class family whose vulgar breeding she feels will impede her acceptance by Cleveland and his family. She is thus hesitant to reveal her engagement. An accidental meeting leads Cleveland's younger brother, Frank, to pursue Eliza and the fortune that will rescue him from debts, while he remains oblivious of Eliza's relationship with his brother. In the meantime, Cleveland finds that his family has called him home to announce an arranged marriage to a Miss Percival, whose fortune will pay off Sir Marmaduke's mortgage. Cleveland's inability to tell Eliza of the arrangement makes him appear unfaithful to her when she sees him with his new intended. Miss Percival discovers Cleveland's previous attachment and schemes with Frank to bring the aristocratic and nouveau riche families together in order to embarrass Cleveland and destroy his match. The result is an evening during which snobbery and rudeness, pride and prejudice succeed in interfering with Eliza and Cleveland's wedding plans. In an effort to spite the Tylneys further, Miss Percival withdraws her dowry, which leads Sir Marmaduke to prepare to ship Cleveland back to India. Cleveland is thus further hesitant to claim Eliza. Mistaken identities are ultimately

Frank (Ian Kelly) falls under the spell of Miss Percival (Juliette Grassby) in *A Busy Day*, Show of Strength production, Hen and Chicken Theatre, Bristol, directed by Alan Coveney and designed by Elizabeth Bowden. Courtesy of Bob Willingham and Alan Coveney, Show of Strength

cleared up with the help of Cleveland's sister, Jemima, who arranges the exchange of Eliza's fortune for Sir Marmaduke's estate so that the couple's plans can proceed. Frank is left with Miss Percival, and Cleveland's aunt, Lady Wilhelmina, is left lamenting the vulgar family to which she is to be allied. Cleveland delivers the closing message of the play, that "Merit is limited to no Spot, and confined to no Class" (V.907-8) and that the merchant class deserves recognition.

Membership in a family is shown to be both idealized and coercive, at once forcing individuals together romantically and keeping them apart in distinct social classes. This process is powerful for Eliza, whose idealization of family ties leads her to submit financially and emotionally to her parents, and then in turn to limit her personal desire because she feels she cannot escape identification with her family's vulgarity. Eliza's task is to discover a way to remain properly obedient to her family and to gain Cleveland as a marriage partner, which leads her to become characterized in different ways depending on who interprets her social and familial position. She discovers, in a manner similar to Cecilia in The Witlings, that the final key to her marriage to Cleveland is not her individuality, but her money, and that her family's vulgarity will always haunt others' opinions of her.

Eliza Watts is perpetually torn between competing identities. She both idealizes her parents and yet seeks independence from the class, manners, and attitudes they represent. A Busy Day thoroughly questions this aspect of participation in the family: to what extent can familial obligations or membership be chosen or rejected, especially by women? Although Eliza enters the dramatic scene as an independent woman financially, socially, and bodily, over the course of the represented action (one busy day), we see her gradually giving over her autonomy first to her family and then to her fiancé's family. Her losses are material and personal: an £80,000 inheritance, the ease of social interaction, an autonomous marital choice. The process of yielding both self and money is intense because it foregrounds the conflict between what *should be* and what *is* in terms of family connection. Eliza senses the constructed nature of familial ideology—she originally conceives of daughterly submission as a choice—but discovers that this "choice" is illusory. She certainly seems unable to conceive of alternatives to it. Burney critiques familial power by dramatizing the process by which women who are otherwise financially and socially independent of their families force *themselves* into the very submission that their money should render unnecessary.

In the tragedies, Burney emphasizes how the physical occupation of space is indicative of relative powerlessness for female figures. In A Busy Day, she grants a similar iconographic function to the use of stage space in several pivotal scenes, including the opening scene, when she establishes the independence of her heroine. Eliza enters a hotel room with remarkable assertiveness despite her unfamiliarity with London. Although she is supported by her servants, she calms their cries for help by announcing that she is uninjured. Eliza's first gesture is to "*disengag[e] herself*" (I.6) from her maid, Deborah, and then to silence her and make inquiries about her whereabouts. Eliza has already sent her fiancé from her and has parted from a Mr. and Mrs. Brown "who were to have delivered [her] into the hands of [her] Parents" (I.98-99). Financially secure and physically and socially unabashed by her solitariness, Eliza is an unfamiliar female figure, as the anxious remarks made by Deborah and Cleveland, who arrives shortly, suggest. Her unconventionality is further expressed in her efforts to prevent injuries to her Indian servant, who is routinely ignored by everyone else.[9] It is against this initial representation of female self-direction that Burney shows the gradual decline of Eliza's autonomy. Eliza's nonconformity is overcome by a series of gender- and race-specific judgments that privilege the assessment of value based on presumptions about sex, class, and skin color rather than individual merit.

The paradox of Eliza's entrance—developed throughout the play—is that her independence from Cleveland is something she has demanded in order to become appropriately dependent on her family. She tells him that her desire is to be reunited with her family as a single daughter before disclosing her match with him, which has been arranged without prior parental approval. Her greatest fear is that she would be seen to be "triumphing in [her] independence" (I.78); instead, she wishes to "entreat . . . [her family's] directions how to proceed" (I.146) after living and traveling without them for so long. Burney pairs Eliza's attitude with an immediate incapacity for self-direction, as she becomes generally unable to make her demands on the hotel's waiters heard. The opening scene is Eliza's only moment of autonomy, for she is transformed (and transforms herself) into a more typical daughter who needs familial sanction for marriage and whose marital choices thus become less important than financial connections. Frank and his friend, Lord John, who soon encroach on Eliza in this scene, effectively characterize the position she holds now that she is back in London: they speak of her as if she were absent, commenting on her money and on how "Consumed pretty" she is (I.244). The potential suitor, Frank, takes control of the dramatic space through the verbal and physical abuse that he uses in order to assert his desires.

Eliza's view of family life combines a conventional sense of filial duty with a surprising recognition that she will "act" a part that is not entirely authentic. While the ability to feign daughterly respect should downplay the strength of familial ideology, in fact such deception substantiates the power of family ties to mold behavior despite their artificial nature. Eliza discloses to Cleveland that her parents' "claims are so near, and must to themselves seem so complete that the communication [about the engagement] cannot, I think, be made with too much circumspection. A Father,— A Mother—my dear Cleveland! what sacred ties! Even though my memory scarcely retains their figures, my heart acknowledges their rights, and palpitates with impatience to shew its instinctive duty" (I.86-91). Eliza wants her parents to *think* that she is completely tied to them, a disingenuousness that is countered by her investment of biological ties with "natural" and religious overtones, replete with appropriate behavior and emotional avowals. Artificiality and an idea about "natural" ties seem curiously compatible in her mind.[10]

Once Eliza meets her parents and sister, her sense of controlling her relationship with her family fades to a sense of obligation. Although her dialogue indicates a resistance to becoming another Miss Watts (she refers to her family as her "nearest Friends" [III.146]) and despite her clear embarrassment over the family's vulgarity, Eliza resolves that she "never will forsake nor disavow [her] family" (III.310-11). While Doody writes that the play shows a "corrective to filial reverence,"[11] the corrective is

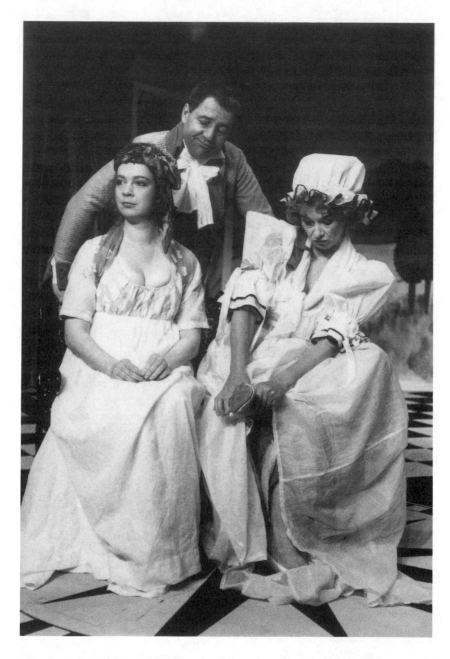

Eliza (Wendy Hewitt) and Margaret (Maggie O'Brien) sit with Cousin Joel Tibbs
(Paul Nicholson) in Kensington Gardens, in *A Busy Day,* Show of Strength
production, Hen and Chicken Theatre, Bristol, directed by Alan Coveney and
designed by Elizabeth Bowden. Courtesy of Bob Willingham and Alan Coveney,
Show of Strength

never fully achieved, for Eliza performs under a sense of obligation throughout. She labors to supply her parents and sister with familial emotions and ties just as certainly as she supplies them with the material baggage of a newly arrived foreigner. Indeed, she is a foreigner in many respects, for she encounters attitudes that surprise her in their novelty: a complete identification of her worth with her wealth, an emotional void, and a comic but important new set of names (her sister pretentiously hails her as "Elizeana," while she is the diminutive "Lizzy" to her mother and "Bet" to her father).

The Watts family reunion is accomplished with a variety of spatial and verbal cues that augment the discomfort and disappointment of Eliza's situation.[12] As she meets Mr., Mrs., and Miss Watts, Eliza runs to greet them, a demonstration of eagerness that is scarcely acknowledged. The greeting to her father, on her bended knee, prompts a "How do do, my dear?" from him, and the observation "I should never have known you!" (I.375-76). Her sister Margaret comments on her hat and her beaux, and her mother responds to her open arms with a caution against squeezing an expensive new handkerchief (I.394-95). In the dialogue exchanged following the reunion, Eliza is shut out verbally as well as emotionally by her family (I.394-528). She speaks only seven times (10 percent of the dialogue), once to have an emotional remembrance of Mr. Alderson interrupted by a request for "Indy muslin" (I.420) and later to defend her bizarre respect for Indian people, among whom her father's money can now prevent both daughters from going. Burney's stage business implies Eliza's peripheral place next to her family and emphasizes how closed their circle is to her (Mrs. and Miss Watts tend to whisper to one another, for instance). This scene physically and verbally confirms Eliza's speculation that the unproblematic inclusion of Cleveland in the family through marriage seems unlikely. Eliza must silence her individuality and construct a place for herself in the context of the family. This opening recognition scene suggests that Eliza is the heroine of a sentimental comedy caught somehow in a comedy that begins rather than ends with reunion, and a disappointing reunion at that.

Although Eliza does not feel joined to her family, she does become identified with them. The Wattses' strongest influence over Eliza is to determine her social status. Her inheritance cannot counteract her identification with nouveau riche relatives, and Eliza soon realizes that her desired match with Cleveland will be unacceptable to him because of the frowned-upon category of her family's wealth and their manners. Burney represents Eliza's disappointment in this fact repeatedly in spatial and verbal terms, when the daughter's inability to separate herself from her family results in general discomfort and distance from Cleveland. When the Wattses take a stroll around Kensington Gardens (act 3), they spy Cleveland, Jemima, and Miss Percival. The latter perpetually renews her bodily contact with Cleveland (despite his protestations), which leaves Eliza silent and constantly moving away from the clinging pair. Eliza's gestures reflect her social unease. Her mind is "too ill at ease for rest" (III.347) and she "*looks down*" (III.425), turns her head away, or, fittingly, has her view of Cleveland "*intercept[ed]*" by her mother and sister (III.472). Margaret Watts at one point takes over her sister's rightful position of responding to Cleveland's attempts to communicate, and Miss Percival vocally disapproves of the Wattses. Eliza "*rises but keeps aloof*" (III.515) or "*walk[s] aloof*" (III.537). Her emotional response to the unexpected and confusing meeting with Cleveland is only verbalized once she is alone: in her family's presence she cannot give voice to it. Alone, she observes that Cleveland's mind must "involuntarily recoil from an alliance, in which shame must continually struggle against kindness, and Pride against Happiness" (III.572-74). Eliza's actions and silence suggest in fact that the attitudes she imagines to be his are similar to her own. Her devotion to her family is nominal only, as she dutifully martyrs herself to an ideal of filial obligation.

A Busy Day is as much about generalized class and racial prejudice as it is about Eliza's own particular experience of the connection between family, class, and marriage. In depicting two families that occupy distinct social positions and who are antagonistic because of them, Burney shows how the affiliations of class and biology are connected. As Barrett and McIntosh note, the family is a prime vehicle for maintaining class prejudice: ". . . far from being a social leveller, forging bonds that cut across the barriers of class and sex, the family creates and recreates the very divisions it is often thought to ameliorate."[13] Each figure in *A Busy Day* comments in some way on class divisions. Mr. Watts laments his failure to achieve recognition along with money, Sir Marmaduke manifests a complete disdain for those "beneath" him, and Lady Wilhelmina is appalled by the idea of a "citizen" entering her family. For Sir Marmaduke especially, the problems of the lower class (fire, starvation, harvests) are significant only if they interfere with his leisure activities. Sir Marmaduke permits Frank's interest in a "citizen" because he is a younger brother, and as such, his marital choices have less influence on the family's integrity. As Sir Marmaduke says, "Who cares about the genealogy of a younger Brother's wife?" (II.351-52). Although Eliza's manners and money are acceptable, they are not influential enough to protect her from the endless stigma of being a Watts. It is significant that the money that solves the conflict (Eliza's) comes from inheritance rather than business (as her father's does), and inheritance that is extrafamilial at that. Margaret Watts, who misunderstands Cleveland's approaches to her in the garden, is "unacceptable" in a number of different ways and she does not have the luxury of *inherited* wealth to help her overcome this fact.

The construction and evaluation of identities according to lineage, inheritance, or earned money create problems for Eliza's self-definition. Her acceptance of family ties leads her to see herself, for the purposes of her proposed marital alliance, as a Watts, and to feel somehow implicated by the Wattses' shameful behavior. She is a woman deeply divided by her loyalties, her ideals, and her shame. Her escape from this division, however, is only partial and requires her to be placed in an economy that equates female worth exclusively with money. While Cleveland is also confined by his family's choices for him, his situation differs greatly from Eliza's. He is never forced into the position of denying his family or separating himself from them. His fear of rejection by Eliza is entirely illusory, because of his higher social claims. Her trepidation, by contrast, is confirmed by Lady Wilhelmina: an alliance with Eliza is an alliance with the Wattses, and unlike Cleveland, Eliza cannot have both her marriage and her family approved.

Eliza's malleable identity is one mark of the play's exploration of the nature/nurture dichotomy: she is a submissive daughter, independent heiress, foreigner, sophisticate, pretty face, financial resource, and orphan. It is no wonder, then, that she cannot enter space and occupy it in a self-possessed and assertive fashion. Burney makes full use of blocking and dialogue in order to communicate this borderline existence once Eliza enters the Tylney home (act 4). She has been summoned here by Cleveland who is not home when she arrives, so she is once more alone. Here she is assumed to be what she is not by birth (a member of the upper class), but she cannot assert who she is: a Watts by birth, an heiress by adoption, and a fully refined lady because of her upbringing. Lady Wilhelmina perceives an "elegant deportment" which "immediately announces [her] own connexions to be in the very first style—" (IV.64-65). Because of Lady Wilhelmina's uninformed acceptance of her, Eliza is then forced to listen to the tales of Cleveland's attachment to Miss Percival and Frank's "disgraceful purpose" regarding a woman from the City (IV.134). Eliza is thus pushed simultaneously into the roles she vacillates between: she is the girl from the City, Frank's advertised but unintroduced conquest, an accepted social peer of Lady Wilhelmina, and Cleveland's unacknowledged fiancée. The misinterpretations render Eliza nearly speechless, or at least unable to make herself heard; she questions Lady Wilhelmina unsuccessfully, stutters, and does not finish her sentences. From her place in the Tylney house "*in a recess at the end of the scene*" (IV.327), she witnesses Frank's awkward petition to Mr. Watts, who has come to the house with the would-be suitor, and the subsequent arrival of Cleveland. Eliza is then forced to observe the confused debate between Cleveland and Frank over her. She becomes the subject of too many intertwined and contradictory conversations. Cleveland does not extricate his real intentions from the morass, and Eliza leaves without hearing his explanations. When social and familial roles become problematic or difficult to fulfill, identity itself is thrown into question.

The meeting of the Tylney and Watts families in act 5 is a marvel of stage handling. The two families have been invited together by Miss Percival, who, spurned by Cleveland, wants revenge. Burney indicates a large number of gestures and movements intradialogically. The act includes a series of entrances and exits that force together different character constituencies, which tend to consist of discrete pairs. Mrs. and Margaret Watts enter *"richly dressed"* and comment on the lavish surroundings (V.178-81). They attempt through their gestures to make themselves a seamless part of the finery, but fail miserably and it is very clear that this is a space that does not welcome them. Margaret accuses her mother of making a "stiff courtsie" (V.186) and proceeds to demonstrate her own superior brand of deference. The second set of novelties enters, Mr. Watts and his cousin, Joel Tibbs, and Miss Percival and Frank mutter between themselves, and then brush by Mr. Watts midbow. This prompts an observation from Mr. Watts, who notes that "The civiler one is, the ruder they be! You'd never believe what a push she give me in going by" (V.221-22).

Significantly, little whispered conversations take place between figures with similar social backgrounds, as in the milliner's shop in *The Witlings,* but seldom is there interchange between those with inherited wealth, and those whose wealth is earned. The short confrontation (conversation would be a misnomer) between the Wattses and Lady Tylney exemplifies the mode of exchange that takes place in this scene:

> MRS. WATTS. Dears, my dear, I wish she'd receive us, like; for I'll be whipt if I can think of an word to say for a beginning.
>
> MISS WATTS. Why ask if she's going to Rinelur. That's the genteel thing to talk about in genteel company.
>
> MRS. WATTS. I will, my dear. Pray good lady, may you be going to Rinelur to night?
>
> LADY WILHELMINA. Sir Marmaduke!
>
> SIR MARMADUKE. Lady Wil.?
>
> LADY WILHELMINA. Did any body—speak to Me?

MRS. WATTS. Yes, it was me, my good lady, as spoke; it wasn't that Gentleman.

LADY WILHELMINA. How singular! (turning away) [V.263-74]

Mrs. Watts has a sense of how fine people behave, just as the witlings understand the concept behind a literary party, but neither can quite pull it off. Vulgar pronunciations announce the status of interlopers and Lady Wilhelmina's aghast response to her husband rather than to Mrs. Watts is excused generously by the latter as a mistake rather than a snub.

It requires Joel Tibbs to pull the mask off of the rudeness expressed by the Tylneys. He observes to Margaret: "What think you of this purdigious fine quality breeding? Walking off one by one, without never a word, except turning up their noses? If this here behaviour's what they call the thing, it's none so difficult. I warrant I could do it as well as they; it's a little more than turning upon one's heel when a body speaks to one; or squeling a tune at 'em; or saying over again their own last word." (V.658-63). Margaret challenges Tibbs to make the attempt and he obliges. He stares at the Tylneys; refuses to respond to their requests, making out as if he has not heard them; and then *throws himself full length upon the sofa* (V.694). The sofa, which Lady Wilhelmina "had thoughts of occupying [her]self!" (V.700) becomes in miniature the territory fought over by these antagonistic parties. Rather than gaining any mutual understanding in the process of spending time in proximity, the members of these families instead have their divisions solidified. The last we hear from Tibbs is his imitation of Lord John's "O the Doose!" and "O the Divil!" (V.748, 51). While different exits and entrances create a variety of meetings on the stage following this, the last arrangement sees all the figures onstage but no closer together ideologically than they were to begin with.

Eliza's own particular antagonism with Cleveland is resolved when Jemima leads her out to explain the situation and the impediments to her marriage are removed at the end of the play, because Jemima intercedes and convinces Sir Marmaduke to take Eliza's fortune to pay off his mortgage. That it is Jemima who petitions for the acceptance of Eliza, without Cleveland's knowledge, underscores how ineffectual Cleveland is regarding his own inclinations. Eliza then makes the arrangement of the marriage with her "friends" and announces that the consent of her family is of the utmost importance to her (V.824-25). However, while Eliza is finally reconciled with the proper brother and their marriage is permitted, she is not completely released from being identified with her family and its vulgar origins. Sir Marmaduke is willing to "hang her Birth!" for the sake of her fortune (V.791), but Lady Wilhelmina is not and her protest perpetuates the racialization of class prejudice evident throughout the play: "Surely Sir Marmaduke, you have not accomodated yourself with a person descended from such a tribe? . . . I can make no compromize" (V.893-96). The marriage and the money are unlikely to relieve the prejudice which is, as Eliza notes, "so chillingly unkind, so indiscriminately unjust" (V.902-3).

Eliza's last speech suggests that she is still caught between her family's power to define her and her desire to be accepted on her own merits. Cleveland's final pronouncement, in fact, actively encourages Lady Wilhelmina not to accept the vulgar Wattses, but to ignore them.[14] He tells his aunt to "look not at the root, but the flower," for "Merit is limited to no Spot, and confined to no Class" (V.895, 907-8). Cleveland's preference for examining the flower rather than the root as much as asserts his contempt for Eliza's genealogy, which he overlooks by superficially clipping Eliza from her roots and grafting her to his own: "from weeds so coarse can a flower so fragrant bloom? How beautiful, o Nature, are thy designs! how instructive is thy study! Avaunt all narrow prejudice; Elegance, as well as talents and Virtue, may be grafted upon every stock, and can flourish from every soil!" (III.599-603). In Cleveland's eyes, Eliza only achieves elegance by being separated from her family and grafted on another. In fact, this is the tale of her upbringing, when she was transplanted to Mr. Alderson's care in the first place. She must achieve this most recent social transplantation by giving up the financial independence that is her only possible source of autonomy. The play ends where others would conventionally begin, in a scene dominated by physical comedy and prejudiced misunderstanding. The reunion of child with family that we expect to close an eighteenth-century play is relegated to the early scenes of Burney's drama, which then reveals the consequences of having to cope with a reunion that is unfulfilling and unhelpful to the woman in question.

Burney shows that wealth is an inimitable social quality; that "breeding," manners, and emotions can be imitated or ignored; but that social divisions predominate because entrance into the Tylneys' circle requires *permission*. Eliza may enter, once her funds are given over to Sir Marmaduke, but the Wattses cannot, despite their money, because they are seen as more inherently "coarse." Mr. Watts in particular regrets having any higher social status at all, because he is generally ignored. Unlike Sir Marmaduke, who wields complete authority, Mr. Watts has lost his paternal power as he has risen nominally in status: "Ever since I left off business, I've never known what to do." His wife and daughter have made him give up old friends, and "as to our new [acquaintances], it's as plain as ever you see they only despise me: for they never . . . get up off their chairs, if I ask them how they do in their own houses; and they never give me a word of answer I can make out, if I put a question to them" (III.275-81). Miss Percival's perpetual flight from the "wigs" (Mr. Watts and Mr. Tibbs) further, and physically, confirms their outcast social state.[15] In their rejection by those within and outside of their families, Mr. Watts and Mr. Tibbs are victims of a social system that has endless criteria for acceptance by the "cultured" and "well-bred." This complete rejection of the newly rich is represented spatially when the families gather at Miss Percival's. Dialogue is not exchanged between the two families, space is only reluctantly shared, and contact is regarded as intolerable by the Tylneys.

Eliza's initial hope that her servant might be treated well and her final awareness that prejudices linger despite nominal acceptance begin and end this critique of gender, class, and racial intolerance.[16] All forms of prejudice coalesce in Eliza; she asks that civility be extended to her Indian servant but she cannot insist on unprejudiced treatment for him or for others deemed inferior for a variety of reasons. She is part of a family from which she feels alienated, loved by a man who cannot find a way to speak to her, and treated as a representative of the vulgar nouveau riche, as a source of income for Sir Marmaduke's mortgage, even as a racially inferior "Other." The proliferation of racially based references and insults ties together ideas about money, class, race, and sex, as Burney shows groups alternately oppressing and being oppressed by others. For instance, the Wattses express their fear of the "Indins" and find solace in the protection they believe their money will grant them. Miss Watts exclaims, "La, nasty black things! I can't abide the Indins. I'm sure I should do nothing but squeal if I was among 'em." But, as Mr. Watts replies, "There's no need for you to go among 'em now, my dear, for I can give you as handsome I war'nt me, as the Nabob gave your Sister." (I.461-64). This expression of undesirable difference is echoed in the Tylneys' equation of class and racial inferiority as they try to distance Eliza and her family. Miss Percival flees the "wigs" while shouting "O the Savages are bearing down upon us!" (III.528-29) and Cleveland refers to members of the London merchant class as if they are foreign "natives of that noble Metropolis" (V.908-9). Frank persistently calls Eliza his "little City Gentoo" (II.487), marriage to whom is a "barbarous . . . downfall" (II.455) despite the "Gentoo's" money.

Imperialism lurks thematically behind the problems Eliza and Cleveland encounter when they return from a colony, for the problems revolve around the insistence that money properly acquired is the sole motivating force for social contact, but that this contact cannot threaten to be too intimate or be without regulation and the right of refusal. The Wattses are necessary to the Tylneys and to Miss Percival, for they establish a group against which to gauge their own success, just as a colonial "Other" might be used. The Indian servant is at the bottom of all forms of stratification.

The figurative purchase of Eliza is mirrored by the literal purchase of Eliza's servant, Mungo. For him, the price of the body is extreme, because he is literally a commodity that has been, as Cleveland casually observes, "just imported from Calcutta" (I.96-97). He has none of the power assumed by his white male counterparts and he is beneath the other servants' contempt, too, because of his race. His nonappearance on the stage simultaneously symbolizes and perpetuates the idea that invisibility is a preferred status for "undesirable" people who enter an unwelcoming society, city, or family.

Although *A Busy Day* exhibits various momentary challenges to hierarchies (a Watts allies with a Tylney, Tibbs relaxes on Lady Wilhelmina's couch), the hierarchies remain in place at the play's close. The Wattses remain shut out from the social gathering and Cleveland's final speech about merit occludes his hesitation to admit that the "little Gentoo" Frank spied is his fiancée. The female autonomy represented so unusually at the play's opening is replaced gradually by family obligation (illusory but inescapable), misconstrued identities, and finally by the subordination of personal to financial worth. The exchange of permission to marry for money takes place and the aristocratic patriarch, Sir Marmaduke, overrides his wife's objections and accepts Eliza into the family, more as a resource than as a niece.

The tendency for both Eliza and Cleveland to be defined by their place in a family and for a family's social position to be a source of shame and an impediment to personal desire leads to an acknowledgement that class boundaries can be crossed only by metaphorically severing one's family ties, artificial as they might be. The potential for a complete removal of Eliza from contact with her family remains beyond the play's scope, but the attitudes expressed at the end of the play do not deny this possibility. The authority of the Tylneys in determining what families and modes of behavior are acceptable (whether through finance or not) remains unchallenged. Merit is shown to be limited to those chosen by the socially and familially powerful, and it is at their discretion alone that individuals are considered "well-bred" and acceptable. Eliza has been torn by both families between self-definition and imitation, desire and obligation, assertion and submission. In *The Woman-Hater*, this same view of the coercive power of the family is explored, but the family's ability to sanction individual action and attitude is not uniform. Its limitation of personal freedom and desire is complicated by an astonishing female figure who seeks to be known on her own terms, though this does not guarantee complete social acceptance any more than does Eliza's money.

The Woman-Hater also considers the family unit's power to mold individual behavior and attitudes and to transmit behavior deemed appropriate to gender, family, and class roles. The oppressive mechanism of membership in a family is not definitely challenged in *A Busy Day*, and by the play's resolution, familial and patriarchal power reign securely. *The Woman-Hater* sees one family simultaneously dis- and reassembled. Burney depicts in this dual moment a variety of ordeals experienced by this family's members. These experiences include submission to the severity of misogyny and paternal authority and the exuberance of escaping this constrictive authority. In the play's resolution, Burney draws attention to a family circle enclosing Wilmot, Eleonora, and Sophia, and potentially stifling the female members of this unit. In opposition to this is Joyce's emancipation from the circle and her potential for self-determination.

The Woman-Hater resurrects some of *The Witlings* to which Burney bid farewell at the start of her career as a playwright. The new figures include Joyce, Sophia, and Eleonora. The remaining figures nearly all evolved over a long period of time. While an exact date of composition for either of the two copies of this play is uncertain, there are indications that Burney was working on the foul copy at least up to 14 November 1801 (as indicated on a postmarked scrap). The fair copy bears a watermark of 1800. The exact process of evolution is also unclear. While the fair copy suggests that Burney's final cast list includes Old and Young Waverley, Sir Roderick and the others, a scrap in her notes for revision, watermarked after 1800, still refers to Codger, a remnant from *The Witlings*. This scrap could post-date the fair copy, which may indicate that she continued to rework the play after making a fair copy.

There are numerous fragments boxed with the fair copy in the Berg Collection that at least partially indicate the gradual transformations that produced *The Woman-Hater*. An intermediary play may have existed, which included characters from *The Witlings*, *The Woman-Hater*, *Love and Fashion*, and *A Busy Day*: Codger, Sir Marmaduke, Censor, Beaufort, Cecilia, and Jack all appear in some scraps, Sir Marmaduke and Dawson in others. In one fragmentary version, Cecilia is Sir Marmaduke's niece, given "new fangled notions" by a literary set. In another, a "Noble Exile" and his children appear along with Lady Esprit, The Persecutor, and others. It would appear that as the final version of *The Woman-Hater* evolved, the following name changes occurred. Sir Roderick replaces Sir Peppery and Sir Marmaduke, Dawson no longer appears, Codger is now Old Waverley, Sophia and Eleonora replace Domina and Adonia/Cedonia respectively, Wilmot was formerly Kembolton, and Joyce replaces Lora.[17] Bob Sapling, Lady Smatter, and Jack all have changed only slightly from *The Witlings*.

Many manuscript fragments of scenes from this long-evolving play are not boxed with the play, but like those for many other plays, can be found in the five folders labeled "Miscellaneous Pieces of Manuscript,

1772-1828." These fragments include versions of Eleonora's first meeting with Lady Smatter, Roderick's antimarital proscription for Jack, Old Waverley's meeting with Sophia and her mother, the disguised Jack's meeting with his father, Joyce's desire to escape her father with Bob, Wilmot's discovery that his wife and a daughter (in one version: Bastardella) reside nearby, many versions of Sir Roderick's woman-hating, a character sketch of the nurse's relationship with Joyce, Joyce's frolicking, the steward's enlistment of Bob as an heir for Roderick, and the original story of Eleonora's sudden flight from Wilmot while they are abroad. None of these fragments indicates an order to Burney's composition, or a date for the final version. It is clear, however, that Burney abandoned the finance and Esprit plots of *The Witlings* in favor of this tangled story of familial rupture, mistaken identity, and eventual reunion.

In *The Woman-Hater*, Lady Smatter's false learning has been recast into a less threatening affectation that interferes with her romantic attachments but does not dominate the play's action. As a young woman, Lady Smatter rejected Sir Roderick in favor of another man who pleased her by wooing her in verse. At the time of the action, Sir Roderick—a confirmed woman-hater—has vowed to avenge himself by willing his fortune to Young Waverley ("Jack") on the condition that he never marry. Lady Smatter and Roderick are also at odds because Roderick's sister, Eleonora, married Lady Smatter's brother, Wilmot, without their approval. Wilmot has just returned from the West Indies with a daughter, to request Lady Smatter's financial support now that she is widowed.[18] Wilmot is without his wife, because she left him and his infant daughter years ago to pursue a licentious affair, in a double abandonment of marital and maternal duty. Miss Wilmot, who quietly observes her father's demands in his presence, is rambunctious when she is left alone with her nurse and servants or with Aunt Smatter.

Wilmot's wife, Eleonora, was denounced by Roderick because of her marriage. She, too, has returned to England to seek Roderick's or Smatter's financial help, and she has a young woman, Sophia, with her. Eleonora claims that Sophia is Wilmot's daughter, with whom she departed because of her fear of Wilmot's jealous rages. Sophia and Eleonora are spied in their cottage in the woods and the former is wooed by both Young Waverley and his father. Identities become confusing when Sophia and Miss Wilmot arrive at Roderick's in order to petition him for support. After complications that include Wilmot's discovery of Eleonora and his horror when he believes she has had a daughter out of wedlock, the Wilmots are reunited as a family unit and the woman thought to be "Miss Wilmot" is discovered to be Joyce, the nurse's daughter, who was substituted for Sophia when Eleonora originally departed. Joyce resolves to take up the life of a ballad singer and marry the dunce Bob Sapling, a "witling" now under the thumb of his sister, Henny, rather than of the overbearing Mrs. Voluble of *The Witlings*.

The story of usurpation and substitution is of course Evelina's story as well. In both *A Busy Day* and *The Woman-Hater*, Burney revisits many of the situations she explored in her first novel, most particularly where the intermingling of social classes and the depiction of class-based anxieties are concerned. Both plays include scenes that are familiar to readers of *Evelina*: embarrassing meetings in Kensington Gardens, the discovery of vulgar relatives, and the horror at finding an impostor in one's family. The different genre permits Burney to foreground, via the *mise en scène*, anxieties about class distinctions, which were becoming increasingly fluid at the end of the eighteenth century. Dramatic actions give an immediacy to the gestural and verbal codes of speech and behavior that mark membership in different classes and that create conflicts between them. Burney reminds us that anxieties about a new social order are felt most when we must share our dressing rooms and sofa with those formerly beyond our doors and our thoughts.

Epstein suggests that the transition from a patronage and patrimony system to bourgeois capitalism and "the uneasy emergence and mingling of distinct social and economic classes" this implied are preoccupations of Burney's novels. Burney "offer[s] a powerful critique of the superficial codes of behavior that condemned the working classes to social inferiority and promoted the landed gentry to a supercilious sense of its own moral aristocracy."[19] When the possession of money by itself could not be used as a justification for social separation, behavior continued to be a marker of social acceptability and refinement. Evelina is intensely anxious about behavior and social position. She is surrounded by social climbers who include her own grandmother, a former "waiting-girl at a tavern;" Polly Green, who takes Evelina's social and familial place; and several other Pollies Madame Duval speaks about: girls who after a time abroad are "so much improved, that [they have] since been taken for [women] of quality."[20]

Evelina's main task is to discover the proper way to "act" when she is with genteel company, so that she might claim her birthright without embarrassment. Her experience with the theater provides a touchstone for her evolving sense of social place. Her second lengthy letter to Villars describes repeatedly her discovery that she must act a new part if she is to fit in with the "quality" and, in this process, she moves from the position of spectator (viewing Garrick's acting and the fine people in St. James's Park), to that of an actress costumed in new silks and a hairdo, to a female spectacle observed at the ball and evaluated by a large, male audience. Evelina eventually becomes a "natural" at the part that her patrilineage finally allows her to claim legitimately.

Evelina's control of most of the novel's narrative draws attention to her own attitudes about class and behavior, especially when she describes her cousins, the Branghtons. As Staves points out, Evelina must "dissociate herself in her own mind from the Branghtons by branding their behavior as rude, pretentious, and unfeeling," and when her connections to them threaten to be too public, Evelina experiences real anxiety.[21] Her contempt for her family demonstrates the mental distance she has traveled from the country and, because we never directly hear from the objects of her ridicule, we might consider the relentless commentary on the family's vulgarity as a rhetorical and narratological gesture that shores up Evelina's claims to Lord Orville and his gentility. Although new to fashionable society, she does not hesitate to pass judgment on the Branghtons and their "extreme want of affection, and good-nature" and their "folly and their want of decency."[22] To Evelina's dismay, her relations run around, fight, laugh out loud, and tease and threaten each other. She finally blames "all the uneasiness" accompanying her departure from London upon them and their "forwardness and impertinence."[23] The Branghtons, in their insistent physicality, may coexist with those above them, but their behavior does not allow them to "fit in" successfully.

Evelina's letters describe for us the mixture of anxiety, ridicule, humor, and dismay that accompanies the mingling of members of different social classes. Far worse than the Branghtons' impertinent use of Evelina's name in claiming Lord Orville's carriage, of course, is Polly Green's assumption of Evelina's rights and name as Belmont's daughter. In the novel, Evelina struggles to *tell* her readers of the trials of fitting in; the play renders the tangible side of emotional and intellectual fears about vulgar behavior and class encroachment, *showing* us some of the prejudices that try to maintain a rigid social structure.

Many of the figures and plot movements in *The Woman-Hater* are conventional elements of eighteenth-century comedy. However, while mistaken identities, impersonations, and reunited families are commonplace, Burney's particular combination of them merits attention because the stock comic situations—an older, undesirable man's courtship of a younger woman, a severed marriage, or a pursuit of the fortune that will assure security—all depend to some extent on the ways in which female figures are perceived. This emphasis on gender is an element of *The Woman-Hater* that unites its separate plots, including Old and Young Waverley's wooing of Sophia, Sophia's and Joyce's petitions to Sir Roderick, the separation and reunion of Wilmot and Eleonora, and the reunion of Sir Roderick and Lady Smatter. While Burney may use conventions that she saw or read about in other plays, she adapts and then reexamines the ways in which male and female figures interrelate, especially in a family setting.

Doody writes that this play (and the other late comedies) examines "injustice, separation, and inadequate or inappropriate responses," particularly as they relate to the Burney "Family Romance."[24] *The Woman-Hater* represents, like *A Busy Day*, the problems that emerge when individuals are expected to fulfill social and familial roles in accordance with a narrow range of predetermined emotional responses and deportment. In *A Busy Day*, Burney's concentration is on the role of the daughter, Eliza. In *The Woman-Hater*, the range of familial identities is expanded to include daughters and wives, and the figure that holds familial power, the husband/father, is examined more carefully and developed more fully than the shadowy Belmont is in *Evelina*. The process by which the behavior of wives, mothers, and daughters is defined—and deviations from this behavior are punished—is represented in physical, verbal, and spatial terms. As the title suggests, misogyny underlies the evaluation and punishment of female figures and is manifested in a variety of forms that include physical confinement, accusations, threats of violence, presumptions of guilt, and enforced silences. This play, more than Burney's other comedies, carries tragic undertones and severely criticizes gender-specific circumscription.

Burney scrutinizes the set of clearly understood emotions, actions, and attitudes that govern the way individuals fulfill the roles of father, mother, and daughter. Actions are categorized by the play's figures as either definitively approved or disapproved, as "natural" and expected, or unnatural and deviant. A normative view of mothers and daughters is that they are obedient, subservient, and "naturally" inclined to meet the demands of fathers and husbands. The paternal role is one defined by strict authority and an assured ability to pass judgment on others, but it threatens to teeter into violence. Perspectives on each of these three roles emerge from different figures, so that Burney does not simplify conflict or make easy assumptions about how men and women should perform socially or familially. She represents instead the complex ways in which people respond to the normative expectations of others, demand actions from themselves, and conceive of their places within families and the larger community. What is clear is that an insistence on rigidly governed behavior or a "natural" hierarchy of father/husband over wives and daughters is especially dangerous for women and leaves for male figures little to choose between authoritarianism and antagonism.

The value of maternal love and responsibility is a prominent element of *The Woman-Hater*. Burney depicts the predominance of maternal ideals and social evaluations of mothering as they relate to two female figures: Eleonora and the nurse. She suggests that appropriate maternal behavior is established and sanctioned by male figures with the aim of limiting female sexuality within the bounds of familial duty. A misogynistic view of unbridled female desire underlies the need for women to be contained within the purview of the family. Apparent deviations from a maternal ideal of devotion and selflessness lead women to be refashioned by negative male judges who identify, in the apparent absence of motherly love, shameless prostitution, adulterous abandonment, or opportunism. Once again, the spatialization of female figures is apparent. Eleonora as mother *should* provide Wilmot with the vessel he might fill with legitimate heirs. He is incensed because he believes she has substituted for his heirs the offspring of her own adultery and has thus foiled his view of himself as the unchallenged male authority in her life.[25]

Eleonora claims for herself, when alone with Sophia, the strongest of maternal inclinations. In depicting maternal devotion, Burney creates a figure who acts in the interests of keeping the mother-child bond intact against the influence of outsiders: "yet how could I bear to leave thee? Not alone to be torn from the joy of thy loved sight—the charm of thy look, the fascination of thy infantine carresses, but to know that thou wouldst be bred to blush for me, and tutored to abhor me . . . I thought myself authorized by maternal duty to prevail with thy Nurse clandestinely to relinquish thee" (III.ii.45-51). Although Eleonora is without community support either emotionally or financially, her sense of performing a duty preserves her from complete despair. She observes, "To what may I lay claim, if not to maternal tenderness? Even the wrong—the sole wrong of which thou canst justly accuse me, sprung it not from that source? Have I not been bereft of all else?" (V.xiv.64-67). A mother's attachment to her child becomes the source of her punishment for apparent wrongs because the mysterious daughter is assumed to be the evidence of her adultery.

The conceptualization of women as social, biological, and narratological spaces has its counterpart in the dramatic space of *The Woman-Hater*. Eleonora and Wilmot are not shown in the same scene until late in the play, which emphasizes Eleonora's attachment to Sophia (with whom she is most often seen) and, by contrast, underscores the vacancy in the Wilmot family. This empty female space is especially emphasized in Burney's use of the stage area and dialogue in the play's opening scenes. When we first see Wilmot, he is consumed by the gap left vacant by his wife and by the *idea* of her. Although his daughter is present, Wilmot's extended speeches are addressed to the absent Eleonora, who he apostrophizes a half dozen times. Although Wilmot accepts partial responsibility for her initial departure, he nonetheless feels that maternity dictates that the suffering wife should have no recourse to self-preservation: "How couldst thou abandon [your child], Eleonora? Did no voice plead within for so sacred a charge? Because offended thyself, didst thou deem thy own duties cancelled?" (II.i.19-22). His wife haunts him, "darkens [his] views, confuses [his] intellects" (II.i.34). Beneath Wilmot's ostensible forgiveness of Eleonora lurks a lament for his own suffering and a longing for the ideal wife and mother: "while my heart recoiled from her iniquity, it clung to her idea! and while I renounced her sight, I doated on her remembrance!" (II.i.75-77). The husband's vacillation between forgiveness and suspicion marks all of his mental and physical interactions with Eleonora and suggests that at no point is he entirely satisfied with explanations given to him. Wilmot renders Eleonora responsible somehow for his negative views of her, and therefore responsible for any punishment she might receive.

The emphasis on the seamless union of ideal marital and maternal devotion is apparent in the evaluations of Eleonora that come from elsewhere in the community as well. Codgerly Old Waverley suggests that Eleonora deserved "no better" than rejection by her family because "She played naught, and ran away from her husband, and forsook her Child—" (I.i.64-65). When he sees Eleonora with Sophia, but does not know her true identity, he assumes that Eleonora is a "vile old Hag" and a "sad Jade" who prostitutes her daughter (III.v.129, 153). There is no room in the realm of community standards for extramarital maternal affection. Lady Smatter similarly berates Eleonora for "absconding, then, from [her] husband and family" and, despite Eleonora's explanations, continues to insult her "who ought to be bowed down to the Earth, and begging for mercy" (II.viii.36, 43-44).

The extremity of Wilmot's view of the hideous, self-indulgent, and dangerously sexual mother is more readily apparent once he knows that Eleonora resides nearby with what seems to be an illegitimate daughter. On the basis of appearances, he hastily envisions the falsely accused wife as an adulteress whose "pledge of lawless love" has led her to live with the "Child of her shame" rather than the "offspring of wedded Honour" (IV.x.39, 44-45). It is clear that ideals of maternal devotion demand not only a requisite class position (see below), but also careful adherence to the ideal of marriage. Maternal devotion is clearly no recompense for questionable sexual or marital morals. When Wilmot finally confronts Eleonora, his sense of having been wronged dominates his view of maternal duty. He mocks Eleonora for claiming "maternal tenderness" (V.xiv.59) as her motivating emotion when he accuses this "perfidious woman" (V.xiv.52) once again of dissolving "every chaste duty, every legal tie" through her "cherished infamy" as a "dauntless criminal" (V.xiv.71-72). He asserts his role as arbiter by calling on his own sense of "retributive Justice" (V.xiii.10), a role he assumes by virtue of his authority as husband. In his resolve to part from Eleonora "the Child of [her] licentious fondness" (V.xiv.73), Wilmot chastises maternal devotion because of its apparent replacement of wifely devotion with uncontrollable female sexuality.

Wilmot's propensity for violence, remarked upon by Eleonora and the nurse, reminds the audience of the possible consequences of deviating from an ideal that is always-already subject to patriarchal standards of value. Eleonora's repeated statements about Wilmot's violence suggest, as Doody notes, that Wilmot is the play's main "woman-hater" and confirm that the hierarchal organization of the family and its eventual restoration is accommodated only by tolerating male domination: "Mr. Wilmot represents the more normal forms of woman-hating in the world Frances Burney knew: disapproval of feminine wishes; dictatorship over feminine conduct; censorship of female utterance; fraternal, filial, and marital coldness." However, I question how "essentially banal" Wilmot's conduct is;[26] his coercive behavior, if Gothic exaggeration, is nonetheless a source of real fear. Kemble was wishfully cast by Burney to play Wilmot. Given the actor's preference for tragedy and his prowess in representing, in Walter Scott's terms, "characters with 'a predominating tinge of some over-mastering passion,'"[27] Burney's casting seems designed to emphasize the jealousy and threatened violence that characterize Wilmot.

Although Eleonora suggests that Wilmot's extreme behavior is a result of his jealousy ("till this fatal warp of jealousy, not more noble than gentle was his nature" [III.ii.60-61]), her genuine fear of him dominates her meditations and likely would not go unnoticed in a performance, especially one presented by Siddons (Siddons's more frequent portrayal of tragic heroines also substantiates the menacing undercurrents in *The Woman-Hater*). When Eleonora hears that Wilmot is nearby, she cries that he "comes but with confirmed hate, and determined belief in my unworthiness!—or comes but to claim the last treasured tie—Name me not to him! . . . Ah, let me, then, begone! not here, not thus must I risk a meeting upon which hangs life or death!" (II.viii.112-22). She questions his possible erratic behavior in a "cruel uncertainty of his state of mind and intentions" (III.ii.36). What Eleonora dreads are further displays of violence, like those which led to their original parting: "O Wilmot!—in what temper of mind com'st thou at last? Is it utterly to demolish me, by snatching away my Child? or to call back my lost happiness, by restoring me thyself?—" (III.i.3-6). Eleonora's attempted forgiveness is admirable, which suggests that Wilmot's repeated rejection of her is all the more unreasonable.

The mortal Gothicism of the tragedies is shown to be only narrowly averted in *The Woman-Hater*. The final meeting of Wilmot and Eleonora confirms that her fear of violence is justified. Importantly, when Eleonora receives Wilmot's original petition for forgiveness, before he turns on her yet again, she is willing to agree that he is more insane than barbarous (a distinction that holds little comfort). Wilmot's immediate presumptions about Eleonora's guilt the moment she mentions her child, however, prove that his erratic nature persists. It is no wonder that Eleonora dreads his passion: "once enraged, inflamed, how terrible!—O from his Eye in wrath protect me, Heaven!" (V.xiv.8-9). That she questions if it is his "intention, then, to deposit [her] in some place of secret horror?—some dungeon?" attests to the coercive power of her husband (V.xiv.23-24). Eleonora does fear the unthinkable and she screams when she sees him.[28] Burney enlists the devices of Gothic tragedy—entrapment, villainy, and punishment—in order to demonstrate the trials suffered by mothers and wives in *The Woman-Hater*.

The nurse, too, is an object of Wilmot's rages and her fear that he will kill her when he discovers her trickery further attests to his menacing reputation. Burney's new version of *Evelina* draws attention to the lower-class woman whose efforts on her daughter's behalf originate the confusion about the identity of the "real" daughter. *The Woman-Hater* is a tale of two mothers' devotions to their daughters' welfares. While Eleonora's actions are finally, if grudgingly, accepted, similar actions on the part of the nurse are not and it becomes clear that maternal instincts and motivations are evaluated differently depending on the status of the mother involved. The nurse is a version of the monstrous maternity I discussed in chapter 3 in connection with *Elberta*. Her substitution of Joyce for Sophia, though intended to secure her child financially, is viewed as a usurpation of class privilege rather than acceptable maternal behavior. She tells her daughter she is the one "that did it all for your sake, that hoped you'd have got a rich husband before it was found out, that let you have your own way in every thing" (IV.viii.69-71). While even the impostor, Joyce, is assured of Wilmot's continued financial interest, the mother behind the daughter is never exonerated. Wilmot rejects the nurse's maternal devotion by making usurpation the main issue, calling her a "miscreant" who has "develloped her fraud" (V.xxi.18). Significantly, the nurse does not reenter the final scene of reconciliation following Joyce's revelation of her "real" identity. Instead, she departs, fearing criminal prosecution that will find her "sent to Botany Bay" and exclaiming that she must "run!" because Wilmot will "kill [her]!" (V.xvi.4, 21). The nurse, like Eleonora, fears Wilmot's physical and juridical power. In presenting a matrix of class, gender, and familial roles, Burney offers a complex view of the relationship between authority and maternity. Paternal or male authority predominates, supported by misogyny. Where maternal authority is concerned, the nurse is most damningly evaluated. Without a proper name, defined only by her profession and, significantly, without a proper husband, the nurse is literally and figuratively forced outside the circle of reconciliation and power at the close of the play.

The negative effects of Wilmot's view of his authority are only one form of misogyny scrutinized in *The Woman-Hater*. Wilmot may be the play's most threatening woman-hater, but he is not its only one. A backdrop of antifeminism includes all of the local men, each of whom expresses negative opinions about motherhood and women in general. Bad mothers are considered to be solely responsible for male failure and all women are seen by the male figures as potentially corrupt. Old Waverley has a strong dislike for female assertiveness (he describes women as "wheedling" and "sly" [I.i.71, 84]) and he counsels his son against involvement with them on these grounds. Young Waverley's dismissal of Sir Roderick as a woman-hating "brute" is also suspect (I.iii.101), given that at one point he courts Lady Smatter for her money alone.

Sir Roderick's misogyny is certainly more openly expressed than that of Old Waverley or Wilmot. He makes sweeping condemnations of women: "A poor sickly, mawkish set of Beings! What are they good for? What can they do? Ne'er a thing upon Earth they had not better let alone" (I.ix.26-28). He is particularly eager to denounce female education as superfluous for beings who would have nothing to say in any case: "If you meet with e'er a one, by accident, that i'n't a wicked hussey, it's only because she's such a cursed fool, such a dawdle, such a driveler, such a mince-mouthed, lisping Ideot, that she don't know how to set about it" (I.ix.30-33). For Sir Roderick, female education should extend only to the practical needs of household management, the cooking and sewing that barely compensate for a perceived inability to plough, build, navigate, or fight (V.xxiii.56-59). His woman-hating is ultimately exposed as an activity based on stereotypes and emerging from a sense of male insecurity. It is Joyce who lights upon this discovery. She demystifies Sir Roderick's antagonism towards women as being a response to a lack of power and control: "I have learned . . . what is meant by a Woman-Hater! It is,—to hate a woman—if she won't let you love her: to run away from her—if you can't run to her: to swear she is made up of faults—unless she allows you to be made up of perfections: and to vow she shall never cross your Threshold,—unless she'll come to be mistress of your whole house!" (V.xxiii.103-9). Sir Roderick's misogyny originates in his inability to control Lady Smatter and in her failure to live up to the patriarchal, oppressive version of the submissive and deferential woman.

This hatred of subversive women parallels Roderick's fears of usurping servants, both of whom threaten his sense of his "rights." Sir Roderick is preyed upon by those who want to be his heir and figures manipulate each other in order to jockey for his favor. His power to bestow a fortune announces his social authority but also makes him anxious about anything that erodes his power. As Roderick declares, he has a right to be angry at his servants: "A'n't I your Master? A'n't you all my hirelings? Who pays for the house that shelters you? Who pays for the cloaths that cover you? Who pays for the food that crams you till you are all sick? Why I, I, to be sure" (I.vii.35-38). His search for control over others—control that is always slipping away—betrays his fears about the "lower orders" making free with his possessions, or worse, women presuming to move beyond their proper (limited) spheres. Joyce is precisely the figure most to be feared: a woman of low birth who comes into contact with Roderick because of a scheme for social betterment.

Patriarchal authority exercises itself over daughters, as well as mothers, wives, and servants. Doody writes that "*The Woman-Hater*, of all Burney's works, most fully expresses discontent at the daughterly relationship, and most openly asks whether something has not gone grievously wrong."[29] By splitting the character of the daughter into two—Sophia and Joyce, legitimate and usurping daughter—Burney can examine the various ways in which daughterly behavior is defined by genealogy, self-direction, and duty. The doubling of the daughter figure also allows for an especially strong criticism of familial and paternal power, in that Sophia, who is reunited with her father, becomes immediately subject to his dictates and remains nearly completely silent, while Joyce, who has no legitimate family position, rejoices in her freedom from this same authority. "Illegitimate" emerges as perhaps the most attractive designation to assume.[30]

Sophia is arguably a rather uninteresting character. She is deferential and obedient, willing to pursue on her mother's behalf Sir Roderick's financial assistance. *The Woman-Hater* shows, however, that even the woman who most successfully lives up to a behavioral ideal can be the object of accusation. When Sophia and Joyce arrive at Sir Roderick's asking for financial support, both are seen as morally dangerous in their efforts to be self-determining. Sophia is accused of having an "impudent frolic" at Sir Roderick's expense (V.viii.16-17), and he forces Old Waverley to deny their acquaintance because the boldness of the "little plague" makes him appear improper (V.viii.58). She is the "impudentest baggage that ever entered a house" merely because she cannot distinguish between old men (V.viii.60). She is left pardoning her unintentional offense (V.viii.21)—a family trait, considering her mother's willingness to blame herself for denying Wilmot his paternal joys—and, like Evelina, she is accused of being the impostor. Eleonora rightly laments, "Is innocence no guard? Virtue, no bulwark?— And can Man alone from Man protect us?" (IV.xiii.95-96). Sophia's good behavior only secures the reward of Jack Waverley at the play's close, a union determined by a father who is completely unknown to her. Her silence confirms that she is not consulted on this alliance. Significantly, her last action is to kneel to her father, asking for his blessing. Eleonora's final statement—"Suffer not retrospective sadness to usurp the place of grateful Joy" (V.xxiii.100-101)—can be interpreted symbolically, for Sophia's silence suggests that her "rightful place" in the family is a submissive one to an authoritarian, violent, and erratic father. "Grateful Joy(ce)" is permitted to escape this final position.

The figure of Joyce is perhaps the most intriguing element of Burney's play. When she is introduced, she is the submissive and silent "Miss Wilmot" whose relationship with her father seems to amount to little more than acceptance of his reading assignments. Joyce shows an adeptness at gauging her behavior to the company she keeps. Burney's use of movement and dialogue is telling when "Miss Wilmot" and her father are together. In these scenes, the daughter does not openly challenge paternal authority. She is demure and obedient, referring to Wilmot repeatedly as "sir" and uniformly agreeing with his statements. Wilmot's repressive idealization of female roles extends to his "daughter," who he has educated to be "simple and unpolished, fearful as the Hare, who in every shadow sees a pursuer, invincibly shy, pensive, and nearly mute" (III.viii.20-22).[31] It is no wonder that this ideal of the silent and frightened woman is intolerable to Joyce, or that it emerges from the husband Eleonora fled years earlier.

Any absence of Wilmot leads to a transformation in "Miss Wilmot," who rejects her father's "stupifying learning" (II.iv.34) and later claims, "I'm kept in such subjection, I've no comfort of my life. . . . There's nothing but ordering, and tutoring, and scolding, and managing . . . and reading!" (IV.vii.22-26, second ellipsis in original). When freed of her father's oppressive presence, Miss Wilmot sings and dances, questions and makes demands of others, and generally asserts her own desires and her ability to speak for herself: "Why, Nurse, Papa's so dismal dull! always setting one to study! I wonder what's the use of Books, Nurse? If Papa had as many words of his own as I have, he would not be always wanting to be poring over other people's so. I can find enough to say of myself. And I'm sure that's cleverer." (II.iv.88-92). Doody emphasizes Joyce's physicality, writing that "Joyce insists that women have physical urges, bodies to be satisfied, appetites."[32] Joyce is also characterized by a mental assertiveness that exults in exercising power over others at the same time as she asserts her ability to direct herself and her future. For Joyce, being alive means being *original* rather than following old rules and regulations.

The physicality and exuberance of Joyce, in their stark contrast to the demure actions of "Miss Wilmot," make full use of drama's unique quality of active embodiment. The actress Dorothy Jordan was noted for such roles. I have already noted Reinelt's observation about the political power of drama in representing resistant, alternative modes of existence and Cixous's comments about the necessity of the body to drama (see chapter 1). In showing the silence and bodily confinement of a properly submissive daughter, and the delightful movements of a woman who leaps up from beneath her father's thumb, *The Woman-Hater*, more than any other of Burney's plays, most contradicts critical assessments of Burney's view of female experience. Epstein, for instance, writes that Burney's heroines struggle "to weigh the risks of rebellion against the humiliations of submission" and Cutting-Gray remarks that Burney's "heroines seek for a legitimating patronym to lend them substance."[33] Joyce risks rebellion and asserts her physical and mental substance beyond the circle of the Wilmot family, at least momentarily, and does so by rejecting the patronym and by embodying resistant modes of behavior.

It is in Joyce's actions that Burney makes a strong point about the relationship between class and behavior: "breeding" is shown to be less a matter of biology than behavior, because genteel actions can be imitated even if a "reputable" genealogy is lacking. The dramatic medium allows us to see the physical, behavioral components of membership in a particular class, which for Joyce are overwhelmingly combined with those of a gender hierarchy as well. Burney underscores the physical confinement expected of a gentlewoman when the nurse reminds "Miss Wilmot" that a lady "can't be supposed to be as free and easy" as a serving girl and should not act out "before them low people!" (II.iv.26-27, 55). When Joyce is left in her Aunt Smatter's care, a similar contrast between a demure lady and a hellion is evident. Blocking and dialogue provide the audience with a sense of the physical encroachment and control that a chameleon like Joyce threatens because she can transform herself and negotiate successfully both refinement and rebellion. Joyce takes a place intended for quiet study and manufactures from it a playground. Yet another sofa is taken over, as she "*throw[s] herself upon a sofa*" (III.x.15) and interrogates Lady Smatter, allowing her few words in response, until in exasperation Lady Smatter seeks to "make [her] escape!" (III.x.105).

Other uses of the stage space emphasize Joyce's physical and ideological path toward revolution when she transforms Smatter's dressing room into the meeting place of the servants. She invites herself to devour the bonbons she finds and invites Bob Sapling and Miss Henny to watch:

MISS WILMOT. . . . . Mrs. Prim, pray call up Bob.

PRIM. Ma'am!

MISS WILMOT. Call up Bob. I want to speak to him.

PRIM. Call up Bob?—Into my lady's Dressing room?

MISS WILMOT. Well, then, I'll call him myself! I won't be kept
in a prison, so! never doing any thing I have a mind. I am quite
tired of it, I am so. (calling) Bob! Bob! [IV.vi.17-24]

Joyce then sings that she is "all for Liberty!—Liberty, Liberty, Bob!"
(IV.vii.29).[34] The dressing-room Bastille is fully in Joyce's hands and a
young woman who would otherwise be subservient orders others around
and takes over the territory of house and class. The figure who should
command our attention in this scene, the Lady of the House, is absent, replaced by those who do not belong against such a backdrop. Surely Joyce
conjures up both the ideals and upheaval of the French Revolution and
provides a comic and (possibly) less dangerous version of the social dis-
ruption the Revolution enacted.

Lady Smatter, in her self-important but misguided support of local
writers, is a representative of the decaying patronage system to which
Epstein refers. Smatter's depleted resources and her error-laden "knowledge" of the classics are suggestive of a bygone era in which money and a
classical education secured gentility. Such marks of leisure are attacked by
Joyce and the play's other employees and schemers who try to better themselves. The point of Joyce's triumph over Aunt Smatter is, I think, not only
to show Joyce's relief in emerging out from under her father's thumb, but
also to show a space clearly intended to signify the trappings of gentility
being reorganized and controlled by one who under "normal" circumstances would be unacquainted with such luxuries, one who is even scornful of them. The play, especially in this scene, depicts a moment of extreme
social flux: a shoemaker's daughter is in control, the classics are dismissed
in favor of candies, and a figure who should be a bastion of intellectual
and financial strength, Aunt Smatter, has seen her resources dwindle because she has no ability to judge good from bad poetry.

Joyce's sense of self-determination and her dismissal of the values of
Lady Smatter's world include a curious mix of assertive control over
others and a charitable view of their right to act independently, too. She
fantasizes about rescuing a beggar child and bringing it up for her own,
ironically imagining a reenactment of her own story but replacing the
secret crime of usurpation with benevolence (III.x.34-37). Her desire, as
she tells Smatter, is to "talk or be dumb, as much as I will for my own
amusement, and to let you scold, or look bluff, as much as you will for
your's. Now that I think fair play" (III.x.81-83). At different times Joyce
seizes the power that adults usually exercise over her, ordering (unknowingly) her mother around, or assuming the assertive role of wooer usually
reserved for men. When Joyce hears of her real parentage, she says she
"want[s her] liberty" (V.xii.25): "Don't contradict me, I say, for I'll marry
Bob!—I shall like that a great deal better than always studying Books; and

sitting with my hands before me; and making courtsies; and never eating half as much as I like,—except in the Pantry!—And I'll make Bob do every thing I bid him; and you shall be my house-keeper!" (V.xii.27-31). Joyce's desire to tell the truth about her parentage, having "lost two Papas" (V.xxiii.103), is not entirely altruistic, for the legacy she transfers to the "real" daughter includes responsibility for "all the Books!" (V.xxii. 7-8).

Joyce's act of rejecting the paternal family establishes for her a new, maternal-only family that is in fact under her control, rather than her mother's. She removes herself from the Wilmot circle before Wilmot has an opportunity to initiate such action, and in so doing, continues her re-fusal of the stereotypical roles and behavior of daughters, especially upper-class daughters: submission to parental authority; deference to others' decisions, particularly where marriage is concerned; and generally unob-trusive behavior. As Doody notes, "Joyce recovers her real name (a mater-nal name, a first name only) by losing the (false) paternal name. . . . Joyce is in an enviable position in that she can *generously* and of her own accord cast off the Father."[35] Although Joyce retains the financial interest of Wilmot, she is no longer claimed by him, but has a lineage of occupations rather than names, "nobody's but old Nurse's, and a shoe-maker's" daugh-ter (V.xvi.16-17).[36] (Altered lineage is reflected in the script of the play, for the nurse's daughter appears as both "Miss Wilmot" and "Joyce.") Joyce also rejects the shame that might otherwise attend such a loss of social po-sition. She instead announces, "who cares for work, if it's followed by play?" (V.xii.34). Retirement and learning, signs of class privilege, are ex-changed for activity. The fact that she is not devastated by the news that she might have to be a ballad singer both announces her "natural" affinity for the work at the same time as it undercuts the class-based abhorrence of female work and female play that Burney was to explore later in *The Wanderer*.

Joyce's exuberant calls for self-control and freedom surely make her an admirable figure. However, behind the depiction of her joyful literal and figurative usurpation of an upper-class position lurk stereotypes about class distinctions that are quite conservative. While Burney's characteriza-tion of Joyce suggests that gentility can be successfully imitated, it also re-veals a sense that there is a "natural" class identity that specifies Joyce's social place as closer to that of the nurse than to Sophia, Wilmot, or Lady Smatter. Throughout the play, for instance, it is clear that the members of the lower class have an affinity for each other that goes beyond words. Bob tells of a spark he alone sees in Joyce's eye even before he meets her (I.xvi.7), and by the end of the play Joyce resolves to marry Bob and become a ballad singer. Burney makes further references to the natural affinities between people of the same class when Joyce announces that she has "always loved [Nurse], and . . . could never abide Papa" (IV.viii.72-73). The qualities of lower-class people are repeatedly characterized here as predominantly physical and almost belligerently anti-intellectual. Joyce announces her unending hatred of books and reading and states emphatically: "I hate thinking" (III.x.109). While Joyce privileges originality over rote learning, rejecting books, she also rejects any mark of education. Joyce finally wins over Sir Roderick by offering to make a bonfire of all Smatter's books. She prefers Bob to all others because he can skate, swim, and fight and because the "great Dunce" hates reading too (II.iv.94). The two share a conversational bluntness as well. She asks Sir Roderick to "be so kind, and so good-natured, as to give [her] a few of [his] thousand pounds—" (V.iv.66-67); Bob tells Sir Roderick that if he needs "a body to leave [his] fortune to, upon [his] dying . . . [he] should like it very well" (IV.xvii.76-80). Although it is "pleasant to see [Joyce] burst through the folly and negativity and exclusiveness around her,"[37] social hierarchies are confirmed by the play's constant presumptions about the mutual interests of people within a class and the lack of correspondence between those of differing ranks. *A Busy Day* tackles this same issue, but there the notion that prejudice supports class distinctions is at least voiced, even if it falls on deaf ears. *The Woman-Hater* is only implicitly critical of a firm social hierarchy. All the talk in the play of the books that represent "culture" implies that class positions are constructed rather than inherent, yet we are reminded that Joyce is able to take on the physical trappings of gentility, but few of the intellectual ones.

On the other hand, Sophia's name and behavior imply that her "nature" is gentle, noble, and wise, something that her reunion with her father will confirm in terms of social class and familial "normalcy." Jack is attracted to his future mate, Sophia, as surely as Bob is enticed by Joyce's eyes, and he comments on the mother and daughter he has spied in a nearby cottage: "the Daughter is all softness and sweetness, the Mother has a grace, a manner, so dignified, yet so winning—" (I.iii.45-47). As is so often the case in the literature of the period, gentility manifests itself in manners and appearance that might be temporarily but not permanently feigned. After all, Evelina's face is finally what confirms her as her father's heiress.

When Joyce celebrates her success in gaining Roderick's money, she sings "Rule, ye fair ones,—Ye fair ones, rule—the Men!" (V.vi.4). Her song parodies James Thomson's "Rule Britannia," from the masque *Alfred* (1740). "Rule Britannia," set to music by Thomas Arne, is listed in *The London Stage* just eight times between 1776 and 1793, but performances multiplied in the last eight years of the century to reach approximately fifty-nine. Many of these performances were joined with "God Save the King" and were prompted by the king's presence in the theater, or by naval victories against the French. Each of the eight years between 1792 and 1800 saw at least four nights on which the song was performed, but the number rose to seventeen in 1794, the year after the French king was executed and during the Terror.[38] The ode proclaims British supremacy across the globe and declares in its nationally, racially, and economically charged refrain an unending British liberty: "Britons never will be slaves." The ode's increasing popularity in the century's last decade might indicate a strengthened nationalism in the face of war and events in France, or a need to compensate in undeniably public and collective ways for a shaken faith in the endurance of political or national institutions. A postrevolutionary reassertion of a conservative, rigid, and hierarchical society with a monarch at its head was one counterresponse to the social fluidity that was associated with the Revolution and with social reform generally. Certainly, "equality" was hardly an unambiguously attractive idea and vocal or bodily moves toward it cannot be regarded as uniformly admired.[39] Joyce thus parodies an important musical endorsement of national self-definition.

Given this musical, political, and social context, Joyce can be a difficult figure to read. While we might applaud Burney's creation of a figure who exuberantly rejects old forms of social organization, another way to view the alignment of Joyce with the parodic and the revolutionary, rather than the patriotic and orderly, is to see her as the cause for real anxieties about any wholesale dismissal of custom and convention. The mingling of members of different classes was alarming for many. Joyce calls for female superiority and her actions pose the threat of usurpation that seeks to replace snobbery with charity, intellectual study with work and play, the commands of superiors with self-direction, stasis with movement, and order with upheaval. While Joyce does return to her "place" with money, importantly, she does not retain the social recognition that goes with it. This is the new and still ambiguous social order Burney explores. Joanna Baillie writes that drama cannot reach "the lowest classes of the labouring people," who "can never be generally moved without endangering every thing that is constructed upon it, and who are our potent and formidable ballad readers." Instead, drama reaches the people at the next level of society, and has "over them no inconsiderable influence. The impressions made by it are communicated, at the same instant of time, to a greater number of individuals, than those made by any other species of writing; and they are strengthened in every spectator, by observing their effects upon those who surround him. . . . The theatre is a school in which much good or evil may be learned."[40] If Baillie is right, the people Joyce represents are not the main contemporary audience for *The Woman-Hater*'s lessons. The play does provide a mirror for those members of the audience who feared having to give up territory as small as a sofa or as large as a birthright. What the play suggests is that resting easy in the drawing room is perhaps the first step to being removed from the drawing room entirely. Sir Roderick's sense of being besieged, Joyce's imitation of gentility and her affinity with Bob and with work, or the Wattses' presence in the Tylney apartments can be contextualized as examples of late-eighteenth-century drama's strength as a vehicle for depicting in codified form the uneasy intermingling of members of different social classes. Watkins makes this point when he writes that late-eighteenth-century and romantic drama was especially sensitive to a new social order that marked the transition from an aristocratic to a bourgeois worldview. Plays of the period reveal "the tensions, anxieties, and ideological struggles" of this transition and provided a public forum in which "class struggle and many of the personal and public conflicts corresponding to this struggle played themselves out."[41]

The play's final blocking, with the Wilmots symbolically joined together, depicts a circle that excludes encroachment by the lower classes and simultaneously limits the coercive power of the father to his family members. Eleonora's final words speak of the need to appease Wilmot and the new-found daughter is given in marriage to a man she knows only slightly. This renewed family, under a shadow of violence, undercuts the sentimental reunion of this comedy. Wilmot, upon seeing Sophia, cannot claim his own "forbearance" and continues to see himself as the injured party (V.xv.8). When Joyce arrives and reveals the truth, Wilmot feels caught between this "execrable stratagem—or what unheard of bliss" (V.xvi.11-12), and only then, with the physical evidence of the impostor daughter, does he seem convinced of his wife's purity: "It's full conviction had flashed upon me before my voyage hither; and, impressed with remorse, I came over to publish it: but a new and dreadful deception again wrought my senses into phrenzy:—the Nurse, the miscreant Nurse, has now develloped her fraud,—and—had I been less credulous, less fiery—what a Wife,— what a daughter—might I at this moment claim!" (V.xxi.15-20). Wilmot seems to be just as willing to blame others for their deceit as to blame his own rage, distanced as credulity and fieriness.

The excessive forgiving and forgetting here suggest that filial and nuptial affection must be belabored in order to compensate for sixteen years of separation and accusation. Eleonora does finally claim that her "resentment is gone for ever!" and Wilmot calls her "Wife of my Heart! my esteem! my gratitude! my contrition!" (V.xxi.23-26). The couple resolves to "fly from sorrows" and turn toward a new "compensation for the cruelty of the past" (V.xxi.29, 37). Wilmot tells Joyce, "I am impatient to assure you of my inalterable interest in your welfare—though the parental tie by which I thought it bound, has changed its object" (V.xxii.4-6). The irony of his admission—that his interest in Joyce or Sophia is due only to a binding biological tie rather than affection—is lost on those reconciled in the forest at the play's close. That Wilmot's interest in anyone could be "unalterable" seems unlikely. The ending teeters perilously close to the tragedy of a newly confined wife and daughter. Burney may be rewriting the ending of *A Midsummer Night's Dream*, in which the forces of magic restore reason and a woman gains the suitor of her choice. In the wood at the end of Burney's play, a woman is offered to a man without her consent and the only "safe" woman is the one beyond the father's control. The failure to include all figures in a patriarchal family structure permits a lingering criticism of the relationship dynamics within this sort of "normal" family. Joyce is left out, but it is in her marginal existence as a woman without paternity that she finds her access to autonomy and the satisfaction of desires that she was forced to deny in her father's presence.

Burney's *The Woman-Hater* is perhaps the most difficult of her plays about which to draw conclusions. It can be read as a conservative, cautionary tale to women about the dangers of rebelling against the rules of marital or maternal obedience, for example. At the same time, it exposes patriarchal authority as a prejudicial and physically threatening force for women. The issue of class is a vexed one as well. The nurse's well-meant but unappreciated maternal devotion simultaneously marks a distinction between types of mothers that can be considered unacceptable or appropriate. The exile of the nurse or the portrayal of Mrs. Watts's neglectful attitude towards Eliza in *A Busy Day* reveals that Burney did not uniformly question the class prejudices of her time. While much of her work criticizes the false distinctions that make up class divisions, she also relies on some of these stock attitudes about the differences between people when she depicts the lower-class figures in her drama as unrefined and physical rather than as intellectual beings. While she depicts what for many people was the real threat of social chaos that impostors pose, she does not show *lasting* rebellion or real social change. Joyce resolves to be a ballad singer and the Wilmots are united; Eleonora never was a bad mother, and her imagined transgressions as a bad wife are forgiven. The play features a complex middle way between condemning social order, accepting it, and undermining it. This suggests that it was difficult for Burney to imagine motherhood in any form beyond its patriarchal, middle-class, familial version and that it was equally difficult to leave Joyce or her mother completely and unproblematically accepted by those who had been duped.

Both *A Busy Day* and *The Woman-Hater* examine the relationships between family members, between families allied by financial and marital arrangements, and between families that occupy different rungs on a social ladder. Biological relationships are shown to be tied to social roles that carry with them attitudes about how people should act or think, often to their detriment. In this atmosphere, where a premium is placed on an individual's ability to fulfill a role in a socially acceptable way—or be rejected for the failure to do so—individual freedom is gravely threatened. Eliza Watts is therefore absorbed into the Tylney family because it allows financial wealth to speak where genealogy fails. Personal desire is largely irrelevant and where necessary familial ties can be severed and reassembled at the will of those with social power. The claims of biology reign supreme for Sophia, who must become immediately submissive to both her father and her future husband. Joyce alone, without surname and without the sanction of patrilineage, can assert her individuality and remain outside the family circle, self-determining and oblivious to negative attitudes about members of the lower class. While Eliza must offer to the Tylneys a financial benefit in the place of her family origins, Joyce is free to socialize herself as she chooses, but only, it would seem, once she is beyond the walls of Lady Smatter's library.

What is evidently a topic of *A Busy Day* and *The Woman-Hater* is the idea that female experience at the end of the eighteenth century was largely limited to familial roles (daughter, wife, mother) that were similar in the submissiveness they demanded of women but that varied with social class or marital status. Hilaria Dalton, in *Love and Fashion*, also discovers confinement and regulation in a familial setting, albeit one based on guardianship and advice rather than parental control. While Burney explores in her comedies and tragedies various forms of suffering and the confinement of female desire and choice, in no other dramatic work does she represent such a rebellion against confinement as she does in *The Woman-Hater*. That this representation of challenge and triumph is short-lived and expressive of a certain amount of ambivalence should not diffuse its importance, but instead point to the pervasive female constriction for which Joyce's exuberance is a foil.

7

A Context and Overview
Burney and the Late-Eighteenth-Century Stage

I have argued that Frances Burney's plays reveal a thorough awareness of the conventions of the theater of her day and of the ingredients of a potentially successful production. Her knowledge and love of the theater is also well represented in the novels. Her heroines all attend and comment on plays and other public entertainments.[1] Indeed, in the novels, the theater provides a metaphor for female experience and the performative aspects of femininity: learned appropriate behavior, movement, manners, and speech. Each heroine must discover the proper way to "act" for a given audience, and more often than not, she is performing for a male audience whose watchful gaze is emphasized in the narrative: Edgar Mandlebert is quintessentially the spectator, a quality shared by Lord Orville and the other heroes. In Burney's last novel, *The Wanderer*, Juliet offers her observations about the professional theater and her desire for its reform. She praises drama that, at its most refined, "brings before us the noblest characters, and makes us witnesses to the sublimest actions" and admires those performers who "unite, to their public exercise, private virtue and merit." However, Juliet herself shies from the stage: "I think [acting] so replete with dangers and improprieties, however happily they may sometimes be combatted by fortitude and integrity, that, when a young female, not forced by peculiar circumstances, or impelled by resistless genius, exhibits herself a willing candidate for public applause;—she must have, I own, other notions, or other nerves, than mine!"[2] Juliet's observation reasserts a dynamic that is played out in Burney's plays, that is, the difference in ease of social movement and activity between women of different classes. More genteel women are more constrained in what they can and cannot contemplate professionally or socially. The interaction between gentility and the theater was a concern for Burney herself and was something that plagued the careers of many women writing for the stage in the eighteenth century.

Burney's letter to her father regarding the production of *Love and Fashion* (see chapter 5) implies that her own desire for the publicity required by theater professionals *was* impelled by "resistless genius" despite concerns about the propriety of such activities. But, as Juliet's statements affirm, the theater world was an unusual sphere in which to find female writers. Women who wrote for the late-eighteenth-century stage were challenged, far more than their male counterparts, by demands placed on them concerning the propriety of their works and their "private virtue and merit." As Judith Philips Stanton observes, women were far more likely to write poetry or prose, and even then, to do so in far fewer numbers than their male counterparts.[3] While Burney was surrounded by theater professionals, including such noted figures as Richard Cumberland, David Garrick, Samuel Johnson, Arthur Murphy, Richard Brinsley Sheridan, and of course Samuel "daddy" Crisp, who all offered her encouragement at various points in her career, her participation in the theater world remained almost exclusively private and her literary reputation would rest until recently on her letters, journals, and novels.

The honing of the works and skills of Frances Burney, dramatist, was thus hampered, in a paradoxical way, by her ability to write successfully in another genre. She was not forced to develop her skills as a dramatist as other women writers did, out of a need to make money, though she seems always to have wished that these skills could be acknowledged and she was perpetually returning to her dramatic creations. Despite the private and public atmosphere that discouraged female playwrights, Burney did write more discrete pieces of drama than fiction and her plays demonstrate an unrelenting eye toward the stage. Her cast lists and her creative awareness of contemporary themes, devices, and stage figures reveal an ambition that is belied by the production and critical history of her plays. Burney's drama manifests all of the strengths (and weaknesses) of her contemporaries. It seems appropriate, therefore, to place her work in a context that includes other women who were writing for the stage, some, such as Elizabeth Inchbald, who were also novelists, like herself. Because of the unique history of Burney's dramas—written mainly with production in mind but largely unperformed—no comparison of receipts, production runs, or critical reception is available to us. We can, however, examine the concerns and attitudes expressed in plays by women and study the devices they use to display their ideas. This process offers an opportunity for a brief overview of the concerns in Burney's drama. The predominance and variety of comic plays at the end of the eighteenth century make comparisons of individual plays difficult, so I mention examples of plays by other playwrights in passing where appropriate. These can be added to the references scattered throughout the individual chapters on each comedy.

Because there were fewer tragedies written in the period, especially by women, I have made direct connections between Burney's tragedies and those of some other female dramatists.

Even a casual glance at *The London Stage* reveals that comedies dominated the late-eighteenth-century stage, outnumbering tragedies five to one. Of the twelve most popular pieces staged in the last quarter of the century, over half were revivals of older pieces and one-third of the plays were tragedies (all Shakespearean). Only one play, and this a new one, was by a woman: Hannah Cowley's *The Belle's Stratagem* (1780). Of the female comedic writers producing new plays on the stage between 1775 and the end of the century, Hannah Cowley (1743-1809) and Elizabeth Inchbald (1753-1821) were by far the best known. Susanna Centlivre (1669-1723) continued to be popular, with plays such as *The Busie Body* (1709) and *A Bold Stroke for a Wife* (1718) being played repeatedly throughout the century. Burney saw Cowley's *The Belle's Stratagem* in 1798, and Inchbald's *Such Things Are* in 1787 and *The Midnight Hour* in 1789.[4]

Doody suggests that women were impeded from writing comedy in a time of increased moral fervor because the genre "was thought to require an unabashed knowledge of life and manners which it would ill become a lady to assume—it is a *bold* form."[5] The prologue to Inchbald's *To Marry, or Not to Marry* (1805), by "J. Taylor, Esq.," mentions the problems of women writers:

> Custom to her that range of life denies,
> Which ampler views to lordly man supplies;
> He, unrestrain'd, can ev'ry class survey,
> That mark the myriads of the grave and gay;
> Hence can his talents take a boundless sweep,
> And richest crops of character may reap;
> But, woman, fix'd within a narrow scene,
> What Genius slights, must be content to glean.
> Thus for the suppliant of to-night we plead,
> Lest you should think she brings a motley breed,
> Of local humour, or of magic birth,
> For gaping wonder, or for giddy mirth.
> The passions chiefly have engaged her art,
> Drawn from the nice recesses of the heart;
> Where some just shooting into life she spies,
> And others swelling to a monstrous size:
> In all, her anxious hope was still to find,
> Some useful moral for the feeling mind.[6]

Such an acknowledgement of the narrower purview of female-authored comedy, and of a moral purpose, is an important context in which to place Burney's plays. She for the most part avoids suggestions of sexual innuendo, which do appear in other plays by women who deal with the topics of adultery, flirtation, deception, or divorce. Only in *The Woman-Hater* is there a comical suspicion of sexual impropriety, but this is the mistaken Old Waverley's belief that he is the object of Sophia's advances. Fears about Eleonora's sexual transgression are treated quite seriously, rather than casually. Burney also tends to concentrate on domestic experience and the concerns of individual female figures, rather than couples or the affairs of a larger community. While the comedies feature pairs of lovers, the plays' conflicts tend to separate hero and heroine, rather than pit them together against the world. Burney's "narrow scene," however, certainly contains in microcosm the problems of her society: class prejudice, racism, and misogyny, among others.

Burney's comedies are difficult to place generically and as such they demonstrate Arthur Sherbo's contention that "theatre-goers in the last few decades of the eighteenth century were as eager for variety as those of any other century" and that the assumed distinctions between sentimental and non-sentimental comedies are misleading.[7] Burney mixes her romantic couples' sentimentality, emotional effusions, and idealism with the financial pragmatism of figures of different classes; she combines the farce of locked-away gossips and ghosts with psychologically detailed depictions of emotions and satirical portraits of false intellectuals, curmugeons, and woman-haters. In this mix Burney tends to create static dramatic figures. This is not necessarily an indication of incompetence. Many of her figures interest us *because* they seldom change. Prejudices are often reinforced rather than reexamined, romantic couples do not have to reevaluate their lifestyles, and authorities reign unchecked for the most part in Burney's plays. Humor often lies in the refusal of figures to budge from their attitudes.

Each of Burney's comedies is concerned with the enduring subject of love and its antagonists. *The Witlings, Love and Fashion*, and *A Busy Day* all feature a courtship plot that is arrested by financial worries and the conflicts between families or moral world views. In *The Woman-Hater*, lovers' conflicts must also be resolved, but here Burney concentrates on the problems of marriage rather than courtship, exposing the negotiations and accommodations that must be made given the realities of passion, jealousy, rage, punishment, forgiveness, and financial necessity. The link Burney explores between money and marriage is made repeatedly in plays throughout the century, in Richard Steele's *The Conscious Lovers* (1722), David Garrick and George Colman, the Elder's *The Clandestine Marriage* (1766, read by Burney), Richard Brinsley Sheridan's *The Rivals* (1775, seen by Burney), and Inchbald's *Wives as They Were and Maids as They Are* (1797), to name but a few examples. In many plays, conflicts arise because a lack of money interferes with marital desirability, just as in *The Witlings* or *Love and Fashion*. Often, hostilities are overcome by new-found sources of money. In Inchbald's *Next Door Neighbours* (1791), the device of a discovered fortune and new parentage eases the impediments to Eleonora's marriage to Henry. In *The Wise Man of the East* (1799), modeled by Inchbald on a play by Kotzebue, money is similarly restored to poverty-stricken Ellen so that she might marry young Claransforth. In Burney's plays, love does conquer almost everything, but it is a love that survives because of blackmail and coercion, an old man's pride, or an old man's greed, rather than because of the gift of a benevolent long-lost parent or of a reformed criminal. Love does not, however, conquer class-based prejudices or threats of violence that persist despite a move toward resolution and reconciliation. It would seem that for Burney, human imperfection rather than generosity is most likely to untangle problems.

Financial trials often reveal the period's social double-standards that were based on gender. In Frances Sheridan's *The Discovery* (1763, known by Burney), for example, such a financial inconsistency exists. Lord Medway is happy to marry off his daughter to Sir Anthony Branville because he will take her without a fortune, so her own desires are inconsequential. On the other hand, Medway permits his son, Colonel Medway, to make his decisions about marriage regardless of fortune. Burney shows just such double-standards throughout her comedies. Her male figures tend to suffer less radically from financial worries than the female figures do. It is inevitably the female member of a young couple who is our primary interest in Burney's plays. These figures experience momentary exile from a community, class discrimination, or moral censure. Cecilia, Hilaria, Eliza, and Eleonora face serious decisions because their financial security demands this of them, whether they need money to gain a husband while they are young, or to ensure a comfortable middle age after beauty (the other great bargaining tool) has faded. Financial trials also show a class-based double-standard. The milliners and Innis scoff at the delicacy of their "betters" because the acquisition of money means something different to them. The nurse, who acts very much like Eleonora, is seen as disgraceful. Burney is well aware that freedom of movement and freedom to announce desire vary with social status.

Burney's heroines are for much of the action forced to act solitarily to preserve romance and desire in the face of financial hardship; they are often left on their own by those from whom they should expect succor. Sir Archy's offers of advice are hardly benevolent, after all, and each heroine makes her most honest statements about her situation when she is alone. Cecilia acknowledges her sense of friendlessness and her lack of personal resources. Eliza speaks of her familial shame and Hilaria contemplates the barter of her virginal charms. Eleonora and Sophia act as a pair, but lament nonetheless their lack of protection from the world at large. Only Joyce celebrates a sense of individuality and her unmooring from parental authority. The figure is only alone onstage once, and this is not for a betrayal of her fears, but for an expression of her assertiveness, as she rummages through Smatter's Dressing Room (IV.iii).

Burney's depiction of her heroines evolved over the decades between *The Witlings* and the late comedies. In the early play, Cecilia is a somewhat passive figure, whose sentimental longing for Beaufort and exaggerated assessment of her trials are at times laughable. She pales by comparison to the exuberant Lady Smatter and the absurd but engaging Mrs. Voluble and Mrs. Sapient. Despite her mistaken attributions, pretensions about her knowledge, and her centrality to an incompetent community of artists, Lady Smatter does speak her mind, organize, and promote herself. In the late comedies, female desire, assertiveness, and fear are more evident and the heroines of these plays are more complexly developed. While Cecilia is almost entirely a respondent to action or an ineffectual doer, the heroines of the late comedies take some self-assertive steps toward ensuring their own happiness. These steps are, of course, heavily circumscribed for them. Hilaria must finally make the decision to exchange herself for her lover's freedom and then suggest a further exchange of jewels for marital happiness. She ends up getting her man and a fortune. Jemima makes the gesture that solves the problems of Cleveland and Eliza, by suggesting a similar exchange of fortune for marriage in *A Busy Day*. Eleonora and Sophia make their way to England; Sophia and Joyce petition Sir Roderick for their financial security, even when others have failed; and Joyce asserts at the end of the play that lying and deception must be counteracted by generous admissions and rightful recognition.

Thomas Harris felt that Hilaria was unique on the English stage. The combined charms of her desire for romance, her distaste for an old suitor, and her moral dilemma are certainly attractive. Other comedies of the time do feature even more forceful female figures who seek to control their destinies and somehow achieve a desirable resolution to their problems. Such women include the belle of Cowley's play; Louise Moreton, in Inchbald's *All on a Summer's Day* (1787); Hester in *To Marry, or Not to Marry* (1805); and the plotting sisters in Baillie's *The Tryal* (published in 1798). Louise arranges to avoid a distasteful suitor in order to marry the true love of her life. Hester is an independent woman who has reservations about marriage; these resemble Orwin Mortland's, and they arrange their own marriage. She also reconciles her new suitor to her long-lost father. The sisters Agnes and Mariane in *The Tryal* exchange identities in order to ensure one sister's financial security with her mate and to test the emotional commitment of the other's suitor. They are successful in both cases.

One of Burney's main concerns is to show psychological complexity in her depictions of female dilemmas and trials, especially in the late comedies. Given Burney's successful development as a novelist and the publication of the two novels (*Cecilia* and *Camilla*) that separate the late comedies from *The Witlings*, this emphasis on psychology is not surprising. Her heroines seldom find themselves in morally or sexually compromising situations; they do not test their suitors, run away with them under the cover of night, disguise themselves, or rebel against authority. That is, all but Joyce avoid this. Instead, Burney involves us in the mental lives of her female figures, as they face undesirable decisions or encounter discrimination or ridicule. The heroines of the late comedies all suffer an acute sense of interior division. In these plays, the mental world is almost as important as the material world. While money plays a role in resolving the conflict in *Love and Fashion* and *A Busy Day*, mental attitudes are very important, too, as they are in *The Woman-Hater*. Burney asks not only how such characters would act but also how they would feel and how emotions would be depicted onstage. Although the London theaters at this time mushroomed to capacities that made intimacy and nuance unlikely, Burney does not rely entirely on broad strokes of characterization to communicate ideas to the audience. She often makes her point about female experience by showing her female figures *not* acting, but reacting, listening, observing, or being pushed into silence.

The heroines' positional rather than kinetic physicality (relying on placement on the stage, rather than activity) suggests psychological states aptly. For example, the laughable affectations of the Watts family, heightened by the women's attention to their clothing and Margaret's insistence on calling Eliza by a series of "fine-sounding" names, are placed in stark contrast to Eliza's restrained desire to impress the Tylneys. The interior division between duty and shame is shown in Eliza's silence and in her retreat to a corner of the room. Her movements reflect agitation rather than purpose and she overhears others' prejudices at the same time as she is unable to clarify her own situation. Hilaria, too, is a heroine whose conflict between material satisfaction and moral approval is aptly demonstrated, as she hears the advice of one man or another's condemnation and only voices her own feelings when she is alone.

The Woman-Hater deals memorably and forcefully with the problem of domestic violence and marital discord. Again, Burney shows this mainly by depicting a female figure who is perceived, surveyed, and judged rather than one who acts out (or up) in particular ways, though Eleonora does attempt to secure money from her relatives. Eleonora enters scenes deferentially and hesitantly, with all of the tangible signs of trepidation and doubt. She comes with *"a handkerchief held to her Face, and her Eyes fixed on the ground, [and] courtsies gravely"* (II.viii.1). The psychology of the turmoil she feels when she discovers Wilmot's presence is complex. She is not physically in danger initially. It is the *idea* of Wilmot that frightens her. Eleonora manifests an emotional profile that we might attribute to a battered woman: she wavers between feelings of shame and guilt for having taken Sophia from her father, to genuine fear about Wilmot's violence, to forgiveness for his past wrongs, despite the fact that he "repents" his extreme passion and propensity for snap judgments enough times to make his "conversion" doubtful. Eleonora's call for forgiving and forgetting, for putting on a joyful demeanor at the end of the play, is typical of sentimental resolutions, but is also indicative of the demands placed on a woman for whom there are few choices outside of an undesirable marriage.

Backscheider suggests that some of the stock components of comedy include "hidden auditors and compromising situations and [basing] a play upon a single joke." These "gimmicks, improbabilities . . . , bustle, mistakes, and contrivances . . . [,] mistaken assumptions, awkward situations, and courtship" are said to characterize Inchbald's early plays.[8] Such devices are present in Burney's comedies as well, but with a twist. In *The Witlings*, for example, Mrs. Sapient spends much of act 5 in a closet, but her concealment affords no understanding that alters the plot in any way. Instead, the secrecy of her hiding place is not uniform, and she must listen to Lady Smatter, of all people, insult her intelligence. The device creates very little dramatic irony. It does prepare the audience well for the reappearance of the figure who is described as if she were a locked-away cat. This variation on the screened auditor calls attention metatheatrically to the device by making it obviously contrived. Nothing is private to the witlings—Cecilia's fortune, her misfortune, Lady Smatter's possible shame—just as nothing in drama can really be private, given the generic reliance on what is visible, if only to the theater audience. *The Witlings* plays with this idea of exposure by stripping away literally and figuratively the screens behind which any figure might seek hidden refuge.

Comic writers also often rely on disguise as a device that permits secrecy, revelation (*The Wise Man of the East*), tests of character (*The Belle's Stratagem*), duping (Cowley's 1783 *A Bold Stroke for a Husband*), or surveillance, as in *Love and Fashion*. In Burney's late comedies, the idea of the covert becomes more conceptual than physical, as figures hide behind imposed identities, are seen but not heard, or are assumed to be people they are not. Again, Burney's development as a novelist must have contributed to this change in her perception of character and conflict. In *A Busy Day*, for example, Eliza is put in a position equivalent to being both disguised and screened, as she overhears conversations about Frank's "City Gentoo." The Tylneys effectively screen away Eliza's familial roots, which allows them to discuss the class her family represents openly before her. A device that requires stage props or costume—the hidden or disguised auditor—is replaced here by psychological development that is reflected in blocking and dialogue. There is no willful deception taking place, no covert operation, no denial on Eliza's part; instead, coincidences and the presumptions of the Tylneys provide the disguise and the deception for her. Class prejudice is the most important thing discovered in these scenes, something that itself could be masked, and something very difficult to dismantle.

The Woman-Hater contains scenes that include literal and conceptual disguises that are quite novel. Old and Young Waverley appear at Eleonora's cottage at the same time, with Young Waverley in disguise, but the disguise is entirely transparent, and the humor emerges not from mistaken identity but from Jack's verbal insistence that his "real" self remains indecipherable, though he knows the game is up. The most important use of disguise in *The Woman-Hater* is that which cloaks Joyce as Miss Wilmot. However, this is a disguise and usurpation forced upon the figure rather than one she chooses willfully for devious purposes. And it is not until late in the play that we have access to her "real" identity and to some element of dramatic irony. In this play, multiple facets of identity, especially female identity—obedience, decorum, and the behavior that marks class and refinement—are shown undoubtedly to be learned behaviors rather than "natural" ones, however uncomfortable they are for Joyce. The disguise of "acting" a part is shown to characterize the situations of many or most women. Perhaps Burney is suggesting that the conventional forms of disguise that have often marked comedy can and should give way to more sophisticated perceptions of social roles and interaction that create mistakes and disguises in less tangible ways than a costume and that have far-reaching effects that cannot be cast off with one's physical masks.

Burney's view of disguise can be read as part of a strategy for depicting important social issues in her comedies. Class prejudice (and, in *A Busy Day*, racial prejudice) is a prominent issue exposed by Burney's intermingling of social classes on the stage. At times, such as in *The Witlings*, a gulf between the classes is shown in physical ways in the settings Burney uses, when interaction between classes occurs only when one class employs the other in a place of business. When Cecilia faces a decrease in her status because of her financial loss, she nonetheless cannot feel equal to the milliners from whom she seeks help, because of her sentimental effusions about her problems and because she feels unprepared to fend for herself as the working women do. She remains in practical terms separated from them because her upper-class problems are only financially rather than emotionally relevant to them. Censor's dismissal of those he does not consider his equals, whether they are intellectually, sexually, or economically inferior, informs his entire outlook. He mocks Lady Smatter's pretensions, is dismissive of the milliners' activities, and, as his name suggests, has the sole purpose of evaluating whose causes, speeches, or sentiments are worth acknowledging. In this quite fickle atmosphere of judgment, Jack and Codger are somewhat safe from ridicule and even Dabler is not publicly humiliated, but Smatter does not escape with her dignity. Beaufort makes overtures about the similarities between those who work for a living and himself, but he does not actually undertake physical labor and he cannot even act to preserve his own engagement.

The refinement of Burney's concept of the disguise as she matured as a dramatist is reflected in her problematization of the topic of social prejudice in the late comedies. In *A Busy Day*, Eliza is simultaneously a member of two social groups. Imitation and presumed identities characterize the joining of these groups in one place, an event that fails miserably from the Wattses' standpoint. Via Joel Tibbs, imitation becomes mockery, which is a very different way of assuming identities. However, Burney also participates in perpetuating class stereotypes. If the Tylneys are pretentious snobs, the nouveau riche family is marked by an insistence on the physical rather than the emotional or the intellectual. The Wattses are without the emotional responses one expects from family members, but are interested instead in examining Eliza's clothes and manners and staring at the scenery around them. Like the Branghtons in *Evelina*, they lack refinement because they cannot willfully rein in their physical awkwardness. Such physicality marks Joyce completely, and she is most comfortable singing, moving freely, and announcing her opinions without censorship. While her liberty is admirable, it is also clearly out of step with a social world whose idea of refinement will accept Sophia much more readily.

Burney's male figures are marked by a patriarchal view of both gender and class that is farcically extreme in Sir Roderick but present also in Censor, Beaufort, Sir Marmaduke, Cleveland, Lord Ardville, and Sir Archy. Sir Roderick's statement of authority over his servants is echoed in various ways by these other male figures: "And who the devil may be angry if I mayn't? Ha? Who has a better right? Can you tell? A'n't I your Master? A'n't you all my hirelings?" (I.vii.34-36). Each man fears the encroachment of those below him. For Sir Roderick, this is symbolized by his servants' use of his resources and his constant sense of being under siege by those who do not respect his class and his gender. Sir Marmaduke simply ignores the troubles of the lower class except where they affect his comfortable leisure. When a haystack goes up in smoke, the property loss is more important than the safety of the neighborhood: "I had rather by half the whole village had been burnt!" (II.87-88). Rain only interferes with his ride, though it aids the local crops and eases the trials of the poor. Beaufort and Cleveland, despite their generous gestures toward social equality, celebrate the maintenance of their money and show no genuine interest in *actually* joining the classes below them. Lord Ardville is flattered by Fineer and relies on the inferiority of Litchburn to maintain his superiority. When class and race combine to degrade an individual in the eyes of the onstage figures, as is indicated by the mistreatment of Eliza's Indian servant, only Eliza comes to his defense. That he never appears on stage, however, also indicates the peripherality of the figure to both the on- and offstage observers of Eliza's situation. The white servants do appear, and comment quite particularly about their own enhanced delicacy of complexion, for example, when they compare themselves to the Indian man.

While each of Burney's comedies has the requisite "happy ending" and a restoration of lost money, community, or approval, she reminds us that the generic requirements of comedy ought not to diminish the serious repercussions of social, gendered sources of conflict and punishment. Her mix of the sentimental, satiric, farcical, and laughable allows for a continual series of undercut expectations and a disturbance of an easy evaluation of character or situation. The conventional is challenged by the transgressive and the stereotypical is interrupted by those who insist on uniqueness that must be recognized. Often, what we sense to be justified comic resolutions likewise have the undertones of a newly coerced and undesirable social order, and admirable verbal morals are just as often contradicted by actions and prejudice. Burney's comedies combine many genuinely funny moments—Sapient's confinement with the dirty dishes, Lady Smatter's harried departure from Joyce's antics, or Lady Wilhelmina's horrified glances at the Wattses—with serious observations about how societies are organized and what values underpin the relationships between people of different groups.

The records of plays staged in the last quarter of the eighteenth century reflect a preference for comedy. In the final three decades of the century, new tragedies were written and staged half as often as new comedies, at most. Of both new and revived plays, tragedies never accounted for more than fifteen percent of plays staged in each decade and revivals of Shakespeare were most common.[9] Burney's four tragedies exemplify writing in a time of generic flux, in their mingling of classical elements, the familiar conflict between passion and duty, and popular Gothic devices (see chapters 3 and 4 above). Rather than producing plays that were primarily "private allegories,"[10] Burney wrote tragedies that are comparable to others written by her female contemporaries.

Hannah More (1745-1833) outlines her view of drama and the stage in a preface to her tragedies. She is far from charitable and is especially doubtful about the effects of theater-going on young women. Arguing that drama will be moral only with a thorough purification of both the stage and the theater-goers, More emphasizes the dangers that accompany spectatorship rather than reading: "[i]t is the semblance of real action which is given to the piece, by different persons supporting the different parts, and by their dress, their tones, their gestures, heightening the representation into a kind of enchantment. It is the concomitant pageantry, it is the splendour of the spectacle, and even the show of the spectators:—these are the circumstances which altogether fill the theatre—which altogether produce the effect—which altogether create the danger."[11] She excuses her tragedies on the basis that she wrote them in her youth and suggests that to suppress them would be disingenuous. Given this strong pronouncement about the influence of drama on the spectator, which shares with Baillie's "Introductory Discourse" a recognition of the visceral effects of viewing drama (see below), the fate of the female figures in More's tragedies might be considered cautionary or didactic.

In More's *The Inflexible Captive* (1775), the alternatives presented between personal desire, political duty, and honor are more thoroughly male-centered than in any of Burney's plays. Burney's interest in her tragedies is to consider equally, if not more concertedly, the influence of this type of debate on the female figures close to publicly prominent males. In More's tragedy, the effects of political debate on the protagonist's daughter are depicted, but the message seems to be not that we lament the suffering of women who engage in political strife, but that we lament that they engage in it at all, for More presents Attilia as being entirely unfit for such stern topics. The male protagonist, Regulus, is a political prisoner who refuses, in his country's interest, to be ransomed or exchanged for other prisoners. The incompatibility of his daughter's participation in this heroism is announced from the play's outset, when Licinius suggests that Attilia should not involve herself in governmental affairs. She responds to him by renouncing decorum or romance in favor of filial duty: ". . . I am all the *daughter*, / The filial feelings now possess my soul, / And other passions find no entrance there" (1:513). Regulus sacrifices his paternal role to be fully a citizen, and in the process denies Attilia her personal attachment to him, describing her as his enemy and as a "rash, imprudent girl!" who "little know'st / The dignity and weight of public cares" (1:519).

When Attilia offers herself in her father's place as a captive, this too is denied (unlike *The Siege of Pevensey*), and the return of Regulus to his captors finds him requesting that Attilia be watched over, for "We must not hope to find in *her* soft soul / The strong exertion of a manly courage—" (1:520). Attilia eventually grows to accept the gendered weaknesses that the male figures assign to her, and she seeks only death or madness as her refuge, announcing that as a "poor, weak, trembling woman— / [She] cannot bear these wild extremes of fate—" (1:524). The male virtues of firm resolve and patriotism are triumphant, all of Attilia's protestations go for naught, and she is left physically overcome by the departure of her father. In *The Inflexible Captive*, More seems to draw greater attention to female weakness than to female suffering, and the many pronouncements against a woman's participation in the public sphere of government are unquestioned. Attilia's despair is a "natural" consequence of the political situation and we are invited to ignore this in favor of praising the stoicism of Regulus and his patriotic vision. The play does represent the vicissitudes of female experience, but does not reflect for long on the damaging effects of female subordination, as other plays of the period do.

In More's tragedy, the daughter repeatedly attempts to petition for her father's security or to offer herself in his place. Such filial self-sacrifice is not uncommon in eighteenth-century drama. As Doody notes, the father-daughter relationship was an enduring topic for dramatists.[12] Burney's exploration of this relationship takes two forms in the tragedies. In *The Siege of Pevensey*, the coercive power of the father in the private sphere is replicated by the public power of the sovereign and Adela must submit alternately to these authorities both physically and emotionally. Attilia is explicitly and overtly denied participation in the political realm. Adela, however, is used insidiously by her father and by the other male figures who rely on her sense of filial duty as leverage to gain martial advantages. More seems to lament female weakness, while Burney attends to the forces that construct an ideology of femininity and then use it for public displays of power. Attila is peripheral to the action; Adela's movements *are* the action. In *Hubert De Vere*, daughterly obedience is seamlessly and secretly appended to feminine innocence and gullibility. Cerulia at no time recognizes the familial source of her suffering, De Mowbray, and remains entirely unconscious of the larger political circumstances in which she is caught. Cerulia's death allows Burney to demonstrate in a forceful manner the dreadful possibilities that accompany unthinking obedience and a heart and mind that are so easily swayed by others' commands or exhortations. Because Cerulia is an extremely passive victim of circumstances—and because she is above all obedient—she is Burney's clearest example of how ideals about femininity lead women to perceive themselves in ways that can be quite dangerous to them.

Paternal control and paternal rejection also dominate More's *Percy*, which premiered in December 1777 and was performed throughout the rest of the century. A father's coercion of a daughter's choice provides the background for the play's conflict. Against her will, Elwina broke her engagement with Percy, who her father banished, and married Douglas. Douglas believes Elwina still loves Percy and when her father, Raby, arrives to celebrate the return of successful crusaders, Douglas denounces Elwina to him. Elwina admits that she has told Douglas of her former love, and because of this, her father is enraged. When Elwina hears of Percy's death, she faints and calls out his name; this infuriates Douglas, who resolves to punish Elwina for loving Percy. Elwina, like Elberta, is defined simultaneously by two roles: daughter and wife.

Douglas portrays much the same vacillating view of his wife that Wilmot displays in Burney's *The Woman-Hater*. He alternately resolves to be kind to her, and then seeks revenge against her youthful love on the slightest indication that she has strayed from chastity. Percy is not really dead, and Douglas discovers what he thinks is evidence of Elwina's unfaithfulness and announces his pleasure in tormenting Elwina, "feast[ing] upon her terrors"(1:538). Douglas intercepts a letter to Elwina from Percy that proves to him her guilt. Elwina is caught between indulging her true passion, or remaining true to her marital vows and her husband's honor. She chooses the latter, but not in time to prevent a fight between Douglas and Percy. Percy clears Elwina's name before he dies, and her father admits that he was aware of the meetings and the misconstrued passions. Raby confirms his daughter's spotless name to Douglas, who is willing to ask her forgiveness. Elwina in the meantime poisons herself, becomes deranged, and dies. Douglas stabs himself, and Raby is left to lament his manipulations.

Percy, more than *The Inflexible Captive*, is a tragedy specifically about a female figure, despite its name.[13] Female guilt and immorality are debated throughout the play. Elwina suffers from a process that degrades her just as Elgiva is degraded in *Edwy and Elgiva*. In these two plays, More and Burney show female chastity to be defined by male figures, who thus use the perceived lack of it as a source of libel and punishment. Elwina's apparent guilt is compounded by her own admissions of desire. It is ultimately her desire for Percy, rather than any actions that might manifest this desire, that leads to her downfall. Female desire—especially romantic or sexual desire—is thought to require careful regulation because it threatens to emerge as an excess, something beyond the bounds of male-regulated marriage.

Unregulated female activity threatens community stability. The way female playwrights depict a communal response to the horror of female transgression varies widely. Elgiva and Elwina are both innocent of the crimes of which they are accused. Nonetheless, the forbidden desire that lurks behind Elwina's denial of Percy leads her to suicide. Elgiva is tortured by others' hands. In neither case is the punishment justifiable. In this respect, both plays can be fruitfully compared with a play like Nicholas Rowe's *The Tragedy of Jane Shore* (1714), where Jane's "real" guilt produces a moral example for the community. The closing speech indicates that female suffering is entirely self-created, because of Jane's betrayal of her marriage vows: "Let those who view this sad example know / What fate attends the broken marriage-vow; / And teach their children in succeeding times, / No common vengeance waits upon these crimes, / When such severe repentance could not save, / From want, from shame, and an untimely grave."[14] More and Burney debate instead the power that external disapprobation and presumptions about female guilt have to fill up the vacant space that is female innocence. It is abundantly clear from More's and Burney's tragedies that actual transgression is not really necessary for punishment to be meted out, because paternal and marital authorities see the female figures of the plays as objects to be evaluated rather than subjects who might prove their chastity or lack thereof.

The prologue to More's *The Fatal Falsehood* (1779) gestures toward some of the concerns I have raised in arguing for a woman-conscious vision of tragedy. Here More discusses the importance of "A simple story of domestic woes," which, in her view, appeals more universally than "grander" themes of government and war (1:545). In this play, the Earl Guildford has a son and daughter, Rivers and Emmelina. Guildford's nephew, Bertrand, is the villain of the piece. He would like to marry Emmelina, so he seeks to divide Rivers from his betrothed, Julia, in order to rechannel the family fortune. Orlando, Rivers's friend, also loves Julia, and is beloved by Emmelina in return. Rivers is convinced that Julia loved Orlando before she was betrothed to him, so he doubts her faithfulness. To test Orlando and Julia, Rivers invites Orlando to be an attendant at the wedding. Orlando convinces Julia to delay the wedding upon threats of his suicide and threats to Rivers's safety. Bertrand tells Orlando that Julia loves him, which he "proves" by giving him a letter she intended for Rivers. The letter requests a meeting at the garden gate and he believes she will flee with him. Rivers comes to the garden gate as well, at Bertrand's request. There is a fight in the darkness, and Orlando believes he has killed Rivers and he accuses Julia of betrayal because of the letter. Orlando is seized, but it is discovered that Bertrand, not Rivers, was killed. Despite the reappearance of Rivers, Emmelina cannot believe her brother yet lives, and goes mad, ranting about Orlando's guilt for the murder. She fancies the living are ghosts and does not recognize her own father; she weakens and dies. Orlando, distraught over Emmelina's death, stabs himself and dies.

Emmelina is a corollary figure to Cerulia: both are innocent victims caught up in others' acts of control and both are pushed beyond the realm of sense into madness and finally death. In More's tragedy, Emmelina is one of several victims, but some characters she believes to be dead are saved by mistaken identities, darkness, and coincidence. She thus responds to her sense of a fuller tragedy than we do as the play's audience. While poetic justice is enacted on Bertrand, Emmelina's death spreads the net of punishment to the innocent. Cerulia, by contrast, is a more exclusive victim in Burney's play. While De Vere and Geralda certainly suffer, their love is restored along with De Vere's political position and Geralda's innocence. The only other extensive suffering is experienced by De Mowbray, and his is the suffering of guilt and punishment. I have argued that Burney's tragic heroines serve as evidence against those who wrong them; Emmelina's death does not perform this function as strongly as does Cerulia's, for while Orlando kills himself after Emmelina dies, the deeper source of the villainy (Bertrand) remains unaware of the effect his acts have had (unlike De Mowbray), and Emmelina's raving deterioration is not given the centrality that Cerulia's decay is granted. Emmelina's suffering, while not unimportant, is nonetheless peripheral.

More's tragedies show a range of attitudes towards women. The status of these attitudes as "woman-conscious" varies quite extensively: Attilia wants to assert her ability to help but is left incapacitated; innocent Elwina is pressured to commit the suicidal act of one more guilty, as a testimony to her marriage vows; Julia and Emmelina are manipulated and the latter dies because of this. What links the depiction of these female figures' suffering is that they are punished on the basis of private, personal, and domestic relationships. Perhaps this is the particularly domestic view of the tragic that More refers to in her preface to the last play, and arguably this concentration on the personal and domestic separates *Percy* and *The Fatal Falsehood* from *The Inflexible Captive*'s more classical explorations of honor and more conventional ideas about heroism. Whether these female figures respond to the manipulations of fathers, husbands, or lovers, their experiences of denial seem more contextual than individual. "The Inflexible Captive" faces no dilemma, ultimately: his mind is made up and he asserts his will unquestioningly. His tragedy is derived from his chosen public role and patriotism. The female figures are punished because they love the wrong man, or fail to perform the proper duty expected of them by others. This view of female vulnerability is shared by Burney.

The father-daughter relationship is shown at its most degraded in *The Siege of Sinope*, by Frances Brooke (1724-1789). The tragedy, based on an anonymous libretto from Sarti's opera *Mitridate A Sinope*, ran for ten nights in early 1781 (the opera with music by Sacchini was played opposite it at the King's Opera House). Here, the filial bond has been entirely ruptured. Athridates has recently made peace with Pharnaces, who is married to his daughter, Thamyris. The resentment between the two kings emerged when Athridates broke a long-time engagement between Pharnaces and his daughter. Pharnaces seized her anyway, and made her his queen. Despite the new peace between the kings, Athridates resents the seizure of his daughter, and has a simmering desire for vengeance against Pharnaces because Pharnaces's father, Mithridates, killed Athridates's only son. To exact revenge, Athridates plans to surprise Pharnaces during the feast that celebrates the peace.

The tragedy becomes increasingly focused on the trials of Thamyris, who is eager to see her husband and father reconciled: ". . . Once again / My filial arms shall press a much-lov'd father; / Again his child, his Thamyris, shall see / The smile paternal on his aged cheek, / And hear his voice in blessings."[15] With her father's aggressive and dishonorable declaration of war, however, the daughter must acknowledge in the father a "savage conqueror" (II.v.18) and she pledges to take her own life and the life of her son if her husband is harmed. The torn affiliations of the queen, who is swayed alternately by filial, marital, and maternal responsibility, are emphasized throughout the play. Like Burney's heroines, Thamyris becomes a political pawn because of her familial bonds.

The intense (perhaps unbelievably so) paternal rage that Brooke depicts finds its outlet in declarations that Athridates will not be satisfied ". . . 'till the fierce Pharnaces, / His queen (no more my daughter), and their son, / The bond of their detested union, glut / The ravening vulture's hunger" (III.i.24). Brooke depicts the redirection of male aggression and intermale conflict onto a female object in a manner similar to Burney. While the opening scene establishes the seizure of Thamyris as being beyond her control and not to her wishes, Athridates insists on blaming his daughter for disobedience and abandonment and he establishes himself as a heaven-appointed judge and punisher. The initial meeting between warring father and daughter finds Thamyris having alternately to define herself according to conflicting roles. She renounces the appellation of "daughter" for that of "Queen" and refuses to invest her oppressor with a paternal identity that will weaken her resolve to resist him. She stands as a link between generations, between a warring grandparent and grandchild, and between her father and her husband. Thamyris must simultaneously acknowledge her own maternal and marital tenderness but yet deny her relationship with her father; her own need to protect her child intensifies the incredible failure of parental care on her father's part.

Thamyris's need to keep her child safe is used explicitly by her father as a weapon for discovering where she has her son hidden. When Athridates finally captures his daughter and grandson, she pleads for her child and, trusting her father to protect him, as a last resort turns him over to her father. Athridates decides to send them away with Roman troops as disgraced prisoners. This final insult, worse than death, forces a nearly mad Thamyris to seek her father in order to plead again for her son's safety: "Lead me to him,— / To Athridates, Cappadocia's tyrant, / This scepter'd murderer, this crown'd assassin, / This scourge of trembling infancy, this—father" (IV.i.42). The queen's catalogue of identities makes synonymous Athridates's paternal role and those roles that make him villainous, so that no one can forget the familial bonds that underlie the political conflict. Although Thamyris renounces her daughterly role, it persists in informing her response to all she experiences.

The conflict between father and daughter comes to a head when Athridates offers his daughter an ultimatum. She can either break her marital bond with her husband and permit her son to reign over his father's kingdom, or she can condemn them all to death. Thamyris chooses the sanctity of her marital bond and gives up her son. This scene, in which the daughter must choose between two equally distasteful options, serves to produce some important dramatic irony when Thamyris is reunited with her besieged husband. He discovers that his son has been turned over to the enemy and he immediately accuses his wife of lacking heroic fiber: ". . . wherefore did my fondness trust / Thy woman's heart? The hero's glow of soul, / The generous thought, firm virtue's stubborn purpose, / Thy feeble bosom feels not" (IV.vi.52). The management of the dramatic scenes which show Thamyris alternately in the company of her husband or her father, but not with them both until the play's close, emphasizes her conflicted sense of identity. The audience has access to the extremity of Thamyris's trials by her father, but Pharnaces does not, and he momentarily dismisses her turmoil as lacking heroic dimensions. He just as easily then asks her forgiveness for his rash accusation.

In the final act of *The Siege of Sinope*, Thamyris's powers as an orator allow her to regain her son from the troops, and she shelters him in a temple. When her father and husband meet her there, the men fight. In the culminating scene, after Thamyris has witnessed her father's repeated cruelty and betrayal of her and her son, she still intercedes between husband and father, and pleads that her father be spared. He stabs himself instead and, before dying, blesses his daughter. The family is reunited and Pharnaces reigns triumphant again, but regret for her father's death continues to haunt Thamyris, and "calls, unbid, the tender filial tear" (V.x.69).[16]

Brooke creates a firmly woman-conscious work by concentrating the sense of conflict and dilemma in a female figure, and illustrating the internal discord that arises because of an ideology of filial and wifely obedience and maternal responsibility. In the two "siege" plays, *The Siege of Pevensey* and *The Siege of Sinope*, it is a woman who is under siege as much as a political territory. In both plays, numerous exchanges take place. In Brooke, Thamyris vacillates between three male constituents who hold power over her: her father, husband, and son. She faces giving up allegiances to any of her male-defined roles. In *The Siege of Pevensey*, Adela is exchanged physically because of her male-defined roles, and the physical exchanges accompany a requisite emotional vacillation between personal desire and filial duty.

Cowley's *The Fate of Sparta; or, The Rival Kings* was performed at Drury Lane in January and February of 1788, with Siddons, as Chelonice, playing across from Kemble in the role of Cleombrotus. This play reverses the initial situation of Brooke's, by introducing the daughter in her father's camp. Her husband, Cleombrotus, observes that in his wife,

> . . . the filial principle
> So strongly burns, that easier 'twere to woo
> The murm'ring ring-dove from her unfledg'd brood
> Than her, from him, who gave the charmer life.
> She thinks his safety, too, hangs on her presence—
> Oh, can I blame the cruel, lovely duty,
> Which thus, unwilling, holds her from my arms?[17]

Her father, Leonidas, once ruled Sparta along with her husband, who was deposed. Against his wife's wishes, Cleombrotus now threatens to battle Leonidas with a mercenary army.

Chelonice's dilemma—her choice between warring factions—is more intensely depicted than that of Thamyris, whose loyalty to her husband is aided by the extreme hatred of her father. Chelonice secretly goes to her husband and, with the use of blackmail, persuades him to delay his attack. This makes Cleombrotus look weak in the eyes of his men, who defame Chelonice.

When Leonidas discovers his daughter's subterfuge, he offers her an "option" that is uniformly distasteful to her. Her secret petition to her husband for her father's safety is regarded by her father as a betrayal. He resolves to "test" her "vaunted duty" and if she fails, to see her as "Not a child, / But a false traitor" who will ". . . lose a sire in the offended prince"

Act V. GAMESTER.

Mr KEMBLE & Mrs SIDDONS *in the Characters of*
M.^r & Mrs BEVERLEY.

Mrs Bev: *Look down with mercy on his Sorrows?*

Sarah Siddons as Mrs. Beverley and John Philip Kemble as Mr. Beverley in Edward Moore's *The Gamester* (1783 production). Courtesy of the British Museum

(2:33). Thamyris must give up her son to her father or risk her husband's life; Chelonice must lure her husband to a nearby grove where he will be ambushed and killed by the king's hired assassin, Amphares. She refuses and is put in prison, claiming that she can be both daughter and wife.

The scene following this refusal is a curious one that points to one of the distinguishing features of Cowley's play. Here, the people plead for Chelonice's release, but she intercedes and supports her father's decision. She thus martyrs herself simultaneously to the ideal of filial duty and the state's need to protect itself against other traitors. She even thanks her father for the gift of the chains that imprison her, the outward manifestations of the ties of filial obedience. Chelonice can only warn her husband about the intended ambush via her agent, Nicrates. Nicrates is mistakenly stabbed by his brother, Amphares, who believes him to be Cleombrotus. Cleombrotus seeks his wife and son in the prison, but during their reunion, his army attacks without his sanction. He then turns against his own soldiers and fights to save Leonidas. Leonidas returns this favor with aggression and Chelonice rushes to plead for her husband. Her father relents and offers banishment instead of death. In an odd twist to the conventions of government, Leonidas makes his daughter his queen, a near-incestuous usurpation of the husband's rights. The conflict between husband and father is ended when Leonidas is stabbed by Amphares, and he bequeaths the crown to Cleombrotus. The intertwined roles of daughter and wife are truly difficult to dissociate in *The Fate of Sparta*.

In each tragedy I have discussed, a woman's virtue is imputed. It is important to consider the nature and source of the accusations. In Burney's tragedies, accusations come from a variety of sources. Chester condemns Adela's actions without really understanding them, but he forgives her when she capitulates to him. Arnulph similarly is critical of Elberta's escape from Offa. Elgiva and Cerulia, by contrast, are acknowledged as the innocent victims of treachery and only in the former case does accusation come from the villain, as part of his plan to overthrow Edwy. In Cowley's tragedy, the heroine is decried by her husband's troops but is also self-accusing and she accepts and even invites the punishment of failed filial duty. In this respect, with her more active participation in the action, Chelonice can be further distinguished from Burney's heroines in her refusal of victimization. The implications of this type of characterization for woman-conscious tragedy are provocative. Female survival is depicted by Cowley, but it is survival that permits the female figure to give herself over fully to father, husband, and state simultaneously. As Chelonice says, "The duties of the wife and child, may each, / Without opposing, warm the heart" (2:38). The husband avenges the father's death and protects his body from insult. The father's death, the husband's reign, and the wife's martyrdom and forgiveness all coalesce in the closing scene of reconciliation. Cowley seems to seek a resolution in which a woman's choices can satisfy all constituencies, so her obedience can be complete. Perhaps this ending suggests that a woman can and should encompass all the demands made on her, no matter how antagonistic they might be.

Joanna Baillie (1762-1851) is perhaps the most interesting figure to juxtapose against Burney. Unlike Burney, however, Baillie enjoyed some production and publication success; *De Monfort, Count Basil,* and *The Tryal* were published in successive editions each year between 1798 and 1800. *De Monfort,* with Kemble and Siddons in the leading roles, was staged at Drury Lane from 29 April 1800 to 9 May 1800. *The London Stage* reports that on the evening of the 3 May performance, the epilogue was omitted due to Siddons's fatigue, which was, according to the *Dramatic Censor,* "very favourably received by a drowsy audience, who were happy to find the Tragedy had reached its conclusion."[18] Burney certainly had heard of Baillie's play, but does not indicate that she saw it (*JL,* 4:417).

In the "Introductory Discourse" to *A Series of Plays* (1798), Baillie contemplates some of the motivations and conditions that surround the observation of passionate excitement, horror, torture, and affliction. The effect of viewing such passion is to feel "powerfully excited" by it, because it is familiar to us.[19] Our eagerness for observation is described by Baillie as minute and attentive, even prying and voyeuristic: if a man's passion is not clear by his movements and looks, "would we not follow him into his lonely haunts, into his closet, into the midnight silence of his chamber in order to discover it?" (11). In Baillie's terms, such observations are instructive. By using the "sympathetick curiosity of our nature . . . we are taught the proprieties and decencies of ordinary life, and are prepared for distressing and difficult situations. In examining others we know ourselves. With limbs untorn, with head unsmitten, with senses unimpaired by despair, we know what we ourselves might have been on the rack, on the scaffold, and in the most afflicting circumstances of distress. Unless when accompanied with passions of the dark and malevolent kind, we cannot well exercise this disposition without becoming more just, more merciful, more compassionate" (12). The importance of *witnessing* is explicitly linked to drama, which displays passions without the mediation of narration and is most effective when most "natural." The writer of tragedy may present the variable effects of passion on the great and powerful, who otherwise remain too distant to be discerned. "To Tragedy it belongs to lead [heroes and grand men] forward to our nearer regard, in all the distinguishing varieties which nearer inspection discovers; with the passions, the humours, the weaknesses, the prejudices of men" (29-30).

We are improved by tragedy, because we gain a greater awareness of our own propensities, and this applies as easily to female tragic protagonists as to male, "with some degree of softening and refinement" (36 n). Baillie's scheme for writing tragedy was thus to display in successive plays the influence of a dominating passion on a figure, as an example to "the Monarch, and the man of low degree" (42).

While Baillie's tragedies seem generally preoccupied with the passions of male figures, the interplay between the male and female figures in them is important. In her best-known tragedies, *De Monfort* and *Count Basil*, female figures are depicted as survivors, enduring the destruction of the male protagonists, left either to mourn their passing or to sustain the ruined men. Cox comments on Baillie's depiction of women in her Gothic drama. Typically, female figures are "either terrorized and mad or stoic and indomitable, but . . . always passive." By contrast, Baillie's use of the Gothic is formulated by Cox in feminist terms: "her plays explore the power that literary representations—and particularly dramatic ones—have to fix women within a particular cultural gaze." She "offer[s] a critique of various conventional modes of dramatizing women."[20] In Cox's view, Baillie's plays "embody a sustained meditation upon the roles and plots that constrict women, a meditation not matched in her period by other dramatists or for that matter by the better known Gothic novelists."[21] The potential for Burney's plays to challenge Cox's view of Baillie's uniqueness should be apparent here. Both Baillie and Burney explore the socialization of women by a range of institutions and attitudes that serve to constrict female movement and agency. While Elgiva and Cerulia are certainly typicallly passive Gothic heroines, Elberta and Adela are not. Elberta particularly refuses the role male figures force on her—the prisoner and passive wife—in favor of active mothering.

Baillie challenges conventional views of real women, and of their dramatic counterparts, in many of her tragedies. In *De Monfort* (published in 1798), the male figure resolves to be guided by his sister Jane's efforts to quell his desire for revenge against a former foe, Rezenvelt. De Monfort's passion, however, makes him susceptible to the rumors that his sister harbors a secret love for Rezenvelt. Hate consumes De Monfort and he exacts his revenge by killing Rezenvelt. His remorse and despair kill him. Jane is left to mourn her brother's rashness and she resolves to take up life in a convent. Throughout the play, her voice is the voice of reason and moderation, and she is a guiding and protecting figure, urging conciliation and pledging loyalty. A role-reversal takes place over the course of the play—the passionate brother must be governed by the more reasonable sister—and De Monfort assumes the position usually occupied by the Gothic heroine, startled by sensations of the supernatural and madness.

Cox argues that Baillie cast Siddons in the role of the heroine in order to demand that her audience question the conventionally passive, gaze-attracting, objectified female that Siddons often portrayed. He writes that the "men in the play want Jane De Monfort to be a typical Siddons character: emotionally responsive, powerfully attractive, passive. They want her to be the spectacle at the center of their narrative, the object over which they fight—both in the social realm of flirtation and in actual combat. She, however, simply refuses to play that role."[22] Jane De Monfort demonstrates the division so often experienced by Burney's heroines, as she struggles against the contradictory definitions of herself as family member and as marriageable woman and emerges as a figure of strength.

A similar exchange of conventional roles occurs in *Count Basil* (published in 1798), with the Duke's daughter, Victoria, assuming the more aggressive role of wooer, captivating Basil with her beauty.[23] Over the course of their relationship, Victoria maintains the upper hand, rousing Basil's jealousy by conjuring up an imaginary lover, and leaving Basil to respond by saying, "I'll do whate'er thou wilt, I will be silent; / But O! a reined tongue, and bursting heart, / Are hard at once to bear! will thou forgive me?"[24] However, the conflict faced by Basil—between his honor and duty as a soldier, and his romantic passion—is exploited by Victoria's father, who uses her power over Basil for his own ends. Her father declares that ". . . she is a woman; / Her mind, as suits the sex, too weak and narrow / To relish deep-laid schemes of policy" (1:101). Victoria resembles many of Burney's tragic heroines, who are pawns in a larger political action, though her strength in the private arena is unquestioned. Whatever female agency is achieved in the domestic sphere is counteracted by the political action that consumes the male figures and ultimately alters Victoria's view of herself.

Basil is defeated, not in battle, but because his love distracts him sufficiently so that he does not fight at all. His sense of having failed his martial duty resembles Arnulph's in *Elberta*: both men lament their removal from a community of men joined by fellow-feeling. Arnulph elevates his ideal of public duty over his familial ties. Basil admires the "hallow'd neighbourship" of "social converse" that he is now denied: "But I, like a vile outcast of my kind, / In some lone spot must lay my unburied corse" (1:176). He should have died honorably in battle, where his grave would invite homage from other soldiers. The hero's sense of failure emerges only after a passionate decision has been made, one that counteracts public responsibility. For Basil, it is the failure to attend battle. For Arnulph, it is his momentary choice of family over self. Destruction follows in both cases, instigated by a desire to make amends for others who have been wronged. Basil commits suicide, in a cave deep within a savage wood, and Arnulph turns himself in.[25]

Victoria, like Elberta and Jane De Monfort, survives the impetus toward male martyrdom and suicide. The effect of Basil's actions on Victoria is important, for it conjures up not female power, but the ease with which a female figure assumes guilt for another's lack of self-control. Victoria is cursed by Basil's friend Rosinberg and believes herself guilty of ruining "a brave man's honour!" (1:175). She declares in the final scene that she is responsible for his death and she seems to lament her momentary assumption of control, believing it to have been fatal: "Open thine eyes, speak, be thyself again, / And I will love thee, serve thee, follow thee, / In spite of all reproach" (1:189). Victoria's final posture is remarkably different from her earlier assertiveness when she lured Basil through happier woods. She now submits to the power of his corpse and she announces her devotion to him, because ". . . he lov'd me in thoughtless folly lost, / With all my faults, most worthless of his love; / And I'll love him in the low bed of death, / In horrour and decay" (1:190). She is left clinging to the corpse in grief, and Rosinberg makes the final declaration of the play, one that admires Basil for his virtues rather than his faults and that exposes the Duke's machinations that produced this tragedy.

Our readings of the final scenes of any of these tragedies are all-important: Jane De Monfort's stoic direction of the action, Victoria's prostrate grief and Rosinberg's declaration of Basil's virtue, Hubert De Vere's call for an observation of Cerulia's suffering, Elberta's vow to avoid an emotional indulgence, Aldhelm's declaration of the joint virtue of Edwy and Elgiva, Elwina's suicide, the homage to patriotism as Regulus departs, the plea for peace in Sinope. The closing scenes of these plays establish the variety of resolutions, thematic statements, or *mise en scène* formations that invite or, requisitely, discourage feminist interpretations. The physical and narrative centrality of the suffering woman informs the spectator's evaluation of the powers that punish or torture. It is important, therefore, to ask whose voice brings the play to a close, where the heroine is positioned relative to the other figures, and who is represented as controlling the final space. This type of analysis allows us to make distinctions between plays like *Edwy and Elgiva*, *Hubert De Vere*, *The Fatal Falsehood*, *Almeyda* (by Sophia Lee) and *Orra* (by Baillie), for example. Each tragedy portrays innocence destroyed by greed and manipulation and all feature a variation on a mad scene. In More's play, Emmelina is not a central player in the action and her death seems peripheral to the main action that involves the lovers' triangle. She is the financial/marital object Bertrand seeks, but I doubt that her response to the schemings is a dominant consideration in the final scene. The suspense turns on the outcome of the meeting in the dark garden. Emmelina's death thus has an element of surprise for us and suggests the expansion of the circle of villainy to include peripheral figures. Elgiva's death is united with Edwy's in Aldhelm's final moral about virtue and trial, so that even in death her identity is appended to Edwy's. By contrast, Cerulia's fate is exclusive and we see her progress toward madness over the course of the play, as she becomes distracted and wanders wildly. The move toward her death at some point becomes inexorable. As a central female figure, she occupies a literal and figurative focal point; she is dead center in the closing scene, and De Vere calls for a halt to the political intrigue as her death is observed and spectators (on and off the stage) are asked to be aware of their status as watchers.

Cerulia and Emmelina, to different degrees, provide physical evidence that accuses their corruptors (although Orlando is relatively less guilty than Bertrand, he assumes responsibility for Emmelina's madness and death). However, despite the prominence of these innocent tragic victims, the final voice of the play is that of a male figure who calls attention to them and attempts to provide a context that directs our perception of them. *Almeyda; Queen of Granada* (1796), by Sophia Lee (1750-1824), has a similar ending. Queen Almeyda (another Siddons role) is a ruler of real strength who seeks to be reunited with her true love, Alonzo, but is finally poisoned by her foe and kinsman, Abdallah. The two men who love her, Alonzo and Orasmyn, remain by her side in the final scene, mourning her death. The play ends with a minor figure's observation that "such scenes alone / Can shew the danger of those cherish'd passions, / Which thus can antedate the hour of death, / Or make existence agony!"[26] Almeyda's passions, however, were not the cause of the tragedy, though her body sustains the signs of it. It is the surviving male figures who teach us how to respond to female suffering, but we should sometimes question their wisdom.

Other heroines provide evidence of decay and suffering more directly, by speaking for themselves. In the first half of Baillie's *Orra* (published in 1812), an unusually assertive heroine argues compellingly for marital choice, and suffers physical confinement because of her allegiance to this ideal. She is ultimately defeated by superstition that drives her mad; Baillie's use of a Gothic supernatural resembles Burney's in *Hubert De Vere* because the ghosts feared are the ghosts present only in the woman's mind. The closing scene of the play contains no satisfying resolution but ends instead with Orra's raving and frantic motions. There is no concluding statement from the rational (male) figures who surround her. Instead, the stage directions suggest that Orra's madness dominates the other figures and maintains them in her world, rather than releases them into the world of the sane and protected. She is seen *"Catching hold of* HUGHOBERT *and* THEOBALD, *and dragging them back with her in all the wild strength of frantic horror, whilst the curtain drops."*[27] It is Orra's fate to remain in the world of Gothic entrapment; her interstitial position between living and dead, in the company of both (her hallucinations parallel Emmelina's), and between madness and sanity, is preserved indefinitely at the play's close. Baillie refuses to provide a final moral. Yet another point on this spectrum of woman-conscious resolution is illustrated in *Ethwald I* (published in 1802), also by Baillie, in which the spurned Bertha (not unlike Cerulia), goes mad and pleads for Ethwald to attend to her. She is removed from the stage long before the real crux of the action occurs. The mad scene is no doubt a stock theatrical convention, but the voice of madness may linger, be decorously removed, or be silenced by death. Our own ability as spectators to "make sense" of the concluding events of these plays is aided by voices of authority, or is problematized by ravings.

In one very important manner Burney's plays emerge in relief against this brief background of female-authored tragedies, and this is in her concentration on the vicissitudes of the female body. In other plays, bodily suffering is depicted, often directly on the stage, and this ranges from weakness to fainting, delirium, or suicide. While psychological and physical suffering is ongoing, the dominant scene of suffering is condensed into a discrete moment. Burney emphasizes the *progress* of enduring decay, whether it is caused by torture or madness. Only in *The Siege of Pevensey* is this not the case (though the possibility of Adela's starvation is mentioned), and there Burney replaces physical torture with imprisonment and persistent bartering. Physical anguish is drawn out by Burney over the course of a full play. Elgiva, for instance, is not once but repeatedly seized and tortured, and we witness her deterioration as her wounds become increasingly mortal and her body and mind weaken. This play alone is remarkably different from a play like *Percy*, which features Elwina's mental anguish throughout and culminates in her suicide. Her death is a temporally discrete examination of bodily agony. In other plays, mental anguish is often ongoing and is severe (*The Siege of Sinope* comes to mind), but physical suffering passes swiftly. This is not the case with Elgiva. Cerulia likewise circles back and Burney repeats scenes that refer to her madness, her wandering, and her progress toward death. Elberta, too, suffers repeated losses. These female bodies bear tangible signs of drawn out physical and mental suffering that ultimately deny existence itself.

Burney's tragedies focus strongly on the female figure in each, despite their titular acknowledgment (in *Edwy and Elgiva* and *Hubert De Vere*) of the hero. While she emphasizes that these women's social positions are somehow peripheral to some locus of power (they are not governors, generals, or leaders), this marginal position is not perpetuated in the plays themselves. Her heroines are not Ophelia-like in their occasional appearance as instances of a widening circle of deterioration. Instead, it is the fate of the female figure that dominates our interest. Burney reexamines the usually supplementary nature of female figures—they are often mere appendages to male figures, are in effect "bonus" figures for the purposes of political intrigue, are conduits of action rather than agents—by making central the damage inflicted by male-dominated greed and authority on such figures of "excess."

Conclusion
Really a Genius for the Stage

The figures, situations, and voices in Burney's plays linger long after a reading of the texts, especially one that is supported by an imaginative sense of their presence onstage: the tortured and imprisoned bodies of Elgiva, Cerulia, and Adela; the piteous desire for food expressed by Elberta; the ridiculous banter of the witlings; the farcical battles between Sir Archy and Valentine; "Margarella" Watts's curtsey lesson; the declaration of Joyce for "liberty, liberty, liberty!" We need not read Burney's plays as mere sideline curiosities of a successful novelist or diarist, or apologetically, as unspectacular and unsuccessful attempts in a new genre. Burney's dramatic work is complex and substantial, growing out of her awareness of an established dramaturgy. She adapts and modifies conventions of the late-eighteenth-century theater in a manner that offers insights into her view of the stage as a site of questioning, probing analyses of contemporary social situations. The plays in turn tell us much about Burney's attitudes towards women and their position in and experiences of late-eighteenth-century British society. Her dramatic works deserve to be studied along with those of other female dramatists such as Inchbald or Baillie, and the more familiar male writers such as Sheridan or Goldsmith.

I have drawn attention to Burney's language occasionally throughout the chapters above, noting particular points where the dialogue indicates movement or is used symbolically to represent the relationship between figures or the relative power of one figure when compared to another. I would like to conclude with some further general comments about Burney's use of language, because the language in the comedies is one of the plays' real strengths, and in the tragedies is one of the drawbacks of Burney's style. This may quite simply be due to the different conventions for dramatic dialogue. It is not surprising that as an accomplished novelist Burney is more astute when working with comic prose. The clear dramatic style of the novels and many sections of her journals and letters, which prompted Burney's friends and mentors to encourage her to try drama, makes the dialogue of the comedies and novels stylistically similar.

In the comedies, Burney uses language carefully in order to mark her figures generically and socially. Throughout the four plays, the heroes and heroines are distinguished by their elevated and exaggerated pronouncements. Cecilia and Beaufort are expansive in their declarations:

> BEAUFORT. . . . I have seen the vanity of my expectations,—I have disobeyed Lady Smatter,—I have set all consequences at defiance, and flown in the very face of ruin,—and now, will you, Cecilia (Kneeling), reject, disdain and Spurn me?
>
> CECILIA. Oh Beaufort—is it possible I can have wronged you?
>
> BEAUFORT. Never, my sweetest Cecilia, if now you pardon me.
>
> CECILIA. Pardon you?—too generous Beaufort—ah! rise. [V.590-97]

Hilaria and Valentine, like Cecilia and Beaufort, can reconcile only with language that announces the desperation they have felt over their trials. Valentine expresses his emotions with great difficulty: "Amazement—admiration—and the acutest sensations, silence—agitate—entrance me!—But I will not abuse her goodness, her nobleness, No!—let me fly!—(V.283-85). Valentine's distracted search for the right word to describe his state of mind (emphasized by Burney's use of dashes) is highly comic, given his assured pronouncements on Hilaria's moral decrepitude. Hilaria tells him, "O Valentine, You have drawn me for-ever from the vortex of dissipation and Fashion—" and he responds by embracing her "in the bosom of conjugal Love!" (V.301-3). Cleveland declares upon the resolution to his trials, "I have nothing left to wish! every hope is surpassed and my felicity is complete!" (V.811-12). Eleonora and Wilmot in *The Woman-Hater* continually use "thee" and "thou" in their addresses to each other and to Sophia, and their commentaries on the states of their mind and body are extreme. Eleonora tells Sophia to "Do what thou wilt! I have no life left but thine!" when she sends her off to get help (III.ii.108). Wilmot declares to Eleonora when they are reconciled: "Wife of my Heart! my esteem! my gratitude! my contrition! Can my whole life's devotion pay this generous pardon?" (V.xxi.25-27).

The language of Burney's heroes and heroines marks them generically as more sentimental than the dramatic counterparts with which they appear. They are surrounded by other figures who rarely speak in such elevated phrases or exclamations. The social status of the newly rich figures is evident in their pronunciations and their bad grammar:

MR. WATTS. Well, Bet, my dear, what say you to Kinsington Garden?

MISS WATTS. La, Pa, now you're calling her Bet again!

MR. WATTS. Well, my dear, don't scold. I can't never remember that new name.

MRS. WATTS. Why no more can I, my dear, as to that. Not that I mean to 'scuse your Pa' in the least. (to eliza) Why, my dear, why you look no how? What's the matter?

ELIZA. My long voyage has a little fatigued me. Nothing else.

MR. WATTS. Why I told you so! bringing her out before a bit of dinner, after crossing all them seas!

MISS WATTS. La, Pa', would you have her be as stupid as you? I'm sure I would not have lost such a morning for Kinsington Gardens for never so much.

MRS. WATTS (to miss watts). Dear, my dear, do but look at your Gownd! Only see how it trails! [III.1-15]

Eliza is alienated from her family because of their garish movements, outlandish appearance, and conversation. Only Joyce moves between classes; her lower-class self sings, dances, and scolds. Her upper-class persona is "silent as a hare." The ability to speak is one of the central signs of a figure's ability to be self-determining.

Burney also skillfully uses language to demarcate numerous comic figures that might otherwise remain wholly unremarkable and undifferentiated from one another. In *The Witlings*, for instance, Mrs. Sapient and Mrs. Voluble occupy very similar positions in terms of the plot, observing rather than participating in the events that surround them. They are comic in very different ways because of the manner in which they participate in the dialogue, as their names suggest. Mrs. Sapient's observations on the action amount to nothing more than cliché or statements that are painfully obvious: "to *me*, nothing is more disagreeable than to be disappointed" (I.309). Burney calls for just the slightest pause when she invites the actress to emphasize "*me*." This quite deftly signals how ridiculous Mrs. Sapient is, because she implies that disappointment may not be disagreeable to others, though by definition this cannot be true. Her effort to distinguish herself with the most undistinguished comments makes her presence on the stage fully comic, though she is for the most part just an onlooker. Similarly, Mrs. Voluble speaks all the time, gossiping about everyone, but says very little. Her constant stream of language fills the air but is productive of little useful information for the audience on- or offstage, except in a few instances. She, like Sapient, announces things that are clearly not true, or are too true to be remarked upon. At other times she contradicts herself, as when she tells Cecilia, "I'm sure, ma'am, I don't mean to be troublesome; and as to asking Questions, I make a point not to do it, for I think that curiosity is the most impertinent thing in the World. I suppose, ma'am, he knows of your being here?" (III.482-85). Figures who without this absurd dialogue might be merely superfluous to the action are granted a prominent part in the creation of the comic effect.

In *Love and Fashion*, as well, a "hanger-on" figure contributes little to the play's plot, but a great deal to its humor. Litchburn loiters around the rich Lord Ardville in hope of some mark of preferment. Litchburn, like Codger or the Lady Wattses, is difficult to insult because he cannot perceive metaphor:

> LORD ARDVILLE. May I take the liberty, sir, to ask what it was brought you to my house just now?
>
> LITCHBURN. What brought me, my lord? I never come but on foot.
>
> LORD ARDVILLE. I did not mean to enquire about your equipage, Sir! (half apart) What an empty fellow!
>
> LITCHBURN (over hearing him). Empty? I'm sure I have eat as good a dinner— (aside) but great folks always suspect one comes to eat! [II.ii.23-29]

The momentary absurdity caused by Litchburn's literalness, Mordaunt's sighs and preoccupation with his dress and his leisure time, Lady Smatter's literary pretensions, and Lord John's repeated "O the D——l" are all memorable efforts on Burney's part to use conversation as well as action in order to enhance the individuality of each figure.

Burney's language in the tragedies is often, by contrast, quite inelegant. Shuckburgh is an early, unimpressed critic of the verse of *Edwy and Elgiva*: ". . . no alterations could have made the play other than ludicrously bad. It is not so much the defect in plot and the absence of movement and action, as the incurable poverty of its stilted language, its commonplace sentiments, and its incorrect and inharmonious versification."[1] Certainly, Burney's verse in the tragedies is often convoluted, as she manipulates words in order to fit the poetic rhythm. The unusual syntax may also be partially explained as an effort to impart a sense of antiquity to the expressions, given the settings of the tragedies. Its effect, however, is often merely awkward. The scene in which Edwy explains his feelings to Aldhelm presents the actor with a difficult mouthful, given the awkward syntax and the combined "th," "f" and "s" sounds: "Thou thinkst Me futile—fickle—worthless—Go!— / Add me not penitence to what I suffer,— / Let me not speak thee ill, howe'er thou movst me!—" (IV.xix.45-47). The real possibility exists that an actor would lisp his way through these lines, making Edwy indeed sound like the driveler mentioned in the play's epilogue.

Generally, the verse in the tragedies has the appearance of being less refined or edited than the dialogue in the comedies. In the case of *Elberta*, of course, this is due to the unfinished nature of the piece. This lack of refinement is evident when Burney tries to represent extremes of emotion, and she often displays an effort to make language conform to mental states with accuracy. For example, she frequently uses the dash in order to emphasize battered nerves, lost sense, or frantic confusion. Arnulph says of himself, "Destruction—Infamy!—a Robber!—oh!—" (IV.vii.5). At other times, it is the brief exclamation of surprise that fills the dialogue excessively. When Adela meets with her father following her secret plan to marry, "O" dominates her expression of horror at what he might think. In act 4, scene 5, she speaks about thirty times, and says "O" in all but seven speeches, even repeating her shocked "O" on several occasions: "O cease! o cease! / O my lov'd Father! rend not thus my Heart!" (IV.v.110-11). Cerulia's mad scene is likewise punctuated by dashes and exclamations: "I shriekt—I knelt—I prayed!—" (V.130). Dunstan, in *Edwy and Elgiva*, asks, ". . . What are these men? / They shrink—they know—or fear me—Hah! a Corpse" (V.xviii.5-6).

The examples we can find throughout Burney's tragedies of stilted phrases and inelegant verse are, however, countered often by passages that show a strong use of images in a meditation on a state of mind. There are several scenes in which a figure is alone onstage, speaking his or her mind and commenting on the action. Hubert De Vere considers his love for Cerulia in a soliloquy:

What touching Beauty! what affecting softness!
What purity of Innocence and Love!
Bright is the view of Honour thus innate
Glowing untutor'd in the uncultur'd mind.
How happy might I prove with that fair creature
Had my deluded soul not fixt its faith
On its own object of elected worship!
Still are we blest—or curst—but by our fancies!
Repining Man, impatient of controul,
Blind to himself, short-sighted to events,
And darkly ignorant of Cause, Means, Purpose,
Judges of All by that inept criterion,
That slave of Impulse, wayward, sickly Self;

Deems Right, or Wrong, what flatters, or disgusts it,
And balances Creation by its wishes.
Self!—various, partial Self!—Thou Thing of Storms!
Blown by conflicting Passions, struggling Vices,
Wild Projects, vain Desires,—resisting Virtues,—
Or, all-enthralling humours of Occurrence
That, by their fond Dominion, chace alike
Advantage or Destruction; Thing of Storms!
Blown, like the Winds in elemental strife
From adverse points, by whirl encountering whirl:—
I marvel at—I scorn—yet bear thy sway.— [II.367-90]

The wind of the passion, vice, projects, and desires that buffet individuals is a fitting image in a play that features chance arrivals on an island and the luring manipulation of figures, especially those "ignorant of Cause, Means, Purpose." This statement befits a romantic hero who is before his time in his Byronic musings.

The language of Burney's comedies and tragedies shows an artist who reached different levels on her way to perfecting her craft. I have suggested throughout this study that Burney's real strength lies in her depiction of gender-specific forms of social experience. Burney's plays meditate on how gender is constructed and transmitted through ideology and social institutions and what the effect of divisions between the sexes is on relationships and social interaction. Burney's emphasis on what it means to be female, feminine, and feminist in late-eighteenth-century society establishes her dramatic works within the purview described by Jean E. Howard and Marion F. O'Connor; she writes texts that "produce, reproduce, or contest historically specific relations of power (relations among classes, genders, and races, for example)."[2] The relations between men and women, dramatized on the stage in the mock-Gothic, Gothic, tragic, and comic fashions of Burney's plays, draw attention to social constructions of gender, behavior, and role-playing. While Burney does occasionally naturalize some of the gendered roles that she dramatizes (the role of mother in *Elberta*, for example), she more often depicts the "unreal" nature of many social ties, such as those between parents and children, an old suitor and a young and uninterested woman, or husband and wife. The similarly artificial nature of social divisions, as opposed to connections, is also an enduring topic in her plays.

In addition to providing critics of late-eighteenth-century literature with an additional perspective on the society from which these plays emerged, these works also offer a largely unexplored contact with Burney's attitudes toward women and female experience. Generalizations about Burney's novels or journals are often contradicted by the plays. Martha G. Brown, for instance, argues that Burney's main interest is in economic, physical, and psychic dependence and that she "clearly disapproves" of the liberated female figures she creates in her novels: Mrs. Selwyn, Lady Honoria, Mrs. Arlbery, and Elinor Joddrel.[3] For Eva Figes, after *Evelina*, Burney "struggled to avoid anything contentiously 'political', even though her later work shows a growing awareness of social injustice."[4] Rogers writes that in her journals, Burney "never openly suggests that injustice toward women was built into the institutions of her society" and Straub suggests that Burney's work shows no "explicit social critique" of "the debilitating effects of male-centered ideology on women's lives."[5] Each of these assertions is difficult to reconcile with the situations found in Burney's drama, whether one considers the debilitating effects of paternalism in the tragedies and comedies, Elberta's surviving strength, Eleonora's depth of fear and forgiveness, the liberation of Joyce from the family circle, or the injustice shown in family situations generally throughout the plays.

This study could easily have been titled "The Family and Frances Burney's Feminist Drama" because the concept of the family is such an important part of most of Burney's dramatic representations of women's lives, whether the family is absent and its role filled by guardians, or is newly rejoined with disappointing results. As Doody's study of Burney demonstrates, familial relationships were often troubling for Burney, particularly when the force of paternalism asserted itself. The paternal role is always present in the plays, in the guardian figure whose force is largely benign, as is Lord Exbury's over Hilaria, or the coercive biological father such as Wilmot or Chester. Mother figures are few in Burney's plays (no hero has a mother, either), and they are rarely unambiguously positive or negative. Mrs. Watts has little to offer in terms of the traditional maternal qualities of nurturing or emotional display, while Eleonora is subject to public ridicule because of her apparent failure as a mother, though her relationship with Sophia seems to be mutually satisfying. Elberta is Burney's only maternal figure who concentrates solely on the physical safety of her family, to the exclusion of other considerations, including her marriage.

Female figures are manipulated in various ways by their family roles, largely because of the contradictions inherent in familial ideology. While it is apparent that filial subordination and duty are deemed appropriate and "right" for daughters, expectations of "natural" affection, support, and appreciation for these same daughters are revealed to be a sort of false consciousness. The myth of the family as a refuge for the individual is exposed as misleading and dangerous; in Burney's plays, the family unit demands that daughters act against their private desires. This is certainly the case for Eliza Watts, Joyce (as Miss Wilmot), Sophia, and Adela. Cerulia is pushed into madness and death by her father. Only in *Elberta*, again, is the family shown to be a refuge for its members, but this too is short-lived, given the departure of Arnulph in pursuit of heroism, sacrifice, and martyrdom.

Burney also suggests that the family as a basic social unit is integrally connected with all other forms of social relations, whether these relations involve the exchange of women in marriage, or the cementing of class and racial distinctions. Eighteenth-century women occupied an interstitial position between families, potentially aiding an alliance with another family that might promote their own relations' financial or social status. Women could also bring into the family undesired children or suitors. In many cases, Burney suggests that the idea of female choice in marriage is as mythical as the succor optimally provided by the family. While forms of choice are presented to most female figures in the plays, these choices are exposed as devices of paternal or familial manipulation. For Cecilia, who does not have a biological family, participation in a family unit is regulated by her potential as a source of money. Beaufort is rendered impotent because of his submission to Lady Smatter's control. Cerulia's desire for Hubert is something constructed for her, and her choices when it comes to pursuing him or leaving him to Geralda are never autonomous, interwoven as they are in the political intrigues and manipulations of De Mowbray. Adela's desire for De Belesme must compete with her sense of the obligation to protect her father and of the potential power that her marriageable status gives to her king and De Warrenne. Hilaria is offered the "choice" of Valentine or Lord Ardville, but the family situation of the Exburys and Valentine's moral chastisement of her serve to confine her choice. Eliza's desire to marry Cleveland is countered by her own family's "vulgarity" and the Tylney family's class-based prejudices. Sophia is given to a man she does not know, by a father she knows even less. Female choice is shown to be at best something achieved by strenuous negotiation and submission to parental dictates, and at worst something completely unavailable, however often it is conjured up rhetorically.

The marriages Burney explores in her drama provide an insight into male-female relations that is largely absent from the novels. In *Edwy and Elgiva*, marriage is shown to have devastating, even fatal effects on Elgiva, because Edwy's relationship with her is inseparable from his relationship with his political subjects. It is thus that Edwy's opponents can use Elgiva's position as unsanctioned wife against her, constructing her as impious and transgressive. Elberta and Arnulph are similarly severed by political and martial events. In a fashion similar to Edwy, Arnulph is torn between the personal and private and the political and public. In the case of both male figures, attention to public images and heroism ultimately sacrifices the safety of their female partners. Elgiva is tortured, banished, and killed, while Elberta is left to fend for herself in a hostile world. Eleonora's marriage to Wilmot, the Watts marriage, and the Tylney marriage are the only prominent ones shown in the comedies. The Watts marriage is defined only by the conventional antimarriage statements on behalf of Mr. Watts and the alienation of Mr. Watts and Mr. Tibbs from Mrs. and Miss Watts. In the Tylney marriage, Lady Wilhelmina can voice her preferences for a niece-in-law, but Sir Marmaduke easily silences her. The Wilmot reunion is a highly troubling element of the resolution to *The Woman-Hater*, given Eleonora's real fears of Wilmot's violence and the frequent misogynistic statements that permeate the play's atmosphere. Marriage is represented in Burney's plays as an institution fraught with trials that are gender-related; female figures are evaluated according to their sexual identities and their ability to fulfill the roles of wife and mother properly. Usually, they are found wanting and are punished for their inadequacy or their challenges to conventional and expected behavior.

The idea of punishment plays a large role in Burney's dramatic works, though its enactment varies according to the generic conventions of tragedy and comedy. This is a particularly important point to consider in relation to the plays, for drama's basis in embodiment serves as a strong semiotic resource for Burney's evaluations of the punitive potential of social institutions such as marriage and the family. The female body, physically present or absent from the stage, becomes a site of the oppression, submission, and control of a woman by male figures or male-dominated institutions like the church. In the tragedies, the female body is physically under siege, threatened as it is by seizure, imprisonment, torture, banishment, starvation, and death. The mangled, bleeding, or maddened bodies and minds of female figures serve as accusations against their punishers, who may be political enemies, or family members, or both. In the comedies, punishment also plays a role, and this too is often physical. Women in the comedies are punished by exile from their communities, as is Cecilia in *The Witlings*, by moral accusations or public ridicule (Lady Smatter, Hilaria, and Eleonora), by public embarrassment (Eliza and Sophia), or by enforced silence and submission (this includes all the heroines, but particularly Joyce, as Miss Wilmot). These punishments are occasionally expressed in terms of the denial of self-expression, as in Miss Wilmot's regulated speech. More generally, though, the suffering depicted in the comedies is mental and emotional, ranging from disappointment over an inability to be a dutiful daughter, to the fear of transgressing established codes of behavior or the fear of being poor and obscure.

Burney depicts versions of female experience in order to analyze sources of gender-specific oppression, whether they be governmental, religious, familial, or marital. At the same time as the oppressed female figure urges us implicitly or explicitly to reconsider institutions, institutionalized behavior, or ideas related to gender, the liberated female body is likewise a challenge and a prompt to reconceptualize the ways in which we conceive of gender and gendered behavior. The most striking example of this challenge is Joyce, once she is released from the confinements that accompany her existence as Miss Wilmot. Joyce's exuberance at being beyond Wilmot's control, along with her fearless determination to be self-directing and optimistic about her future, is an open challenge to the forces of control and oppression that have predominated in *The Woman-Hater*. That her release is coupled with a reduced social status simultaneously points out the confinement enforced on more "genteel" women and asks questions about our view of social stratification. Our fears about a figure like Joyce might alternately raise or abate when she moves about the stage singing and dancing; in either case, much can be learned about what we consider to be normative or desirable conduct.

Other less assertive examples of challenge exist in Burney's plays as well. They include Cecilia's defiant, if somewhat ineffectual, refusal to submit to Lady Smatter's control and her departure from the home; Eliza's initial self-direction when she arrives in London, in control of her seemingly perilous situation; and both Sophia's and Joyce's petitions to Sir Roderick for his financial support. Elberta is also a remarkable figure, refuting the authority of Offa by escaping from his castle and defending her family against starvation and seizure. A late-twentieth-century feminist sensibility might lament that these instances of autonomy are often short-lived and are replaced by a reabsorption of women into patriarchal structures of control. However, the very existence of these dramatic moments can expand our notion of the extent to which late-eighteenth-century female playwrights worked toward important reconceptualizations of gender relations in their society. All of these factors—Burney's representation of social and gender relations, her view of punishment and confinement, and her use of stage space, dialogue, and movement—indicate that Burney's drama is a remarkable body of work that rivals her fiction in the depth of its social commentary. In *The Rakish Stage*, Robert D. Hume writes that "[p]lays with genuine social commentary . . . either contradict the commonplace or at least ask the audience to think more seriously about it."[6] Such exposures and contradictions of the commonplace occur throughout Burney's drama, in relation to the concepts of family, marriage, class, and race, but predominantly in relation to concepts of gender.

I end where I began, by asking "what if" Burney's plays had received greater attention in her time, what if more had been put on the stage, what if she had more publicly pursued her career as a dramatist? With a fully annotated modern edition of the plays, we now can read what she did produce in the genre, and imaginatively reconstruct her plays as if they were before us on a stage. In some cases, productions have made the conjectural real, as in the twentieth-century versions of *The Witlings* and *A Busy Day*. Her drama is expansive in terms of genre, situation, and depth of psychological portraiture and emotional complexity. Burney asks us to think seriously about how notions of gender are influenced by traditional conceptualizations of human relationships and social organization, and how these views of gender in turn have physical, emotional, and mental effects on both male and female subjects. Burney's dramatic work attests to the expanding uses to which theater was being put in the late eighteenth century. These plays also should prompt us to reevaluate our own sense of this writer's astute awareness of the complexities of the world around her, and her ability to convey these complexities in her work.

Notes

Introduction

1. I say "notoriously" because Dr. Charles Burney's interference in Burney's playwriting is a focal point of most discussions of Burney's plays. Margaret Anne Doody, in *Frances Burney: The Life in the Works* (New Brunswick: Rutgers Univ. Press, 1988), and more recently Ellen Donkin, in *Getting into the Act: Women Playwrights in London 1776-1829* (London: Routledge, 1994), have both discussed the interference of male figures in Burney's life and career. Donkin describes the same letter from Burney to her father quoted here as a document of self-assertion and strength (156-58).

2. See Donkin, *Getting into the Act,* 132-58. Percy A. Scholes mentions the suppression of *The Witlings* and the production of *Edwy and Elgiva,* which he dates inaccurately, adding that "[l]ike some other good novelists Fanny was, then, no great playwright. And yet one is not sure. Plenty of successful playwrights have failed in their first attempts, and when one reads the sparkling dialogues of the diary entries and the narrative letters Fanny was so fond of writing, one thinks that perhaps if she had been willing to throw herself into the dangers of the stage, to take the rough with the smooth, and to 'try, try again' (as playwrights *have* to do), she might have left us something very amusing—a little in the Goldsmith or the Sheridan vein. The failure of her tragedy in 1794 may be little to the point; comedy was clearly her natural line." *The Great Dr. Burney,* 2 vols. (London: Oxford Univ. Press, 1958), 1:361.

3. Jeremy Brien, *The Stage and Television Today,* 11 Nov. 1993. For a discussion of the reception of the first production of *A Busy Day,* see Sabor, 1:xi-xii. *The Witlings* was performed at the Willowbrook Campus of the College of Staten Island, City University of New York, 9-13 Nov. 1994, under the direction of Robert Hulton-Baker.

4. A contesting view of Burney's feminism is available from Martha G. Brown ("Fanny Burney's 'Feminism': Gender or Genre?," in *Fetter'd or Free? British Women Novelists, 1670-1815,* ed. Mary Anne Schofield and Cecilia Macheski [Athens: Ohio Univ. Press, 1986], 29-39), who asserts that the label of "feminist" in Burney's case is a misnomer and issues read by contemporary critics as "feminist" (economic dependence, mistreatment by male characters, or the nuptial resolutions

to the novels) are actually matters attributable to the romance genre and as such are found in most eighteenth-century novels by both male and female authors.

5. Rogers, *Frances Burney: The World of "Female Difficulties"* (New York: Harvester Wheatsheaf, 1990), 4.

6. Straub, *Divided Fictions: Fanny Burney and Feminine Strategy* (Lexington: Univ. Press of Kentucky, 1987), 5.

7. Epstein, *The Iron Pen: Frances Burney and the Politics of Women's Writing* (Bristol: Bristol Classic, 1989), 4.

8. Cutting-Gray, *Woman as "Nobody" and the Novels of Fanny Burney* (Gainesville: Univ. Press of Florida, 1992), 4.

9. Hill, *The House in St. Martin's Street* (London: Lane, 1907); Delery, ed., *The Witlings* (Ph.D. diss., City University of New York, 1989 and East Lansing: Colleagues Press, 1995); Rogers, ed., *Meridian Anthology* (New York: Meridian, 1994); Benkovitz, ed., *Edwy and Elgiva* (New York: Shoe String, 1957); and Wallace, ed., *A Busy Day* (New Brunswick: Rutgers Univ. Press, 1984), and "Fanny Burney's Comedies" (M.A. thesis, University of Toronto, 1975).

10. Hemlow, *The History of Fanny Burney* (Oxford: Clarendon, 1958), and "Fanny Burney: Playwright," *University of Toronto Quarterly* 19 (1950): 170-89; Thaddeus, *Frances Burney: A Literary Life* (London: Macmillan, forthcoming); Adelstein, *Fanny Burney* (New York: Twayne, 1968); Devlin, *The Novels and Journals of Fanny Burney* (New York: St. Martin's, 1987); Dobson, *Fanny Burney (Madame d'Arblay)* (London: Macmillan, 1904); Morrison, "Fanny Burney and the Theatre" (Ph.D. diss., University of Texas, 1957); and Mulliken, "The Influence of the Drama on Fanny Burney's Novels" (Ph.D. diss., University of Wisconsin, 1969).

11. Browne, *Feminist Mind* (Brighton: Harvester, 1987); Davidoff and Hall, *Family Fortunes* (Chicago: Univ. of Chicago Press, 1987); Hill, ed., *Eighteenth-Century Women* (London: Allen and Unwin, 1984); Jones, ed., *Women in the Eighteenth Century* (London: Routledge, 1990); Kelly, *Women, Writing, and Revolution* (Oxford: Clarendon, 1993); Nussbaum, *Torrid Zones* (Baltimore: Johns Hopkins Univ. Press, 1995); Poovey, *The Proper Lady* (Chicago: Univ. of Chicago Press, 1984); Rogers, *Feminism in Eighteenth-Century England* (Urbana: Univ. of Illinois Press, 1982); and Staves, *Married Women's Separate Property* (Cambridge: Harvard Univ. Press, 1990).

1. Gender and the Stage

1. Freedman, "Frame-Up: Feminism, Psychoanalysis, Theatre," in *Performing Feminisms: Feminist Critical Theory and Theatre*, ed. Sue-Ellen Case (Baltimore: Johns Hopkins Univ. Press, 1990), 60.

2. See Susan M. Flierl Steadman, "Feminist Dramatic Criticism: Where We Are Now," *Women and Performance: A Journal of Feminist Theory* 4, no. 2 (1989): 118-48; and Elaine Aston, *An Introduction to Feminism and Theatre* (London: Routledge, 1995), 151-62, for excellent bibliographies of resources on feminist analyses of theater.

3. Cixous, "Aller à la mer," trans. Barbara Kerslake, *Modern Drama* 27, no. 4 (1984): 547.

4. See Linda Walsh Jenkins, "Locating the Language of Gender Experience," *Women and Performance: A Journal of Feminist Theory* 2, no. 1 (1984): 5-20; and Karen Malpede, *Women in Theatre: Compassion and Hope* (New York: Drama Book Specialists, 1983).

5. Curb, "Re/cognition, Re/presentation, Re/creation in Woman-Conscious Drama: the Seer, the Seen, the Scene, the Obscene," *Theatre Journal* 37, no. 3 (1985): 302.

6. Keyssar, *Feminist Theatre: An Introduction to Plays of Contemporary British and American Women* (New York: Grove, 1985), xi.

7. Dolan, *The Feminist Spectator as Critic* (Ann Arbor: Univ. of Michigan Press, 1988), 3.

8. Staves defines ideology as "'articulated forms of social self-consciousness,' the explicit public ideas [people] have about human relationships, especially those ideas that serve to justify the power relationships between people, and to explain why it is right and good that different people should have different roles and entitlements to power, wealth, and other social goods" (*Married Women's Separate Property*, 6).

9. The semiology of theater, in a nonfeminist context, is discussed by Keir Elam, *The Semiotics of Theatre and Drama* (London: Methuen, 1980); and Manfred Pfister, *The Theory and Analysis of Drama*, trans. John Halliday (Cambridge: Cambridge Univ. Press, 1988). Both theorists comment on the semiology of dialogue, blocking, space, and time, all of which are relevant to how gender is signified in the theater. I have tried to maintain Pfister's terminological distinction between character and figure throughout this study. He writes that the word "figure" "hints at something deliberately artificial, produced or constructed for a particular purpose" (161). See also Elaine Aston and George Savona, *Theatre as Sign-system: A Semiotics of Text and Performance* (London: Routledge, 1991); and Erika Fischer-Lichte, *The Semiotics of Theatre*, trans. Jeremy Gaines and Doris L. Jones (Bloomington: Indiana Univ. Press, 1992). Laurence Senelick suggests that gender receives an "iconic value" on the stage: "gender roles performed by 'performers' never merely replicate those in everyday life; they are more sharply defined and more emphatically presented, the inherent iconicity offering both an ideal and a critique" (introduction to *Gender in Performance: The Presentation of Difference in the Performing Arts* [Hanover: Univ. Press of New England, 1992], xi). Sue-Ellen Case also discusses the special status of the signifier onstage, imprinted by "the set of values, beliefs and ways of seeing that control the connotations of the sign in the culture at large" (*Feminism and Theatre* [London: Macmillan, 1988], 116).

10. Case, *Feminism and Theatre*, 117-18. According to Dolan, "[f]emale bodies inscribed in the representational frame offered by the proscenium arch, and the frame created simply by the act of gazing through gender and ideology, bear meanings with political implications" ("Personal, Political, Polemical: Feminist Approaches to Politics and Theatre," in *The Politics of Theatre and Drama*, ed. Graham Holderness [London: Macmillan, 1992], 49).

11. Case, *Feminism and Theatre*, 132.

12. Dolan, "Feminists, lesbians, and other women in theatre: thoughts on the politics of performance," in *Women in Theatre*, ed. James Redmond, Themes in Drama Series, vol. 11 (Cambridge: Cambridge Univ. Press, 1989), 204.

13. Reinelt, "Feminist Theory and the Problem of Performance," *Modern Drama* 32, no. 1 (1989): 52.

14. Reinelt, "Feminist Theory," 50.

15. Jones, introduction to *Women in the Eighteenth Century*, 4, 6. Mary Poovey's *The Proper Lady* also provides an excellent analysis of the constricted position of women at the end of the eighteenth century.

16. A useful discussion of tragedy and narrative can be found in Linda Kintz's introduction to *The Subject's Tragedy: Political Poetics, Feminist Theory, and Drama* (Ann Arbor: Univ. of Michigan Press, 1992). Kintz writes specifically about the "tragic oedipal story, which associates man with subjectivity, activity, and force and woman with objectivity and passivity and constructs her as matter or medium" (6).

17. My discussion of dramatic narrative is strongly informed by Teresa de Lauretis's work on "the inherent maleness of all narrative movement" (*Alice Doesn't: Feminism, Semiotics, Cinema* [Bloomington: Indiana Univ. Press, 1984], 108). De Lauretis describes the woman's position in narrative (particularly cinematic narrative) in spatial terms: they are the "abstract or purely symbolic other— [like] the womb, the earth, the grave . . . mere spaces" out of which "the human person creates and recreates *himself*" (121). She argues that "the movement of narrative discourse . . . specifies and even produces the masculine position as that of mythical subject, and the feminine position as mythical obstacle or, simply, the space in which that movement occurs" (143). See also Laura Mulvey, "Visual Pleasure and Narrative Cinema," *Screen* 16, no. 3 (1975): 6-18. De Lauretis and Mulvey have had a tremendous influence on the field of feminist performance criticism.

18. As Aston writes, "the 'female' is enclosed within the male narratives of realism, is most commonly defined in relation to the male 'subject' (as wife, mother, daughter, etc.), is unable to take up a subject position . . . , and is used as an object of exchange in an heterosexual, male economy" (*An Introduction to Feminism and Theatre*, 40).

19. In a dialogue with Catherine Clément, Cixous writes that "ideology is a kind of vast membrane enveloping everything. We have to know that this skin exists even if it encloses us like a net or like closed eyelids. We have to know that, to change the world, we must constantly try to scratch and tear it. We can never rip the whole thing off, but we must never let it stick or stop being suspicious of it. It grows back and you start again." Cixous and Clément, *The Newly Born Woman*, trans. Betsy Wing (Minneapolis: Univ. of Minnesota Press, 1986), 145.

20. Political, feminist readings of Shakespeare, for instance, are too many to mention. See Aston for a brief discussion (*An Introduction to Feminism and Theatre*, 19-23). Of Restoration women playwrights, Aphra Behn has garnered the most attention. Again, see Aston (26) and the essays in Heidi Hutner, ed., *Rereading Aphra Behn: History, Theory, and Criticism* (Charlottesville: Univ. Press of Virginia, 1993). Rogers's *Meridian Anthology* is listed in my introduction. Fidelis Morgan has edited a collection of Restoration plays by women, *The Female Wits: Women Playwrights on the London Stage 1660-1720* (London: Virago, 1981). See also Jacqueline Pearson, *The Prostituted Muse: Images of Women and Women Dramatists 1642-1737* (New York: St. Martin's, 1988).

21. Straub's *Sexual Suspects: Eighteenth-Century Players and Sexual Ideology* (Princeton: Princeton Univ. Press, 1992) discusses the power of the spectator as it served to define and confine the people who performed roles on the stage, suggesting ways in which the sex, gender, orientation, class, and race of players were constructed by the players' presence within a framed spectacle. Straub's analysis of the physical pains of acting is interesting, but not immediately related to the question of characters' pain rather than that of players. *The first English actresses: women and drama 1660-1700* (Cambridge: Cambridge Univ. Press, 1992), by Elizabeth Howe, is not directly relevant to this study, but she does address the question of the influence that a female stage presence had on the content of drama. For

example, she notes that "[t]he presence of women's bodies on the stage encouraged lurid, eroticised presentations of female suffering, and was designed to tantalise, rather than to attack violent masculine behaviour" (176). Her observations about she-tragedy echo my own (chapter 3) when she suggests that it represents the ideal of the victimized virtuous woman suffering passively (176).

22. This is certainly true of Allardyce Nicoll's *A History of English Drama 1660-1900*, 2d ed., vol. 3, *Late Eighteenth-Century Drama 1750-1800* (Cambridge: Cambridge Univ. Press, 1969) and of Michael R. Booth et al., 1750-1880, vol. 6 of *The Revels History of Drama in English* (London: Methuen, 1975). Part 5 of the invaluable resource, *The London Stage 1660-1880*, edited by Charles Beecher Hogan, 3 vols. (Carbondale: Southern Illinois Univ. Press, 1968), is of limited help on points of politics. See L.W. Conolly, *The Censorship of English Drama 1737-1824* (San Marino, Calif.: Huntington Library, 1976) for a discussion of censorship and the politics contemporary with Burney's plays.

23. Qtd. in Linda Kelly, *The Kemble Era: John Philip Kemble, Sarah Siddons, and the London Stage* (London: Bodley Head, 1980), 31.

24. Jeffrey N. Cox, introduction to *Seven Gothic Dramas 1789-1825* (Athens: Ohio Univ. Press, 1992), 18.

25. Qtd. in Cox, introduction to *Seven Gothic Dramas,* 18. There have been a number of studies on the impact of the French Revolution on English theater. See Cox, "Romantic Drama and the French Revolution," in *Revolution and English Romanticism: Politics and Rhetoric*, ed. Keith Hanley and Raman Selden (New York: St. Martin's, 1990), 241-60; and Gillian Russell, *The Theatres of War: Performance, Politics, and Society, 1793-1815* (Oxford: Clarendon, 1995).

26. Cox, in "Romantic Drama," discusses these strategies as they relate to the French Revolution and British politics.

27. Donkin, "Mrs. Siddons Looks Back in Anger: Feminist Historiography for Eighteenth-Century British Theatre," in *Critical Theory and Performance*, ed. Janelle G. Reinelt and Joseph R. Roach (Ann Arbor: Univ. of Michigan Press, 1992), 276-90. See also Pat Rogers, "'Towering Beyond Her Sex': Stature and Sublimity in the Achievement of Sarah Siddons" in *Curtain Calls: British and American Women and the Theater, 1660-1820,* ed. Mary Anne Schofield and Cecilia Macheski (Athens: Ohio Univ. Press, 1991), 48-67.

28. Cox, introduction to *Seven Gothic Dramas,* 3. His arguments about the nature of neglect can similarly be applied to tragedy, I think, and to the work of the female playwrights of this period. Joanna Baillie is currently experiencing a revival, however, and Inchbald's status as novelist and actress has granted her an audience that Burney has not as yet shared. Daniel P. Watkins, in *A Materialist Critique of English Romantic Drama* (Gainesville: Univ. Press of Florida, 1993), deals with ideology and the stage, but only with writers conventionally considered "romantic," a context that seldom includes Burney. See also Julie A. Carlson, *In the Theatre of Romanticism: Coleridge, Nationalism, Women* (Cambridge: Cambridge Univ. Press, 1994); and Marjean D. Purinton, *Romantic Ideology Unmasked: The Mentally Constructed Tyrannies in Dramas of William Wordsworth, Lord Byron, Percy Shelley, and Joanna Baillie* (Newark: Univ. of Delaware Press, 1994) for discussions of the drama of the major romantic figures.

29. Judith Philips Stanton, "'This New-Found Path Attempting': Women Dramatists in England, 1660-1800," in *Curtain Calls*, 325-54.

30. Cotton, *Women Playwrights* (London: Associated Univ. Presses, 1980), 210.

31. Carlson, *Women and Comedy* (Ann Arbor: Univ. of Michigan Press, 1991), 6, 15.

32. Backscheider, *Spectacular Politics* (Baltimore: Johns Hopkins Univ. Press, 1993), xii.

33. Backscheider, *Spectacular Politics,* 238.

34. Backscheider, *Spectacular Politics,* 232.

35. Case, *Feminism and Theatre,* 114-15.

2. Censored Women

1. See Epstein, *Iron Pen,* 93-122.

2. Hemlow, *History of Fanny Burney,* 129-30.

3. Sabor describes the initial reactions of this family audience, including Susanna Burney's admiration for the play's sentimentality (1:xxxviii-xxxix).

4. Doody writes that "Burney's portrait of her witlings is indebted to Molière's *Les femmes savantes*" (*Frances Burney,* 80), as well as to the depictions of pseudointellectuals in Congreve's *The Double Dealer* (1693), Gay and Pope's *Three Hours after Marriage* (1717), Colman's *The English Merchant* (1767), and Kelly's *The School for Wives* (1774). Wallace lists Molière's play and others by him in her list of plays seen or read by Burney (*A Busy Day,* 197).

5. Burney met Elizabeth Montagu while she was at Streatham and Crisp cautioned Burney against Montagu's interference if she were to see Burney's new comedy in progress (*EJL,* 3:155-60, 239).

6. The scraps are among the material in five folders entitled "Miscellaneous Pieces of Manuscript, 1772-1828." The date is inaccurate, as these folders contain manuscript fragments from as late as 1837. While these folders are catalogued as 1-5, there are two folders numbered IV, and no folder III. I have designated the folders labeled IV as IVa and IVb. As Sabor (1:4) and Doody (300-302) note, an intermediary play between *The Witlings* and *The Woman-Hater* exists in fragments. Its characters include Sir Marmaduke, Dawson, Cecilia, Beaufort, Codger, Censor, Jack, and Lady Smatter.

7. Sabor, 1:4.

8. *The Witlings* has received more attention than Burney's other drama. Discussions of the play focus on the circumstances of composition and suppression, on Burney's satiric look at female learning (see note 17 below), and generic considerations. Both T.B. Macaulay, in an early commentary ("Madame D'Arblay," *Edinburgh Review* 76 [January 1843]: 523-70), and Austin Dobson seem to agree with Dr. Burney and Crisp's suppression. Macaulay "congratulate[s] Crisp for 'manfully' counselling Burney against production of the play" (Sabor 1:xxvi) but never seems to have read the play itself. Dobson says that Dr. Burney and Crisp "were right; though they do not seem to have borne in mind how material a part the acting bears in the success of a piece" (*Fanny Burney [Madame d'Arblay],* 104). Hill admires the play's "bright dialogue"; however, she recognizes in the play "some of the drawbacks which struck Dr. Burney and Mr. Crisp so forcibly" (*The House in St. Martin's Street,* 153). Her transcription is the first of any parts of Burney's plays to be published. Adelstein, too, feels the suppression was "just as well because a performance of the play would have marred Fanny's personal life. The formidable Mrs. Montagu would have retaliated by lampooning and ridiculing Fanny in various ways. Such an experience would have been highly injurious to the sensitive young woman" (*Fanny Burney,* 60). Ellen Moers, in

Literary Women: The Great Writers, echoes this view of Burney's transgression, writing that "[h]ad Dr. Burney allowed *The Witlings* to go on the boards, his daughter would have been convicted of a tasteless gaffe" ([New York: Oxford Univ. Press, 1985], 117). Rogers calls the play "hilariously funny." She tells us, however, that Burney "willingly participated" in her father's restrictions of her (*Frances Burney,* 19, 20). Straub agrees that Burney's "feminine sense of subservient relationship with masculine authority made her genuinely, sincerely obedient" (*Divided Fictions,* 109).

Hemlow is critical of Burney's characterization, which pales when compared to *Evelina* because it contains characters who are only "aggregates of foibles, failings, humours, or pretensions, somewhat inadequately clothed with human flesh and spirit" ("Fanny Burney: Playwright," 172). Morrison emphasizes a lack of unity and coherence in the play. She sees Censor as the moral center of a play that preaches the "joys of self-dependency" ("Fanny Burney and the Theatre," 95). For Mulliken, the play "does not hang together very well, and so the ingredients out of which it was made are more discrete and readily visible than they would be in a finished work of art." It therefore "lacks smoothness and credibility" but does show that Burney "could handle contemporary techniques of dramatic characterization and action" ("The Influence of the Drama," 30, 36). Doody concentrates on the function of ideas of finance, commodification, and reputation in the play and establishes a context in which to read Burney's adaptation of the comic form. She discusses the structural use of time-wasting, inaction, clutter, frustration, incompleteness, and anticlimax. Dabler and Frances Burney are compared as artist figures, and Censor is seen to resemble Dr. Burney and Samuel Crisp (*Frances Burney,* 77-98).

9. Hester Thrale observed on 18 August 1779 that Burney "pleased [her] today—She resolves to give up a Play likely to succeed. . . . She makes me miserable too in many Respects—so restlessly & apparently anxious lest I should give myself Airs of Patronage, or load her with Shackles of Dependance—I live with her always in a Degree of Pain that precludes Friendship—dare not ask her to buy me a Ribbon, dare not desire her to touch the Bell, lest She should think herself injured" (*EJL,* 3:352, n. 85).

10. For a discussion of the novelty of this initial setting, see Doody, *Frances Burney,* 77-79.

11. Doody, *Frances Burney,* 78.

12. For a related discussion of act 1 and Cecilia's delayed appearance, see Doody, *Frances Burney,* 79.

13. See Aston and Savona, *Theatre as Sign-System,* 52-55, for a discussion of speech act theory and dramatic dialogue.

14. See Doody, *Frances Burney,* 90, for a discussion of the play's themes. Burney seemed particularly attuned to the idea of time-wasting where her efforts of composition were concerned. She commented after the daddies' suppression of the manuscript that her greatest regret in abandoning it was "throwing away the *Time,*—which I with difficulty stole, & which I have Buried in the mere trouble of *writing* (*EJL,* 3:347).

15. Hemlow, "Fanny Burney: Playwright," 172; and Morrison, "Fanny Burney and the Theatre," 89-90. One of Burney's reports to her sister about her Streatham activities includes her remark that, after listening to the follies of the company playing cards, she is "to pass for a censor*ess* now!" (*EJL,* 3:205).

16. For Doody's view of Censor as "punisher," see *Frances Burney,* 90.

17. Several critics concentrate on the Esprit Party and the issue of female learning. Rogers discusses the satire which she sees as "singularly perverse, since the

main object of satire is intellectual women" (*Frances Burney*, 19). Judy Simons (*Fanny Burney* [Totowa, N.J.: Barnes and Noble, 1987]) also sees Burney as anti-feminist. She is disturbed by the "biting satiric comedy" that attacks "the pretensions of scholarly women" and writes that "Burney is clearly suspicious of the motives" behind a Bluestocking project (9, 126). Hemlow is the only critic to make the important distinction that *The Witlings* is "a satire on pretences of many kinds, but chiefly on the affectation of wit and learning" rather than a satire on learning itself, particularly female learning ("Fanny Burney: Playwright," 174). Figures whose affectation of learning has rendered them unable to communicate with those around them, or made them objects of ridicule, appear in Cowley's *Who's the Dupe?* (1779) and *More Ways than One* (1783). The most popular manifestation of such a character is likely Mrs. Malaprop in Sheridan's *The Rivals* (1775), a play Burney knew. Mrs. Malaprop's inappropriate use of language resembles Mrs. Sapient's problems with logic, and the tendency to fill the atmosphere with inaccurate statements and attributions is of course shared by Lady Smatter.

18. Doody, *Frances Burney*, 90.

19. Doody's unpublished paper, "Age and Youth in *Evelina*: Sexual and Social Chronology" (presented at the general meeting of the American Society for Eighteenth-Century Studies, Austin, Tex., March 1996), comments on the relationship between gender and age in Burney's works, particularly in *Evelina*.

20. Sabor comments on Burney's satirizing of such romantic and sentimental expressions (1:xxxviii-xxxix).

21. The constant, mutual undermining of one by the other that characterizes the relationship between Lady Smatter and Mrs. Sapient is an example of what Susan Carlson describes as the erasure of community through women's aversion to other women (*Women and Comedy*, 80). Lady Smatter, for instance, initially believes that it is Mrs. Sapient, not Censor, who has been defaming her character.

22. Doody, *Frances Burney*, 90. I disagree with Doody's statement that Cecilia and Beaufort truly seek independence, rebel against authority, and decide on poverty, though Cecilia has been looking for a job.

3. Politicized Bodies and the Body Politic

1. Morrison, "Fanny Burney and the Theatre," 171, 105. Devlin writes that the tragedies "are not, like the novels and some of her other autobiographical writings, imaginatively accurate reconstructions of the position of woman in society" (*The Novels and Journals of Fanny Burney*, 60). Simons finds that these plays depict "[m]orbid women" who "are unfairly treated, misjudged, confined, suffer and die in dreary circumstances. *Edwy and Elgiva* survived one disastrous performance only and we should perhaps be grateful for the natural demise of the rest" (*Fanny Burney*, 133). Adelstein's analysis touches each of these points: "Fanny's tragedies, like most of those in the eighteenth century, may be disregarded by all except the specialist. Her three completed plays contain little literary value" and all are interesting only because of what they tell us about Burney personally (*Fanny Burney*, 87). Mulliken writes that the tragedies show Burney's "obedience to the forms and conventions of a genre for which she had no natural aptitude" ("The Influence of the Drama," 48). Doody describes the tragedies as lacking the "completeness, force, and life of [Burney's] novels or her comic plays." She treats them primarily as "psychological documents in Burney's emotional history" and

finds little of merit in these works beyond the psychological profile they help to complete, or their contribution to Burney's later work (*Frances Burney*, 178). This discussion of *Edwy and Elgiva* is reprinted in part from the *Journal of Dramatic Theory and Criticism* 10, no. 2 (1997): 3-23.

2. Doody, *Frances Burney*, 150; Hemlow, *History of Fanny Burney*, 169.

3. Doody puts the composition of *Edwy and Elgiva* two years later than Hemlow, who suggests it was started in October 1786 (*JL*, 3:98 n. 2). Sabor agrees with the former's dating (2:7).

4. For a full account of the biographical circumstances of these years, see chapter 5 in Doody's biography, and chapters 7 and 8 in Hemlow's.

5. A decade later, Burney was to refer to her sister Susanna's miserable marriage in similar terms: "true Tragedy!" (*JL*, 3:74). In October 1799 Burney wrote of the possibility of her sister's "lingering death in *that* prison with *that* geoler" (*JL*, 4:348). Doody notes the tendency for terms of conflict to dominate Burney's diaries and letters during the period in which she wrote her tragedies: "'conflict,' 'monastic,' 'captivity,' 'tyranny,' 'shackles,' 'rebel'—also 'annihilation,' 'deadened'" (*Frances Burney*, 177).

6. Bevis, *English Drama* (London: Longman, 1988), 201.

7. Wikander, *The Play of Truth & State: Historical Drama from Shakespeare to Brecht* (Baltimore: Johns Hopkins Univ. Press, 1986), 129, 131, 135. J. Douglas Canfield discusses Christian tragedy in the context of Nicholas Rowe's works. It is clear that the world view offered in Rowe's tragedies, where suffering and evil are part of a traditional Christian solution, is not found in Burney's works. In Canfield's view, Rowe offers as "the solution to the problem of suffering innocence . . . trust in the providential care and justice of God" (*Nicholas Rowe and Christian Tragedy* [Gainesville: Univ. Press of Florida, 1977], 4). In Burney's tragedies, suffering innocence abounds and divine justice is mentioned at the end of *Edwy and Elgiva* and *Hubert De Vere*, but the heroines, unlike Rowe's Jane Shore, do not take much comfort from this or acknowledge the spiritual component of their suffering.

8. Nicoll, *A History of English Drama*, 3:73, 74.

9. As Bevis's survey and bibliography indicate, there are few books dealing specifically with eighteenth-century tragedy, and none that focuses on the late eighteenth century. Both Nicoll's *A History of English Drama* and *The Revels History of Drama in English* describe the physical components of the theater; other nations' influence on English drama; the impact of morality on characterization and plot; acting style; and specific genres (comedy, tragedy, farce, opera, pantomimes, burlesques, etc.).

10. Bevis, *English Drama*, 288.

11. See Nicoll, *The Theory of Drama* (London: Harrap, 1931; reprint, New York: Blom, 1966), 103-45 (page citations are to the reprint edition).

12. Ibid., 156-58.

13. Kintz, in her introduction to *The Subject's Tragedy: Political Poetics, Feminist Theory, and Drama*, writes compellingly about the repercussions that Aristotle's privileging of the Oedipus story has for theories of gender, performance, tragedy, and epistemology: "[t]he generic features of tragedy produce a dramatic and theoretical discourse that in many ways requires that there be no female agency as it guarantees the masculinity of both the protagonist and the theorist" (1). "Aristotle considered *Oedipus the King* to be 'the most nearly perfect tragedy.' . . . Oedipus' drama *is* the species called tragedy, just as Oedipus *is* the species called

human being. This ironic story of a universal human experience which very few people are entitled to have organizes an aesthetic and epistemological concept of subjectivity in which the tragic subject sets the stage for Western reason and aethetics" (28).

14. Cox, introduction to *Seven Gothic Dramas,* 4-5, 32.

15. Epstein, *Iron Pen,* 7.

16. Sedgwick, *The Coherence of Gothic Conventions* (New York: Arno, 1980), 13.

17. In a paper presented at the American Society for Eighteenth-Century Studies Conference in Charleston, S. C., in March 1994, "'Sulphurous Sparks of Fire': Frances Burney's Gothic Tragedies," Sabor notes the Gothicism of these plays, Burney's interest in other Gothic dramatists and novelists, and the Gothic elements of her own fiction: "[g]iven Burney's immersion in literary Gothicism, it should come as no surprise to find her writing Gothic tragedies in the late 1780s and early 1790s, when the vogue for such drama was at its height" (7). Sabor's reading of Burney's use of the Gothic does not explore the particularly feminine and feminist elements of her Gothicism, which are magnified by the tragic situations in these plays.

18. Scarry, *The Body in Pain: The Making and Unmaking of the World* (New York: Oxford Univ. Press, 1985), 56.

19. In this respect, while Epstein does not deal with the dramas, her view of Burney's obsession with "violence and hostility . . . [which] emerges in scenes of assault and moments of disguised anger" (5) is relevant. Burney insists on physicality: "Burney does not merely report or mirror institutions of oppression; she posits and dramatizes violence as an effect—the inevitable effect—of oppression. . . . Burney and her heroines experience social oppression with and through their bodies" (*Iron Pen,* 32-33).

20. Rubin, "The Traffic in Women: Notes on the 'Political Economy' of Sex," in *Toward an Anthropology of Women,* ed. Rayna R. Reiter (New York: Monthly Review, 1975), 174.

21. Rubin, "The Traffic in Women," 177.

22. Sedgwick, *Between Men: English Literature and Male Homosocial Desire* (New York: Columbia Univ. Press, 1985), 25.

23. This view of the feminist Gothic diverges from the view of Gothic drama put forth by Backscheider in *Spectacular Politics.* I agree with her assertion that, "[a]s social subjects [the heroines] are positioned, motivated, constrained within (subject to) social networks and cultural codes that exceed their comprehension or control" (199). She goes on to suggest that heroines in Gothic works are objectified, "the incarnations of the most elemental of male desires, economic and political as well as sexual" (200). Her conclusion, however, that "there may be no gothic plays written by women," is puzzling (200). Perhaps she feels that women would not use Gothic conventions because they are antifeminist or misogynist. However, as Burney's plays—and those by other female writers—illustrate, the objectified female can be a vehicle for social commentary. The possibility that the depiction of confined women is a literary form of protest should be considered, however undesirable such situations may be to a feminist sensibility.

24. Gellrich, *Tragedy and Theory: The Problem of Conflict since Aristotle* (Princeton: Princeton Univ. Press, 1988), 241.

25. Sabor, 1:xiii; for a list of the other actors involved and for details about the period leading up to the production, see Sabor, 2:7-9.

26. Qtd. in Hemlow, *History of Fanny Burney*, 247.

27. Sabor, 1:xiv. For summaries of the reviews, see Sabor, 1:xiv-xv and *JL*, 3:98-99, 366-67.

28. *European Magazine* 27 (April 1795): 272; *Morning Chronicle* (March 1795). The reception of *Edwy and Elgiva* has improved little since its eighteenth-century debut. Evelyn Shirley Shuckburgh wrote of the play's "stilted language, its commonplace sentiments, and its incorrect and inharmonious versification" ("Madame d'Arblay," *Macmillan's Magazine* [February 1890]: 294). Dobson suggests that despite "a certain stir and action, the plot generally lacks incident and movement" (*Fanny Burney [Madame d'Arblay]*, 185). Benkovitz, the play's first editor, does little to encourage reading the play at all because it "possibly marks the very point of decline in the career of a woman of real literary achievement" (*Edwy and Elgiva*, xiv).

29. Donkin, *Getting into the Act*, 146.

30. The prologue, written by Burney's brother, is a rather long discussion of the different ages of religion, which see the gradual replacement of papal authority with monarchical. Its conclusion is nationalistic: "Teach us to love our Country and her Laws / To glow united in her sacred cause / And boast with swelling hearts and loud acclaim / Our Faiths Defender and our King the same" (lines 53-56). The epilogue pokes fun at the play and its characters, laughing at Edwy and Elgiva as if they were stock comic characters in a satire about marriage: "What shall we say to Edwy and his Rib? / The Boy was sure a Driv'ler—a mere bib, / To make a rout that cost him Crown and life, / To keep a Horse?—a mistress?—no, a Wife!" (lines 11-14).

31. For a complete analysis of d'Arblay's suggestions for revisions to this play, see Sabor, "'Altered, improved, copied, abridged': Alexandre d'Arblay's Revisions to Burney's *Edwy and Elgiva*," *Lumen* 14 (1995): 127-37.

32. Sabor, 1:xvii.

33. Sabor, "'Altered,'" 132.

34. Ibid., 130.

35. For a discussion of Siddons's popularity, see Kelly, *The Kemble Era*; Donkin, "Mrs. Siddons"; and Rogers, "'Towering Beyond Her Sex.'"

36. Henry, *The History of Great Britain, from the first invasion of it by the Romans under Julius Caesar*, 6th ed., 12 vols. (London: Hodgson, 1823), 3:102-104.

37. Smollett, *A Complete History of England, deduced from the Descent of Julius Caesar, to the Treaty of Aix la Chapelle, 1748*, 9 vols. (London: Rivington and Fletcher, 1757-58), 1:162-63. Burney's reading of Smollett is documented in *EJL*, 1:134.

38. Carte, *A General History of England*, 4 vols. (London, 1747), 1:325-28.

39. De Thoyras, *The History of England*, trans. N. Tindal, 3d ed., 5 vols. (London: Knapton, 1743-47), 1:105.

40. Hemlow, *History of Fanny Burney*, 206.

41. Hume, *The History of England*, 6 vols. (Indianapolis: Liberty, 1973-85), 1:93-96. Burney's journal reference to this history is in *EJL*, 1:40.

42. Ellis, *The Contested Castle: Gothic Novels and the Subversion of Domestic Ideology* (Urbana: Univ. of Illinois Press, 1989), 46.

43. Pfister, *Theory and Analysis of Drama*, 200.

44. Ellis, *Contested Castle*, 46.

45. While Sabor notes that Burney was unlike her contemporaries in keeping scenes of violence offstage, she does depict, rather than just describe, the results of such violence (Sabor, 1:xxxii).

46. Scarry, *Body in Pain,* 56.

47. That Elgiva enters "tottering" may indicate that she has been hamstrung, as the historical sources suggest, though Burney makes no reference to this. See Sabor's note to this line (2:70).

48. One reviewer, quoted by Donkin, notes that Elgiva's retreat seemed to be "very accommodating" because "the wounded lady is brought from behind [the scene] on an elegant couch, and, after dying in the presence of her husband, is carried off and placed once more 'on the other side of the hedge.' The laughter which this scene occasioned, although supported by the dying words of Mrs. Siddons, was inconceivable" (*Getting into the Act,* 148).

49. Elisabeth Bronfen, *Over Her Dead Body: Death, Femininity, and the Aesthetic* (New York: Routledge, 1992), 44. The spectator in Bronfen's discussion is the male art historian. The violence of the "fragmentation and idolisation of the body—i.e. a severing of the body from its real materiality and its historical context ('fetishism')—is always built into such images" of death, especially female death (44).

50. Baillie, "Introductory Discourse," in *A Series of Plays,* by Joanna Baillie, ed. Donald H. Reiman, 3 vols. (New York: Garland, 1977), 1:12.

51. The stage directions on this point are quite ambiguous. Figures continue to refer to the corpse, though Eltruda and two peasants remove the dead body.

52. Lindenberger, *Historical Drama: The Relation of Literature and Reality* (Chicago: Univ. of Chicago Press, 1975), 9. A variation on temporal distance is geographical distance achieved by setting plays in ancient Rome or Greece, Spain, or France, for example. See Cox, "Romantic Drama," for a discussion of the relationship of distant settings and times to contemporary politics. Domestic tragedy, conversely, tended to depict contemporary settings. See Lillo's 1730 *The London Merchant* (revised by Colman as *The Fatal Curiosity* [1782]) and Cumberland's 1783 *The Mysterious Husband* for examples. Ellis argues that Gothic writers set their novels in the past in an effort to create for themselves a larger space in which to explore female agency (*Contested Castle,* 17).

53. Lindenberger suggests as well that "[t]he continuity between past and present is a central assertion in history plays of all times and styles" (6).

54. Sabor, 2:232. Where necessary to aid readers in locating my quotations, I have included notations of textual variants, Berg Collection fragment numbers (cited, following Sabor, as "El." followed by fragment number), and page numbers in Sabor.

55. Sabor, 2:233. The Berg manuscript is #4327.

56. Sabor, 2:233. I also thank Janice Farrar Thaddeus for clarifying this for me.

57. While there are no precise historical narratives that relate to this play, it is clear that Burney is once again adding a female perspective to historical events. Edgar Atheling and Malcolm, King of Scotland, are historical figures. The account Arnulph gives of succor in Scotland is accurate (variants III.viii; El. 113). Edgar Atheling is referred to by Hume (*History of England,* 1:41), de Thoyras (*History of England,* 1:187), and by Carte (*General History of England,* 1:463-65), who recounts Malcolm's invasion of England. The variants provide contradictory plot details at times.

58. Sabor, 1:xxxv.

59. Jones writes about the usefulness of a maternal ideal to a middle class that was expanding and required protection from lower-class encroachment (*Women in the Eighteenth Century,* 59). See also Nussbaum, *Torrid Zones;* Marilyn Francus, "The Monstrous Mother: Reproductive Anxiety in Swift and Pope" (*English*

Literary History 61, no. 4 [1994]: 829-51); Mary Abbott's *Family Ties: English families 1540-1920* (New York: Routledge, 1993); Elisabeth Badinter's *Mother Love: Myth and Reality* (New York: Macmillan, 1981); Hill's *Eighteenth-Century Women;* and Jane Rendall's *The Origins of Modern Feminism: Women in Britain, France and the United States 1780-1860* (New York: Schocken Books, 1984) for other discussions of eighteenth-century motherhood. G.J. Barker-Benfield writes that "[c]entral to the purpose of the culture of sensibility was the aggrandizement of the affectionate family and, at its heart, mothering, because it generated traits (the happy energy of social affections) that society needed" (*The Culture of Sensibility: Sex and Society in Eighteenth-Century Britain* [Chicago: Univ. of Chicago Press, 1992], 276). My analysis of Burney's depiction of motherhood is reprinted in part from "Frances Burney's Dramatic Mothers," *English Studies in Canada* 23, no. 1 (1997):41-62.

60. In "Colonizing the Breast: Sexuality and Maternity in Eighteenth-Century England," (*Eighteenth-Century Life,* n.s., 16, no. 1 [1992]: 185-213), Ruth Perry writes that, during the eighteenth century, the conceptualization of motherhood increasingly idealized female sexuality as solely reproductive and devoted to the nourishment of children, who were important resources for England's colonial project. She suggests that "maternity came to be imagined as a counter to sexual feeling, opposing alike individual expression, desire, and agency in favor of a mother-self at the service of the family and the state" (188). Mothers were to be "loving but without sexual needs, morally pure, disinterested, benevolent, and self-sacrificing" (190). This resulted in what Perry describes as a "colonization of women" that relegated them to the domestic, the private, and the personal spheres. (193)

61. Nussbaum, *Torrid Zones,* 24.

62. Wollstonecraft, "To M. Talleyrand-Périgord," in *A Critical Edition of Mary Wollstonecraft's "A Vindication of the Rights of Woman, with Strictures on Political and Moral Subjects,"* ed. Ulrich H. Hardt (Troy, N.Y.: Whitson, 1982), 20-21.

63. Nussbaum, *Torrid Zones,* 48.

64. Francus, "Monstrous Mother," 845.

65. Doody, *Frances Burney,* 24, 177. *Evelina* garners a great deal of attention on the subject of fathers and daughters. See David Oakleaf, "The Name of the Father: Social Identity and the Ambition of *Evelina*," *Eighteenth-Century Fiction* 3, no. 4 (1991): 341-58; and Irene Fizer, "The Name of the Daughter: Identity and Incest in *Evelina*," in *Refiguring the Father: New Feminist Readings of Patriarchy,* eds. Patricia Yaeger and Elizabeth Kowaleski-Wallace (Carbondale: Southern Illinois Univ. Press, 1989), 78-107.

66. De Lauretis, *Alice Doesn't,* 143, 121.

67. Analyses of the suspicion that surrounds female sexual transgression can be found, with variation, in More's *Percy* (1777), Jephson's *The Law of Lombardy* (1779), Cowley's *Albina* (1779), and Hayley's *Marcella* (1789), to name a few instances.

68. The maternal-based impetus for female agency and self-direction can be configured within the context described by Ellis in reference to Gothic fiction. A contradiction emerged in the revolutionary times of late-eighteenth-century England "between the demand of an increasingly self-conscious bourgeois class for a pure female ideal to contrast with the dissolute behavior of those above and below it and the need of writers to engage their readers by providing action that would leave them awaiting the next volume eagerly" (*Contested Castle,* 17).

Motherhood bridges the gap between acceptable femininity on the one hand and a suspenseful plot on the other. As a mother, Elberta may actively pursue her own desires in an autonomous fashion that might otherwise be denied a female figure. The suspense lies in the perilous teleology of Elberta's movement, from captivity to the head of a single-parent family that must struggle to consolidate itself after Arnulph's departure.

69. Doody, *Frances Burney*, 191-92. Except for Sabor's discussion of *Elberta* in his edition's headnote to the play, no critic deals with the play as a whole. Hemlow deals with images rather than narrative: "[n]o scrap among the 303 extant memoranda promises any brighter end than gnawing famine, madness, and death. . . . One has the uneasy impression that Fanny herself was not escaping too soon" (*History of Fanny Burney*, 220). Morrison discusses Burney's efforts to depict the pitiful and does well to account for the devices Burney uses, and concludes that "a study of the fragments suggests that it was well to leave it uncompleted, for it is more sentimental and more pathetic than any other of the tragedies" ("Fanny Burney and the Theatre," 134). Both Doody and Morrison take fragment 265 as the play's main image: "A Female is mentioned, who wild and unknown is seen roaming about—no one is informed whence she comes—woe is in her voice, terror in her aspect,—she never weeps, yet frequently wails, tho in terms unintelligible from their wildness—: Her interesting appearance— / Some she affrights—others is derided by— / Her fierce harangues, though wild when offended— / Her gentle supplications to shadows. / Her inattention to pursuit—" (Sabor, 306). Doody describes this woman as "an angrier representation of Frances Burney, whose potential 'Children,' both biological and literary, have indeed been taken from her," which denies her "the simple submission available in different ways" to heroines of the other tragedies (192).

70. Morrison, "Fanny Burney and the Theatre," 124.

71. Kelly and von Mücke, introduction to *Body and Text in the Eighteenth Century*, ed. Kelly and von Mücke (Stanford: Stanford Univ. Press, 1994), 7.

4. The Daughter's Tragedy

1. Knight, *Principles of Taste*, 4th ed. (1808; reprint, London: Gregg, 1972), 232.

2. See *JL*, 3:69-70 n. 1, and 3:258.

3. After the note to these letters, Hemlow does not discuss any further which play might be referred to when transactions between the Burneys and Kemble are mentioned. The suggestion is that by this time it might well be *Edwy and Elgiva* in question. In any case, on 2 September 1794, Burney writes to her father that they "have [received kind] offers & words from Mr K[emble] with the Compts" (*JL*, 3:79).

4. Sabor, 2:93-94.

5. Hemlow, "Fanny Burney: Playwright," 180.

6. There are no clear historical sources for the story, but King John, a notorious tyrant, had many conflicts with his barons. Hume's *History of England* does refer to a Robert de Vere and a William de Moubray (1:447). Carte cites a William de Mowbray and a Chief Justiciary Geffrey Fitz Piers (*General History of England*, 1:784). John's retirement to the Isle of Wight (1:835) is consistent with Burney's vision of the setting. The story of John's opposition to his barons is found

in de Thoyras, where the historian mentions Robert de Ver, William de Munbrey, and William de Beauchamp (*History of England*, 1:275, n. 2).

7. Heilman, *Tragedy and Melodrama: Versions of Experience* (Seattle: Univ. of Washington Press, 1968), 22.

8. See Heilman, *Tragedy and Melodrama*, 38-73.

9. I thank D. Grant Campbell for his suggestions on the point of Cerulia's innocence.

10. The astrologer resembles a figure in Dr. Charles Burney's *The Cunning Man*, which had 14 performances and was published on 21 November 1766. This two-act "musical entertainment," which he wrote in the 1750s, is based on Rousseau's *Le devin du village* (1752). See Scholes, *The Great Dr. Burney*, 1:107-17.

11. Sabor, 1:xxxii-xxxiii.

12. Doody, *Frances Burney*, 191. Doody's view that Cerulia's death is a rebellion is difficult to accept given Cerulia's sense that the cause of her suffering is no more than De Vere's rejection of her in favor of another woman.

13. Epstein, *Iron Pen*, 32-33.

14. Cutting-Gray, *Woman as "Nobody,"* 4.

15. Sedgwick, *Gothic Conventions*, 12-14.

16. Backscheider, *Spectacular Politics*, 199.

17. Doody, *Frances Burney*, 190. Doody draws similarities between Burney and Cerulia; between De Mowbray and Dr. Burney; and between Hubert De Vere and Burney's acquaintances George Cambridge and Colonel Digby. She also makes an interesting comparison between the female pair in the tragedy, Geralda and Cerulia, and the pair in *The Wanderer*, Elinor and Juliet (188-91). Morrison focuses on the hero, treating Cerulia's death as matter-of-fact. Hemlow gives little more than a plot summary. She too dismisses Cerulia's death as a matter of course: "there is now nothing for Cerulia the village maid but to die, and she dies" (*History of Fanny Burney*, 219).

18. Cixous and Clément, *The Newly Born Woman*, 91.

19. Qtd. in Aston, *An Introduction to Feminism and Theatre*, 47.

20. Doody, *Frances Burney*, 184. A number of tragedies of the period do portray the coercive effect of the father-daughter bond, however, so the extent of the idealization of this familial bond is debatable. For examples, see chapter 7. Doody makes comparisons between Adela and Frances, and Chester and Dr. Burney. This "rickety allegory" (188) of Burney's situation describes a woman who is "traded off for money and influence" (186). While Doody's reading of the father-daughter relationship implies an interesting link between eroticism, passive aggression, and blackmail, her conclusion about the play is truly confusing: "Adela's mysterious trespass is basically the sin of her own response to her fate; the guilt can be relieved only by complete, if momentary, yielding up of the independent adult mind to infantile dream—but the dramatist, however neurotic, who tries to incorporate the conflict, as well as the infantile dream of union, is not innocent of responding in her own way to her own fate" (188). For Adelstein, the plot here "is superior to those in the other tragedies. . . . [T]he verse is less objectionable although it is thin and contributes little to the emotional effect" (*Fanny Burney*, 87). Morrison's interest lies largely with Chester, whose conflict she elevates over Adela's, which is labeled as "troublesome" ("Fanny Burney and the Theatre," 151). She overlooks the fact that it is Adela's body that suffers because of Chester's decisions. Further, Chester's debate lasts for only part of act 1, after which his daughter is returned to

him. He does not discover her subsequent voluntary imprisonment until later, when his main concern is that she has betrayed his love for her. Chester does bargain his own life for that of his daughter in the last act, but he is easily convinced that her cloistering is the best alternative. Hemlow considers the play to be "swollen" and "melodramatic," best described as a "dissertation on filial piety" (*History of Fanny Burney*, 219). This argument ignores the possibility that Burney questions the forms that filial piety takes, rather than simply urging it as a model for female behavior.

21. Hemlow, "Fanny Burney: Playwright," 180.

22. While Burney has derived her figures largely from historical sources, the main story, unlike that in *Edwy and Elgiva*, is her own invention. As with her other tragedies, Burney adds female-centered stories to more general accounts of historical events. Hume's *History of England* mentions William, Robert, the Earls of Shrewsbury and Arundel, Robert Belesme, Robert de Moubray, the Earl of Chester, William de Warrenne, and Robert Fitz Hammon, but not Adela. He notes the king's siege of Pevensey and Rochester and the famine, which Chester, De Warrenne, and Fitz Hammon prevailed upon him to alleviate (1:230). Carte's characterization of Robert de Belesme, son of Roger de Montgomery, Earl of Shrewsbury, is curious, considering Burney's treatment of the same figure: he "had an head fit to contrive, and an heart capable of undertaking any mischief or enterprize whatever; he was crafty, tricking, eloquent, bold in armes, indefatigable in action, infinitely covetous, cruel, and debauched" (*General History of England*, 1:459).

23. As Lynn Hunt notes, this was a notion popularized in the aftermath of the French Revolution by Edmund Burke, who understood "the connection between filial devotion and the willingness of a subject to obey." See *The Family Romance of the French Revolution* (Berkeley: Univ. of California Press, 1992), 3.

24. Adela is present in fully one-third of the scenes (twenty-five of seventy-four), with Chester being the next most prominent figure (in twenty-one scenes), followed by the king and Adela's suitor, De Belesme. De Warrenne's status as an undesirable suitor is evident in his small participation in the action (in ten scenes), and he appears in only one scene with Adela herself.

25. See Aston and Savona, *Theatre as Sign-System*, 36-41, for a discussion of character function and the terms I utilize in the following paragraphs.

26. Heilman, *Tragedy and Melodrama*, 10.

27. Ibid., 22.

28. Leith, "Voltaire and '*Maman*': Female Sexuality, Maternity, and Incest in the Tragedies," *Lumen* 12 (1993): 68-69.

29. Leith, "Voltaire and '*Maman*,'" 66.

30. Adela's expression of what she most wants to hear from her father is not unlike Burney's tortured rebellion against her own father concerning the withdrawal of her play *Love and Fashion* a decade later. Both women ventriloquize their fathers, unable to ask directly for the support they need. See *JL*, 4:394-95 and chapter 5 below.

31. Doody, *Frances Burney*, 187-88. This scene resembles one in Inchbald's *The Child of Nature* (1788), in which a father tries his daughter's devotion to him in an emotionally coercive fashion, after leaving her to another man's care for years and appearing to her initially in disguise.

32. Sedgwick, *Gothic Conventions*, 13.

33. Morrison, "Fanny Burney and the Theatre," 153.

34. Doody, *Frances Burney,* 178.
35. Lindenberger, *Historical Drama,* 52.
36. See Cox, "Romantic Drama," for a discussion of revolutionary themes in the late-century drama.

5. "Choice" and Evaluation

1. Burney left for France to join d'Arblay, already in France pursuing his family's interests after the Revolution. See Doody, *Frances Burney,* 288.
2. Hogan, *The London Stage,* part 5, vol. 1:clxviii.
3. The *Morning Chronicle* announced on 29 January 1800 that "Madame d'Arblay, *ci-devant* Miss Burney, has a Comedy forthcoming at Covent-Garden Theatre" and *The Times* followed on 29 March 1800 with "Madame DARBLAY, late Miss Barry [*sic*], has turned her attention to the Stage, and gives us hopes of a Comedy" (*JL,* 4:392-93, n. 4).
4. Burney's friend Arthur Murphy wrote *The Upholsterer* (1758), which Wallace suggests Burney knew (*A Busy Day,* 198). Donkin writes briefly about this metaphor and *Love and Fashion* (*Getting into the Act,* 155-57).
5. Sabor, 1:107.
6. Hemlow writes that the play includes a thematic indictment of ". . . the *mariage de convenance* . . . [and the] usual castigation of the vices and follies of fashionable life." In it, Burney condemns "arrogant vanity and selfishness, affectation, ill-nature, and hard-heartedness. In the closing scenes the votaries of fashion are punished and love triumphs" (*History of Fanny Burney,* 274). In her article, she suggests that the characterization is "thin and hackneyed. The plot is obvious, its solution and much of its conduct mawkish" ("Fanny Burney: Playwright," 186-87). Morrison writes that the play "panders to the taste of the time" in its sentimentality, and its praise of virtue, benevolence, and tender-heartedness ("Fanny Burney and the Theatre," 181-82). She does not see any irony in the advocacy of "marrying for love and leading a simple life in the country" (182). She instead flattens the play into a simple allegory of the competition between virtue and vice. Mulliken feels that "the resolution of all difficulties comes from the consistency of Lord Ardville's rigid character rather than from a more sentimental transformation" ("Influence of the Drama," 39). Adelstein writes that the combination of romantic comedy, satire, and comedy of manners was "almost bound to fail" (*Fanny Burney,* 106). Doody describes Hilaria as "good-hearted but volatile, flippant, and worldly" (*Frances Burney,* 289). The play's moral is loosely described as "[i]ndependence achieved through work" (290), which overlooks the irony that independence is not achieved through work, but through a woman's willingness to equate herself with a literal monetary amount. This willingness, along with male pride, achieves the play's resolution.
7. Cox, introduction to *Seven Gothic Dramas,* 12. See Doody's discussion of the ghost and the "Strange Man" (*Frances Burney,* 291). Paul Ranger discusses Gothic drama in *"Terror and Pity reign in every Breast": Gothic Drama in the London Patent Theatres, 1750-1820* (London: The Society for Theatre Research, 1991).
8. The "Strange Man" resembles a figure in Burney's father's *The Cunning Man,* which features a soothsayer who brings together the estranged lovers Colette and Colin. See chapter 4, n. 10.
9. Doody, *Frances Burney,* 290.

10. Holcroft's *Seduction* (1787), which Burney saw in 1789, contains some interesting resemblances to Burney's play in the treatment of fashion's interference with affection. Here, a wife's love of fashion competes with her husband's love of gambling. (Another figure in the play is the virtuous Mr. Wilmot, just returned from the Indies; see *The Woman-Hater*.) This play also contains a strong female figure in Harriet, who wants and gets revenge against Sir Friendly for reneging on a promise of marriage, after she is jailed because of Sir Friendly's lies.

11. Straub, *Divided Fictions*, 25.

12. Ibid., 25.

13. Epstein, *Iron Pen*, 86-87.

14. The rather fragmented nature of the plot of *Love and Fashion* is indicated in the amount of time different figures have on stage. Sir Archy and Innis are present in the greatest number of scenes, Hilaria is next, followed by Lord Exbury, Mordaunt, Davis, Miss Exbury, Litchburn, and Dawson. Lord Ardville and Valentine are on stage for equal lengths of time, but are only slightly more prominent than the "Strange Man."

15. This pastoral contrast to the fashionable life may have been prompted by Burney's own retirement with her family in Camilla cottage. In a letter to her sister Esther, who lives "in the *midst of things*," she asks that a bonnet might be altered: "I live in such complete retirement, that the Fashions do not break in upon me enough by degrees to make me have courage, or inclination to adopt them while yet new. I must entreat some alteration that may render it sufficiently *passée* for such a rustic Hermit as myself to wear it without blushing" (*JL*, 4:302).

16. Doody, *Frances Burney*, 290.

17. Ibid., 293.

6. Family Matters

1. For further details, see Sabor's headnotes to each play. Sabor (1:xi-xii) also discusses the premiere production of *A Busy Day* by the British company Show of Strength in 1993.

2. While Camilla alone, of the novels' heroines, has two living parents, the family's members are separated for most of the time covered in the novel. Eugenia is taken over by Sir Hugh, Mrs. Tyrold is removed from direct interaction with her children, and Camilla ultimately is left with only a written sermon for her parental guidance.

3. Boose and Flowers, introduction to *Daughters and Fathers*, ed. Boose and Flowers (Baltimore: Johns Hopkins Univ. Press, 1989), 3.

4. For a discussion of familial ideology, see Michèle Barrett and Mary McIntosh, *The Anti-social Family*, 2d ed. (New York: Verso, 1991). The organization of society in families determines forms of cultural representations, notions of gender, and sociopolitical policies. The family fulfills a social function as a unit perceived to be intimately connected to social perpetuation, stability, morality, emotional security, and desirable familiarity, yet "the moral and hence socio-political claims of the family rest in large part precisely on its being seen as a biological unit rather than a social arrangement" (26-27).

5. Weedon, *Feminist Practice and Poststructuralist Theory* (Oxford: Basil Blackwell, 1987), 38. Terry Eagleton, in the context of *Wuthering Heights*, writes of the family's power over the individual: "the family, at once social institution and domain of intensely interpersonal relationships, highlights the complex interplay

between an evolving system of given unalterable relations and the creation of individual value" ("Myths of Power: A Marxist Study on *Wuthering Heights*," in *Wuthering Heights* by Emily Brontë, ed. Linda H. Peterson [Boston: Bedford, 1992], 400).

6. Hemlow admires *A Busy Day* for its moral, a "devastating indictment of the bad manners of high and low alike" (*History of Fanny Burney,* 305). She feels that *The Woman-Hater* is the play which would have "best pleased theatregoers of her time" (309). Doody places the late comedies in a context of familial upheaval and death. These plays are said to fulfill a "private allegory as well as . . . public comic statement" (*Frances Burney,* 311). Each shows "the rupture of some bond, and the opportunity to escape from some oppressive or irrelevant demands" (311). She notes that, in "each successive play, the ties binding the heroine become more important, and the breaks more serious" (311). The failed parental figures are important for Doody's psychological readings, which culminate in praise for Joyce (*The Woman-Hater*) who can "cast off the Father" (308). Wallace follows Hemlow in her sense that Burney chastises all classes for their members' selfishness. She provides perceptive analyses of the hero and heroine, but announces that the "social and cultural significance" of this type of comedy is not part of her project (*A Busy Day,* 20). Mulliken describes *The Woman-Hater* in terms of its "manners plots" of the Waverleys, Sir Roderick, and Lady Smatter, and the "low comedy" and "natural vulgarity" of Joyce ("Influence of the Drama," 45). Adelstein writes that Sir Roderick "is portrayed as an absurd stereotype instead of a disturbed human being. The author's own feministic views may have kept her from treating him with any kindness or understanding" (*Fanny Burney,* 111). Still, he feels that the play "succeeds" (110).

7. Doody, *Frances Burney,* 295. Burney's sister Charlotte married her own "nabob," her second husband Ralph Broome, in 1798. This may have furnished Burney with some of her ideas for *A Busy Day.* See *JL,* 4:123 and 174. The returned traveller and the exotic air of foreign life are elements of Steele's *The Conscious Lovers* (1722), Cumberland's *The West Indian* (1771), and Inchbald's *The Mogul Tale* (1784) and *The Wise Man of the East* (1799).

8. Epstein writes that Cecilia is Burney's most financially independent heroine (*Iron Pen,* 156). Eliza Watts's inheritance is more advantageous because it is, as Deborah tells Frank, "all in her own hands at this very minute" (I.312-13).

9. Sabor writes that this figure contributes to *A Busy Day*'s subversive potential and is "one of the most effective characters never to appear on stage" (1:xl).

10. Wallace notes that Eliza "talks of [her parents] having 'relinquished' their power over her, the implication being that she now voluntarily returns it to them; that is, she herself is now in control of her actions, but she chooses to defer to her family" (*A Busy Day,* 5).

11. Doody, *Frances Burney,* 299.

12. Wallace's edition of the play includes an excellent chapter, "Staging *A Busy Day,*" in which she discusses Burney's use of stage directions. Her conclusion, that "Fanny Burney was acutely aware that plays are more than words" (*A Busy Day,* 169), is apt, though she does not discuss the implications of many of the stage directions she describes, particularly where they might indicate an inequality in authority or power between figures. She does note that this encounter "deflate[s] Eliza's rather melodramatic sense of duty and proper affectionate behaviour" (7).

13. Barrett and McIntosh, *The Anti-social Family,* 43.

14. The play's conciliatory moral does not seem to be questioned by Doody, even though she notes the pervasive hardheartedness throughout the play in terms of class, race, and forms of rejection in general (*Frances Burney*, 298). While it is true that Lady Wilhelmina provides "a lonely dissenting voice" against a cross-class marriage (Sabor, 1:xl), I think it is also true that the attitudes behind her voice are shared by other figures.

15. It seems odd to suggest, as Doody does, that Miss Percival's fear of "the wigs" is an objection to "the assumption of phallic power by old men" and thus a rejection of "daddying" in the play (*Frances Burney*, 298). In Baillie's *The Tryal* (published in 1798), which Burney knew, young Agnes and Mariane both express their fear of old men's wigs.

16. See Doody, *Frances Burney*, 298-99 on this point.

17. The names of some of these figures are conjectural. See Sabor 1:4-5 and 193; and Doody, *Frances Burney*, 302.

18. Burney may have named Wilmot for a figure in Holcroft's *Seduction* (1787), in which a Mr. Wilmot is newly returned from the Indies. His demeanor is far from that of Burney's Wilmot, though. His honesty is the solution to the marital and financial problems in the play; he appears to the other figures as "Gabriel," whose angelic qualities are obvious.

19. Epstein, *Iron Pen*, 16.

20. Burney, *Evelina; or, The History of a Young Lady's Entrance into the World*, ed. Edward A. Bloom (Oxford: Oxford Univ. Press, 1982), 13, 67. This discussion of the relationship between *Evelina*, the late comedies, and Burney's depictions of class was presented at the March 1996 conference of the American Society for Eighteenth-Century Studies in Austin, Tex.

21. Staves, "*Evelina*; or, Female Difficulties," in *Fanny Burney's "Evelina"*, ed. Harold Bloom (New York: Chelsea, 1988), 24.

22. *Evelina*, 171.

23. Ibid., 254.

24. *Frances Burney*, 302.

25. See also the discussion of mothering in general, and *Elberta* specifically, in chapter 3.

26. *Frances Burney*, 310.

27. Qtd. in Paula R. Backscheider, ed., introduction to *The Plays of Elizabeth Inchbald*, 2 vols. (New York: Garland, 1980), 1:xxvii. Inchbald's unperformed *A Case of Conscience* (written in 1800) is an excellent corollary to *The Woman-Hater*. The plays' similarities emphasize their tragic undertones. In Inchbald's play, a mother, Adriana, is accused of infidelity by her husband based on flimsy evidence. She, however, stands by him and he discovers that she has been faithful all along and that he has been tricked into his accusations by Cordunna, a former suitor of Adriana. She is thus another innocent wife and mother who is punished on the basis of rumors and solaced only by her love for her son, Oviedo.

28. Morrison suggests that Eleonora's illness on hearing of her husband's return to England is an instance of the "false delicacy seen in sentimental heroines" and that "[t]he encounter between Eleonora and her husband is the big concluding scene, done in the best manner of the sentimental tragedy" ("Fanny Burney and the Theatre," 197).

29. Doody, *Frances Burney*, 302. According to Doody, Burney privileges one version of daughterhood over the other: "[t]here is the shadowy, if lovely and ideally good daughter, Sophia, and the awkward, physical, un-ideal Joyce . . . the most

appealing character in the play" (305). Joyce is a representation of "Burney herself [who] is tired of being prudent wisdom (Sophia) and wants to be joyfulness (Joyce)" (311).

30. Burney's emphasis on the "laughing" versus "sentimental" aspects of the comedy can be seen in the length of time she devotes to Old Waverley's mistaken love of Sophia, Lady Smatter's pseudolearning, and Joyce's antics. The shadowy nature of Eleonora and Sophia is attested to in their relative lack of prominence, appearing less often, as they do, than the usurping daughter and her working-class mother.

31. The father's oppressive manipulation of female education resembles that in Inchbald's *The Child of Nature* (1788). Amanthis's education is controlled by her guardian, the Duke of Mercia, in order that her innocence be maintained to the point where she has no desire for company or communication except with him. The discovery of a young and attractive man, the Marquis Almanza, however, puts an end to her love for Mercia.

32. Doody, *Frances Burney*, 307.

33. Epstein, *Iron Pen*, 86-87; Cutting-Gray, *Woman as "Nobody,"* 4.

34. Joyce's cries for "liberty" may echo the popular outcry over George III's antagonism with John Wilkes, who was imprisoned for publishing libel in *The North Briton* in 1763. In 1768, he again opposed the king, who attempted to have his election in Middlesex nullified and his own candidate elected in Wilkes's place. While R.J. White dismisses an idea of a "working class" in London at the time of Wilkes's imprisonment, the call of "Wilkes and Liberty!" did emerge, as he writes, from handloom weavers, porters, carters, sedan-chairmen, and general riff-raff, "whose faces peep out of odd corners of Hogarth's *Gin Lane* and *Beer Street*" (*The Age of George III* [New York: Walker, 1968], 76). The controversy drew class lines, pitting the lower classes against the king and aristocracy.

35. Doody, *Frances Burney*, 308.

36. Luce Irigaray writes, "[i]n patriarchy, the revival of relations between mother and daughter always creates conflict" (*Speculum of the Other Woman*, trans. Gillian C. Gill [Ithaca: Cornell Univ. Press, 1985], 118). Wilmot is removed from the relationship between Joyce and her mother. This new family's lower social status perhaps makes it less threatening than the husband- and fatherless Eleonora-Sophia pair that is brought under Wilmot's control.

37. Doody, *Frances Burney*, 305.

38. Statistics are from Hogan, *The London Stage*, part 5. Of course, the song may have been performed and not listed in playbills or records.

39. "The Contrast" was a popular binary depicting the difference between England and France, the latter nation serving as a lesson by negative example for England. It was disseminated in prints, pottery, medals, and on the stage. The opposition pits British liberty against French slavery, the former characterized by "religion, morality, loyalty, obedience to the laws, independance [*sic*], personal security, justice, inheritance, protection, property, industry, national prosperity and happiness." France is the place of "atheism, perjury, rebellion, treason, anarchy, murder, *equality*, madness, cruelty, injustice, treachery, ingratitude, idleness, famine, national and private ruin, and misery" (my emphasis). "The Contrast" was sometimes coupled with printed copies of "God Save the King" and accompanied by sets of two pictures. One set, by Thomas Rowlandson, contrasts Britannia (with the Union Jack, the Magna Carta, the scales of liberty, a lion, and a sailing ship) with Discord, as "French Liberty." Discord is depicted next to a hanged man, trampling on a corpse and carrying a pike with an impaled head on it. See David

Bindman, *The Shadow of the Guillotine* (London: British Museum, 1989), 118-22, for illustrations and discussion.

40. Baille, "Introductory Discourse," 1:57-58.

41. Watkins, *Materialist Critique*, 8.

7. A Context and Overview

1. See Sabor, 1:xxiii.

2. Burney, *The Wanderer; or, Female Difficulties*, ed. Margaret Anne Doody, Robert L. Mack, and Peter Sabor (New York: Oxford Univ. Press, 1991), 398-99.

3. See Stanton, "'This New-Found Path Attempting,'" 325-54.

4. See Wallace's edition of *A Busy Day* for a list of plays seen or known by Burney (195-99).

5. Doody, *Frances Burney*, 76-77.

6. *The Plays of Elizabeth Inchbald*, 2:lines 9-26. Taylor is likely Inchbald's friend, journalist and critic John Taylor (1757-1832).

7. Sherbo, *English Sentimental Drama* (East Lansing: Michigan State Univ. Press, 1957), 163.

8. Backscheider, introduction to *Inchbald*, 1:xiii, xix.

9. For statistics, see Stanton, "'This New-Found Path Attempting.'"

10. Doody, *Frances Burney*, 178.

11. More, "Preface to the Tragedies," in *The Complete Works of Hannah More*, 2 vols. (New York: Harper, 1835), 1:508. Subsequent references to More's plays cite this edition by volume and page.

12. Doody, *Frances Burney*, 184. Bevis describes the "father's power over his daughter's hand" as a "recurrent theme in Georgian drama" (*English Drama*, 203).

13. Cowley claimed that More copied *Percy* from Cowley's *Albina*, performed at The Haymarket, 1779. In *Albina*, we find a female villain. Editha is a Lady Macbeth figure who controls Gondibert and prompts him to interfere in the marriage between Edward and Albina. The villains of the piece are banished before the final scene, but return to enact some final havoc. Gondibert comes to Albina's marriage suite and stabs Editha, thinking she is Albina, and then stabs himself. Edward and Albina are saved and the deception plot originated by Editha to capture and punish Albina works in reverse, killing Editha and Gondibert. For a discussion of the plagiarism debate, see chapter 3 in Donkin's *Getting into the Act*.

14. Rowe, *The Tragedy of Jane Shore*, ed. Harry William Pedicord (Lincoln: Univ. of Nebraska Press, 1974), V.435-40.

15. Brooke, *The Siege of Sinope* (London: Cadell, 1781), Act II, scene i, p. 14. Cited hereafter by act, scene, and page number.

16. In Baillie's *The Family Legend* (published in 1810), which I do not discuss here, a daughter's uniting of two warring clans is also the issue. Helen has been given by the Campbells to Maclean and peace is declared, but all of Maclean's vassals suspect her of treachery and betrayal. They force Maclean to cast her off and leave her for dead on the seacoast, but she is rescued by a former lover and returned to her father. When Maclean comes to the Campbells in feigned mourning, the plot is uncovered and the villains are punished. Helen is returned to her former lover, along with her son. This is another work that explores the power of plotters to defame an innocent woman, such as occurs in *Edwy and Elgiva*.

17. Cowley, *The Fate of Sparta*, in *The Plays of Hannah Cowley*, ed. Frede-

rick M. Link, 2 vols. (New York: Garland, 1979), 2:5-6. Subsequent references to Cowley's play cite this edition by volume and page.

18. Hogan, *The London Stage 1660-1800*, part 5, vol. 3:2269.

19. Baille, "Introductory Discourse," 1:10. Subsequent references are to this edition, cited by page.

20. Cox, introduction to *Seven Gothic Dramas*, 52-53.

21. Cox, introduction to *Seven Gothic Dramas*, 57.

22. Ibid., 55. Daniel P. Watkins, in "Class, Gender, and Social Motion in Joanna Baillie's *DeMonfort*" (*The Wordsworth Circle* 23, no.2 [1992]: 109-17), takes a somewhat different view, arguing that the status of the female body that invites the male gaze is central to the play. Watkins argues for Jane's captivating beauty.

23. In *The Dream* (published in 1812), Baillie depicts another strong female figure, Lady Leonora, who assumes an active role in helping her former lover, Osterloo, escape his foes.

24. Baillie, *Count Basil*, in *A Series of Plays*, 1:169. Purinton writes regarding *Count Basil* that "Baillie's play dramatically depicts the dissolving and blurring of gender dichotomies that writers of the 1790s feared might occur as a result of the revolution in feminine manners" (*Romantic Ideology*, 141).

25. Count Basil's and De Monfort's declines are unusual depictions of male deterioration and near madness. More often, as the plays I discuss indicate, the mad scene is devoted to female deterioration. Kintz writes that "[w]omen have been associated with madness in the West because of the isomorphic relation between terms in binary oppositions: reason/madness, men/women, culture/nature, speech/silence" (introduction to *The Subject's Tragedy*, 17).

26. Lee, *Almeyda; Queen of Granada* (London: Cadell and Davies, 1796), 121. See Backscheider's discussion in *Spectacular Politics*, 202-5.

27. Baillie, *Orra*, in *A Series of Plays*, 3:100.

Conclusion

1. Shuckburgh, "Madame d'Arblay," 294.

2. Howard and O'Connor, introduction to *Shakespeare Reproduced: The Text in History and Ideology* (London: Methuen, 1987), 3.

3. Brown, "Fanny Burney's 'Feminism,'" 36.

4. Figes, *Sex and Subterfuge: Women Novelists to 1850* (London: Macmillan, 1982), 40.

5. Rogers, *Frances Burney*, 15; and Straub, *Divided Fictions*, 33.

6. Hume, *The Rakish Stage: Studies in English Drama, 1660-1800* (Carbondale: Southern Illinois Univ. Press, 1983), 29.

Index

Note: Page numbers in italic indicate illustrations; those in underlined type indicate primary references.

Abbott, Mary, 216 n 59
Adelstein, Michael, 6, 205 n 10, 209 n 8, 211 n 1, 218 n 20, 220 n 6, 222 n 6
Aicken, James, 52
Arblay, Alexander Charles Louis Piochard d', the Rev. (son), 52, 80, 84
Arblay, Alexandre-Jean-Baptiste Piochard d' (husband), 53, 54, 83, 92, 95, 112, 114, 130, 214 n 31, 220 n 1
Arne, Thomas, 160
Aston, Elaine: *An Introduction to Feminism and Theatre*, 205 n 2, 207 n 18, n 20, 218 n 19; *Theatre as Sign-system*, 98, 206 n 9, 210 n 13, 219 n 25
Austen, Jane, 120

Backscheider, Paula R.: *The Plays of Elizabeth Inchbald*, 172, 223 n 27, 225 n 6, n 8; *Spectacular Politics*, 20-21, 209 n 32, n 33, n 34, 213 n 23, 218 n 16, 226 n 26
Badinter, Elisabeth, 216 n 59
Baillie, Joanna, 20, 186, 193, 208 n 28; *Count Basil*, 186-89, 226 n 24, n 25; *De Monfort*, 186-89, 226 n 22, n 25; *The Dream*, 226 n 23; *Ethwald I*, 191; *The Family Legend*, 225 n 16; "Introductory Discourse," 63, 161, 176, 186-87,

215 n 50, 225 n 40, 226 n 19; *Orra*, 189-91, 226 n 27; *The Second Marriage*, 117-18; *The Tryal*, 170-71, 186, 223 n 15. See *also* gothicism
Bannister, John, 25, 130
Barker-Benfield, G.J., 216 n 59
Barrett, Charlotte, ix
Barrett, Michèle, 138, 221 n 4, 222 n 13
Behn, Aphra, 20, 207 n 20
Benkovitz, Miriam J., 5, 53, 205 n 9, 214 n 28
Berg Collection, The, ix, 2, 5, 25, 26, 53, 54, 66, 84, 95, 114, 115, *116*, 130, 145, 215 n 54, n 55; "Fanny Burney and family," 1, 110; "Miscellaneous Pieces of Manuscript," 2, 84, 145, 209 n 6
Bevis, Richard W., 46, 47, 212 n 6, n 9, n 10, 225 n 12
Bindman, David, 225 n 39
Bloom, Edward A., 223 n 20
Bloom, Harold, 223 n 21
Bonaparte, Napoléon, Emperor, 107
body, the, 7-21, 49, 51, 80, 94, 107, 108, 191-92, 201-2, 213 n 19, 215 n 49; as corpse, 14, 15, 17, 63-64, 92, 108, 215 n 51; in *A Busy Day*, 134, 138, 140; in *Edwy and Elgiva*, 13, 17, 56-64, 215 n 51; in *Elberta*, 70, 80; in *Hubert De Vere*, 17, 86, 90, 92; in *Love and*

the body *(cont'd)*
  Fashion, 124-25; in *The Witlings,*
  38; in *The Woman-Hater,* 70, 156-
  57, 202. *See also* punishment, sexu-
  ality
Boose, Linda E., 131, 132, 221 n 3
Booth, Michael R., 208 n 22, 212 n 9
Bowden, Elizabeth, *133, 136*
Brien, Jeremy, 204 n 3
Bronfen, Elizabeth, 215 n 49
Brontë, Emily, 222 n 5
Brooke, Frances, 20; *The Siege of
  Sinope,* 64, 181-83, 189, 191, 225
  n 15
Broome, Ralph, 222 n 7
Brown, Martha G., 199, 204 n 4, 226
  n 3
Browne, Alice, 6, 205 n 11
Burke, Edmund, 18, 23, 219 n 23
Burney, Charles, Jr. (brother): and
  Edwy and Elgiva, 53, 54, 214 n
  30; and *Hubert De Vere,* 82-83;
  and *Love and Fashion,* 1, 110-12
Burney, Charles (father), 44, 69, 204
  n 1; and *The Cunning Man,* 218 n
  10, 220 n 8; and *Hubert De Vere,*
  83, 84, 93, 218 n 17; and *Love
  and Fashion,* 1, 110-13, 166, 204 n
  1, 219 n 30; and *The Siege of
  Pevensey,* 218 n 20; and *The
  Witlings,* 2, 23-25, 40, 41, 209 n 8
Burney, Charlotte Ann, later Francis,
  later Broome (sister), 82, 222 n 7
Burney, Esther (sister), 110-11, 221 n
  15
Burney, Frances, later d'Arblay: attitude toward her father, 69, 93, 95,
  112-13; attitude toward playwright-
  ing, 1, 3, 24, 41, 83, 111-13; compared with Adela, 218 n 20, 219 n
  30; compared with Cerulia, 218 n
  17; compared with Dabler, 210 n 8;
  compared with Elberta, 217 n 69;
  compared with Joyce, 224 n 29;
  compared with Sophia, 224 n 29; in
  court, 43-45, 55, 65-66; feminism
  of, 4-5, 204 n 4, 211 n 17, 222 n
  6; in France, 110, 130, 220 n 1;
  mother, 68-69; motherhood of, 52,
  80, 84; retirement in the country,

  221 n 15; and Streatham Circle, 22-
  24, 38, 209 n 5, 210 n 15; view of
  women, 4-5, 9-12, 157, 199. *See
  also* drama, Burney's
Burney, Susanna Elizabeth, later
  Phillips (sister), 1, 23, 38, 44, 110-
  12, 209 n 3, 210 n 15, 212 n 5
Busy Day, A, 2, 25, 35, 69, 89, 108-
  10, 127, 130-44, *133, 136,* 145,
  147, 149, 160, 163, 164, 168, 170,
  171, 225 n 4; composition of, 130;
  critical assessment of, 222 n 6; dialogue in, 137, 138, 140-41, 194-
  96; figures in: Cleveland, 109, 170,
  174, 175, 194, 200; Deborah, 222
  n 8; Eliza, 12, 15, 108-9, 129, 149,
  163, 164, 169, 170, 171, 173, 174,
  175, 195, 200-2, 222 n 8, n 10, n
  12; Frank, 222 n 8; Jemima, 170;
  Lady Wilhelmina, 175, 201, 223 n
  14; Miss Percival, 223 n 15; Mungo
  (Indian Servant), 12, 15, 134, 143-
  44, 175, 222 n 9; Mr. Tibbs, 174,
  201; Sir Marmaduke, 15, 174, 175,
  201; the Tylneys, 162, 164, 173,
  174, 200, 201; the Wattses, 162,
  171, 174, 175, 193, 195, 196, 199,
  200, 201; manuscript of, 130; plot
  of, 132-33; production of, 3, 203,
  221 n 1; production, reviews of, 3,
  204 n 3; publication of, 5, 205 n 9;
  space in, 134, 135, 137-41. *See
  also* the body, casting, class, daughterhood, judgment, motherhood,
  race

Campbell, D. Grant, 218 n 9
Cambridge, George Owen, the Rev.,
  43, 218 n 17
Camilla, 2, 109, 112, 171; Mrs.
  Arlbery in, 199; Camilla in, 22, 69,
  129, 221 n 2; Edgar in, 118, 165
Canfield, J. Douglas, 212 n 7
Carlson, Julie A., 208 n 28
Carlson, Susan, 20, 209 n 31, 211 n
  21
Carte, Thomas, 54, 55, 214 n 38, 215
  n 57, 217 n 6, 219 n 22
Case, Sue-Ellen, 9, 205 n 1, 206 nn 9,
  10, 11, 209 n 35

casting, 2, 16, 25, 166; for *A Busy
Day,* 130, *133, 136;* for *Edwy and
Elgiva,* 52, 213 n 25; for *The
Woman-Hater,* 70, 130
Cavendish, Margaret, 20
Cecilia, 2, 25, 41, 43, 171; Cecilia in,
22, 41, 129, 222 n 8; compared to
The Witlings, 25, 41; Lady Honoria
in, 199
censorship. *See* judgment
Centlivre, Susanna, 167
character, actantial model of, 98-100,
99 (figure), 100 (figure), 219 n 25
Charlotte, Queen, 44-45, 66
Cixous, Hélène, 8, 15, 94, 157, 205 n
3, 207 n 19, 218 n 18
class, 12, 16, 173-75, 223 n 20, 224
n 34; in *A Busy Day,* 12, 132-44,
163, 223 n 14; in *Hubert De Vere,*
87-88; and motherhood, 67-69; in
Love and Fashion, 118, 125; in
The Witlings, 15, 22, 35, 36, 39-
41; in *The Woman-Hater,* 153-55,
157-63
Clément, Catherine, 94, 207 n 19,
218 n 18
Colman, George, the Elder, 118, 168,
209 n 4, 215 n 52
colonization, 12, 67, 68, 127, 132,
137, 143-44, 146, 216 n 60
comedy. *See* drama, Burney's; drama,
eighteenth-century; drama, feminist
Congreve, William, 20, 46, 209 n 4
Conolly, L.W., 208 n 22
Cooke, Stewart J., ix, 5, 66
Cotton, Nancy, 20, 208 n 30
Coveney, Alan, *133, 136*
Covent Garden Theatre, 1, 110, 130,
220 n 3
Cowley, Hannah, 16, 20; *Albina,* 216
n 67, 225 n 13; *The Belle's
Stratagem,* 167, 170, 172; *A Bold
Stroke for a Husband,* 172; *The
Fate of Sparta,* 64, 183, 185-86,
225 n 17; *More Ways than One,*
211 n 17; *Who's the Dupe?,* 211 n
17
Cox, Jeffrey N.: "Romantic Drama,"
208 n 25, n 26, 215 n 52, 220 n
36; *Seven Gothic Dramas,* 18, 19,

48, 117, 187, 188, 208 n 24, n 25,
n 28, 213 n 14, 220 n 7, 226 n 20,
n 21, n 22
Crisp, Samuel, 2, 23-25, 40, 41, 43,
166, 209 n 5, n 8
Cumberland, Richard, 1, 52, 166,
215 n 52, 222 n 7
Curb, Rosemary K., 8, 206 n 5
Cutting-Gray, Joanne, 4, 5, 90, 157,
205 n 8, 218 n 14, 224 n 33

d'Arblay, Frances Burney. *See* Burney,
Frances
d'Arblay, Alexander. *See* Arblay,
Alexander
daughterhood, 177, 178, 181-85,
199-200, 224 n 36, 225 n 16; in *A
Busy Day,* 135, 137-39, 142, 144;
eighteenth-century, 82, 95, 218 n
20, 225 n 12; in *Hubert De Vere,*
82-94, 177; in *The Siege of
Pevensey,* 94-106, 177; in *The
Woman-Hater,* 155-61, 223 n 29
Davenport, Mary Anne, 130
Davidoff, Leonore, 6, 205 n 11
De Camp, Maria Theresa, 25, 130
de Lauretis, Teresa, 63, 70, 207 n 17,
216 n 66
Delery, Clayton J., 5, 205 n 9
de Thoyras, M. (Paul) Rapin, 54, 56,
214 n 39, 215 n 57, 218 n 6
Devlin, D.D., 6, 205 n 10, 211 n 1
Diamond, Elin, 94
*Diary and Letters of Fanny Burney,
The,* ix, 44, 45, 55
Digby, the Hon. Stephen, 44, 218 n
17
Dobson, Austin, ix, 6, 205 n 10, 209
n 8, 214 n 28
Dolan, Jill, 8-10, 206 n 7, n 10, n 12
Donkin, Ellen: *Getting Into The Act,*
3, 16, 20, 53, 54, 204 n 1, n 2,
214 n 29, 215 n 48, 220 n 4, 225
n 13; "Mrs. Siddons," 19, 208 n
27, 214 n 35
Doody, Margaret Anne, 3, 4, 5, 6, 69,
95, 120, 167, 177, 199, 204 n 1,
216 n 65, 225 n 5, n 10, n 12; on
A Busy Day, 132, 135, 222 n 6, n
7, n 11, 223 n 14, n 15, n 16; on

Doody, Margaret Anne *(cont'd)*
the comedies, 222 n 6; on *Edwy
and Elgiva,* 212 n 3; on *Elberta,*
217 n 69; on *Evelina,* 211 n 19; on
Hubert De Vere, 90, 93, 218 n 12,
n 17; on *Love and Fashion,* 118,
124, 126, 128, 220 n 1, n 6, n 7, n
9, 221 n 16, n 17; on *The Siege of
Pevensey,* 103, 218 n 20, 219 n 31;
on the tragedies, 43, 106, 211 n 1,
212 n 2, n 4, n 5, 220 n 34; *The
Wanderer,* 225 n 2; on *The
Witlings,* 41, 209 n 4, n 6, 210 n 8,
n 10, n 11, n 12, n 14, n 16, 211 n
18, n 22; on *The Woman-Hater,*
149, 152, 155, 156, 159, 222 n 6,
223 n 17, n 24, n 26, n 29, 224 n
32, n 35, n 37
drama: gender and, 7-21, 206 n 9;
Greek, 7, 212 n 13; and narrative,
12-14, 63, 207 n 16, n 17, n 18;
semiotics in 4, 9, 206 n 9;
Renaissance, 17, 207 n 20;
Restoration, 17, 20, 46, 207 n 20;
speech-act theory and, 35, 103, 210
n 13; theater as political institution,
9, 18-21. *See also* drama, Burney's;
drama, eighteenth-century; drama,
feminist; sentimentality; tragedy
drama, Burney's: comedies, 3, 11-12,
14, 15, 16, 46, 53, 65, 107, 108-9,
127, 129, 130-31, 168-75; critical
neglect of, 4-5; dialogue in, 193-98;
disguise in, 172-74; family in, 130-
32, 199-200; marriages in, 11, 13-
14, 200-1; punishment in, 171-72,
191-92, 201-2; tragedies, 3, 11, 13,
14, 16, 42, 43-51, 134, 175-92;
tragedies, critical assessment of,
211 n 1
drama, eighteenth-century: approaches to, 17-21; censorship in, 18, 19,
208 n 22; comedy, 20, 65, 115,
118-19, 148, 166-71, 175, 221 n
21, 224 n 30; and genre, 18-19, 21,
46, 168; and periodization, 19;
political status of, 18-19;
Restoration drama, 17, 20, 46, 207
n 20; and revolution, 18, 162, 208
n 25, n 26; tragedy, 12, 45, 48, 64,
65, 70, 106-7, 167, 175-76, 212 n

7, n 9, 215 n 52, 218 n 20; women
and, 3, 16, 19-20, 46, 53, 165-92,
202. *See also* drama, Burney's;
gothicism
drama, feminist, 7-21, 94, 206 n 10;
approaches to, 7-8; bibliographies
for, 205 n 2; definition, 8-9; the
góthic and, 48-49, 213 n 23; movement in, 7-9, 16; and narrative, 7,
8, 12-15, 63, 207 n 16, n 17, n 18;
political power of, 9-10; semiotics
in, 4, 206 n 9; and Shakespeare,
207 n 20; space in, 7-9, 14, 16, 17,
21; techniques of, 7-8, 16-17, 21;
and tragedy, 46-51, 86, 207 n 16,
212 n 13
Drury Lane Theatre, 3, 18, 23, 52,
53, 82, 130, 183, 186

Eagleton, Terry, 221 n 5
*Early Journals and Letters of Fanny
Burney, The,* ix, 2, 23, 24, 38, 41,
209 n 5, 210 n 9, n 14, n 15, 214
n 37, n 41
education, 12, 15, 68, 224 n 31; in
The Witlings, 22, 25, 27, 30, 35-
37, 170, 209 n 4, n 8, 210 n 17; in
The Woman-Hater, 15, 146, 154,
156, 158-61
Edwy and Elgiva, 2, 43, 51-64, 92,
93, 94, 97, 189, 191, 196, 212 n 7,
225 n 16; composition of, 44, 54,
212 n 3; critical assessment of, 196,
211 n 1, 214 n 28; dialogue in, 59,
196-97; figures in: Aldhelm, 189,
190, 196; Dunstan, 11, 13, 197;
Edwy, 4, 11, 13, 97, 106, 185,
189, 190, 196, 197, 200; Elgiva,
11, 13, 17, 50, 72, 79, 86, 90, 95,
97, 101, 108, 179, 185, 187, 189,
190, 191, 193, 200, 201, 215 n 47,
n 48, n 51; manuscript of, 53-54,
in Emmanuel College, Cambridge,
6, 53; in Larpent Collection, 6, 53;
plot, 57; production of, 3, 19, 51-
52, 63, 82-83, 106, 204 n 2, 211 n
1, 213 n 25, 217 n 3; production,
Burney's view of, 52, 83; production, reviews of, 3, 52, 214 n 28,
215 n 48; prologue and epilogue of,
53, 214 n 30; publication of, 5, 53,

205 n 9; revisions to, 52-54; sources for, 54-57, 219 n 22; space in, 60-62. *See also* the body, casting, gothicism, judgment, madness, punishment, sexuality, spectatorship

Elam, Kier, 206 n 9

Elberta, 2, 14, 43, 51, 64-80, 93, 94, 95, 130, 153, 197, 198, 200; Burney's view of, 78; compared to *The Siege of Pevensey*, 66; compared to *The Wanderer*, 66, 72; compared to *The Woman-Hater*, 67, 69-71, 77; composition of, 45, 66, 75-79; critical assessment of, 65-66, 211 n 1, 217 n 69; dialogue in, 76, 197; figures in: Arnulph, 11, 13, 106, 185, 188, 197, 200, 217 n 68; Elberta, 11, 86, 89, 95, 101, 108, 185, 187, 189, 191, 193, 199-202, 217 n 68; Offa, 11, 185, 202; manuscript of, 65-66; plot, 66-67; revisions to, 75-79; sources for, 65, 215 n 57. *See also* the body, gothicism, judgment, madness, motherhood, punishment, sentimentality, sexuality

Ellis, Kate Ferguson, 60, 214 n 42, n 44, 215 n 52, 216 n 68

empire. *See* colonization

Epstein, Julia, 4, 5, 6, 48, 90, 120, 147, 157, 158, 205 n 7, 209 n 1, 213 n 15, n 19, 218 n 13, 221 n 13, 222 n 8, 223 n 19, 224 n 33

Evelina, 1, 2, 22, 23, 37, 43, 120, 147, 149, 153, 199, 210 n 8, 211 n 19, 216 n 65, 223 n 20, n 21, n 22, n 23; Belmont in, 148-49; the Branghtons in, 148, 174; Captain Mirvan in, 37; Evelina in, 22, 128, 147-48, 160; Lord Orville in, 148, 165; Madame Duval in, 37, 147; Mrs. Selwyn in, 199; Polly Green in, 147-48; Rev. Villars in, 147

family. *See* daughterhood, ideology, motherhood

"Fanny Burney and family." *See* Berg Collection

Fawcett, John, 130

feminism, definition, 8-9

Figes, Eva, 199, 226 n 4

Fischer-Lichte, Erika, 206 n 9

Fizer, Irene, 216 n 65

Flowers, Betty S., 131, 132, 221 n 3

Francus, Marilyn, 68, 215 n 59, 216 n 64

Freedman, Barbara, 7, 205 n 1

French Revolution, the, 18, 106-7, 158, 159, 161, 208 n 25, n 26, 216 n 68, 219 n 23, 220 n 1, 226 n 24; "The Contrast" and, 224 n 39

Freud, Sigmund, 7

Garrick, David, 16, 118, 147, 166, 168

Gay, John, 209 n 4

Gellrich, Michelle, 51, 213 n 24

George III, King, 44, 65, 161, 224 n 34

Girard, René, 50

Goldsmith, Oliver, 193, 204 n 2

gothicism and gothic drama, 16, 18, 19, 21, 48-50, 60, 84, 90, 117, 176, 198, 213 n 17, n 23; 215 n 52, 216 n 68, 220 n 7; in Baillie, 187, 190-91; in *Edwy and Elgiva*, 60-61; in *Elberta*, 67; in *Hubert De Vere*, 89-92, 190; in *Love and Fashion*, 117-18; in *The Siege of Pevensey*, 103; in *The Woman-Hater*, 152-53

Grassby, Juliette, 133

Griffith, Elizabeth, 20

Hall, Catherine, 6, 205 n 11

Hanley, Keith, 208 n 25

Hardt, Ulrich H., 216 n 62

Harris, Thomas, 1, 110-12, 115, 170

Hayley, William, 216 n 67

Haymarket, The, Little Theatre at, 225 n 13

Heilman, Robert Bechtold, 86, 99, 218 n 7, n 8, 219 n 26, n 27

Hemlow, Joyce, ix, 6, 205 n 10; on *A Busy Day*, 222 n 6; on *Edwy and Elgiva*, 52, 56, 83, 212 n 3, n 4, 214 n 26, n 40; on *Elberta*, 217 n 69; on *Hubert De Vere*, 83, 84, 217 n 3, n 5, 218 n 17; on *Love and Fashion*, 220 n 6; on *The Siege of Pevensey*, 95, 219 n 20, n 21; on the tragedies, 43, 212 n 2, n 4; on

Hemlow, Joyce (cont'd)
The Witlings, 23, 209 n 2, 210 n 8,
n 15, 211 n 17; on The Woman-
Hater, 222 n 6
Henry, Robert, 54-56, 214 n 36
Hewitt, Wendy, 136
Hill, Bridget, 6, 205 n 11, 216 n 59
Hill, Constance, 5, 205 n 9, 209 n 8
Hogan, Charles Beecher, 208 n 22,
220 n 2, 224 n 38, 226 n 18
Hogarth, William, 224 n 34
Holcroft, Thomas, 221 n 10, 223 n
18
Holderness, Graham, 206 n 10
Howard, Jean E., 198, 226 n 2
Howe, Elizabeth, 207 n 21
Hubert De Vere, 2, 43, 64, 82-94,
99, 115, 177, 189, 190, 191, 212 n
7; Burney's view of, 84; compared
to The Wanderer, 218 n 17; composition of, 44-45; critical assessment
of, 211 n 1, 218 n 17; figures in:
Cerulia, 11, 17, 76, 79, 95, 99,
101, 108, 122, 177, 180, 185, 187,
189, 190, 191, 193, 197, 200, 218
n 9, n 12, n 17; De Mowbray, 11,
95, 177, 180, 200, 218 n 17; De
Vere, 4, 11, 13, 106, 180, 189,
190, 197, 200, 218 n 12, n 17;
Geralda, 72, 79, 180, 200, 218 n
17; dialogue in, 89, 197-98; manuscript of 84; plot, 85; production
possibilities of, 51-52, 82-84; revisions to, 83, 84, 91-92; sources for,
85, 217 n 6; space in, 88-89. See
also the body, class, daughterhood,
gothicism, judgment, madness, punishment, sexuality, spectatorship
Hulton-Baker, Robert, 204 n 3
Hume, David, 54, 56, 214 n 41, 215
n 57, 217 n 6, 219 n 22
Hume, Robert D., 202, 226 n 6
Hunt, Lynn, 219 n 23
Hutner, Heidi, 207 n 20

ideology, 5, 49, 106, 108, 123, 157;
definition, 206 n 8, 207 n 19;
familial, 100, 130-32, 135, 221 n
4, n 5; and gender, 7, 9, 10, 15,
131, 198; maternal, 67-71, 80;

romantic, 120, 208 n 28; and the-
ater, 9, 10, 18, 19, 21, 48, 162,
208 n 28
imperialism. See colonization
Inchbald, Elizabeth, 16, 20, 112, 166,
167, 172, 193, 208 n 28, 225 n 6;
All on a Summer's Day, 170; A
Case of Conscience, 223 n 27; The
Child of Nature, 219 n 31, 224 n
31; To Marry, or Not to Marry,
167, 170; The Midnight Hour, 167;
The Mogul Tale, 222 n 7; Next
Door Neighbours, 169; Such
Things Are, 167; The Wise Man of
the East, 117, 169, 172, 222 n 7;
Wives as They Were and Maids as
They Are, 169
Ireland, William Henry, 107
Irigaray, Luce, 224 n 36

Jenkins, Linda Walsh, 205 n 4
Jephson, Robert, 106, 216 n 67
Johnson, Samuel, 1, 23, 43, 166
Jones, Vivien, 6, 11, 205 n 11, 206 n
15, 215 n 59
Jordan, Dorothy, 25, 130, 156
Journals and Letters of Fanny
Burney, The, ix, 1, 52, 53, 83, 84,
110-14, 117, 130, 212 n 3, n 5,
214 n 27, 217 n 2, n 3, 219 n 30,
220 n 3, 221 n 15, 222 n 7
judgment, 11-15, 179, 216 n 67, 225
n 16; in A Busy Day, 139-44; in
Edwy and Elgiva, 57-64; in
Elberta, 73-74; in Hubert De Vere,
87; in Love and Fashion, 15, 108,
118, 119, 122, 123, 126, 128; in
The Siege of Pevensey, 103-5; in
The Witlings, 15, 22, 30, 36, 37,
38, 40-41; in The Woman-Hater,
15, 149-51, 153

Kelly, Gary, 6, 205 n 11
Kelly, Hugh, 209 n 4
Kelly, Ian, 133
Kelly, Linda, 208 n 23, 214 n 35
Kelly, Veronica, 80, 217 n 71
Kemble, Charles, 25
Kemble, John Philip, 25, 183, 184,
186; and Edwy and Elgiva, 52, 54,

83, 217 n 3; and *Hubert De Vere,*
52, 82-83; and *The Woman-Hater,*
70, 130, 152
Keyssar, Hélène, 8, 11, 206 n 6
King, Thomas, 130
Kintz, Linda, 207 n 16, 212 n 13,
226 n 25
Knight, Richard Payne, 82, 102, 217
n 1
Knight, Thomas, 130
Kotzbue, August von, 117, 169
Kowaleski-Wallace, Elizabeth, 216 n
65

Larpent, John, 18
Larpent Collection, The. *See* Berg
Collection
learning. *See* education
Lee, Sophia, 20, 189, 190, 226 n 26
Leith, Hope M., 100, 101, 219 n 28,
n 29
Lewis, Matthew Gregory ("Monk"),
84, 117
Lewis, William Thomas, 130
Lillo, George, 215 n 52
Lindenberger, Herbert, 65, 106, 215 n
52, n 53, 220 n 35
Link, Frederick M., 226 n 17
Locke, William, 83
London Stage, The, 160, 167, 186,
208 n 22, 220 n 2, 224 n 38, 226
n 18
Louis XVI, King, 161
Love and Fashion, 1, 2, 72, 84, <u>108-
29</u>, 145, 168, 169, 171, 172, 221 n
14; Burney's view of, 114-15; composition of, 109-15, 130; critical
assessment of, 220 n 6; dialogue in,
122-24, 194, 196; figures in: Davis,
221 n 14; Dawson, 221 n 14;
Hilaria, 1, 12, 14, 164, 169, 170,
171, 194, 199, 200, 201, 220 n 6,
221 n 14; Innis, 169, 221 n 14;
Litchburn, 25, 175, 196, 221 n 14;
Lord Ardville, 14, 174, 175, 196,
200, 220 n 6, 221 n 14; Lord
Exbury, 199, 221 n 14; Miss
Exbury, 221 n 14; Mordaunt, 196,
221 n 14; Sir Archy, 169, 174, 175,
193, 221 n 14; "Strange Man,"

220 n 7, n 8, 221 n 14; Valentine,
14, 15, 193, 194, 200, 221 n 14;
manuscript of, 114, 116; plot, 115,
117; production possibilities of, 1,
51, 53, 110-11, 166, 220 n 3;
space in, 121-24; revisions to, 114-
15; suppression of, 1, 2, 110, 112-
14, 166, 219 n 30. *See also* the
body, class, gothicism, judgment,
sexuality

Macaulay, Thomas Babington, 209 n
8
Macheski, Cecilia, 20, 204 n 4, 208 n
27, n 29
Mack, Robert L., 225 n 2
madness, 14, 94, 177, 178, 180, 187,
189-91, 201, 226 n 25; and
Cecilia, 41; and *Edwy and Elgiva,*
62-64, 93; and *Elberta,* 76, 93; and
Hubert De Vere, 85, 89-93, 190,
191, 197, 200; in the novels, 90-91
Malpede, Karen, 205 n 4
manuscripts. *See* Berg Collection
Mattocks, Isabella, 130
McIntosch, Mary, 138, 221 n 4, 222
n 13
"Miscellaneous Pieces of
Manuscript." *See* Berg Collection
Moers, Ellen, 209 n 8
Molière, Jean-Baptiste Poquelin d',
23, 209 n 4
Montagu, Elizabeth, 24, 209 n 5, n 8
Moore, Edward, 184
More, Hannah, 16, 20, 176; *The
Fatal Falsehood,* 179-80, 189-91;
The Inflexible Captive, 176-78,
180, 189; *Percy,* 178-79, 180, 189,
191, 216 n 67, 225 n 13; "Preface
to the Tragedies," 176, 225 n 11
Morgan, Fidelis, 207 n 20
Morrison, Marjorie Lee, 6, 43, 205 n
10; on *Elberta,* 77, 217 n 69, n 70;
on *Hubert De Vere,* 218 n 17; on
Love and Fashion, 220 n 6; on *The
Siege of Pevensey,* 105, 218 n 20,
219 n 33; on the tragedies, 43, 211
n 1; on *The Witlings,* 210 n 8, n
15; on *The Woman-Hater,* 223 n
28

motherhood: in *A Busy Day,* 134, 135, 137, 199; Burney as mother, 52, 80, 84; Burney's mother, 69; and class, 67-70; eighteenth-century views of, 67-69, 80-81, 215 n 59, 216 n 60, n 68, 223 n 25, 224 n 36; in *Elberta,* 51, 64-81, 94, 199, 217 n 68, 223 n 25; and genre, 70-71, 80-81; and narrative, 69-70, 150-51; in *The Woman-Hater,* 146-56, 159, 163-64, 199, 224 n 36; *see also* sentimentality

Mulliken, Elizabeth Yost, 6, 205 n 10, 210 n 8, 211 n 1, 220 n 6, 222 n 6

Mulvey, Laura, 207 n 17

Munden, Joseph Shepherd, 110, 130

Murphy, Arthur, 1, 18, 23-25, 166, 220 n 4

narrative: comic, 12-14; and gender, 7, 8, 10, 12-14, 207 n 17, n 18; and motherhood, 68-70, 150-51; resolutions, 14-15, 142; tragic, 12-14, 63, 77, 207 n 16

Nicoll, Allardyce: *A History of English Drama,* 46, 208 n 22, 212 n 8, n 9; *The Theory of Drama,* 12, 47, 212 n 11, n 12

Nicholson, Paul, *136*

Nussbaum, Felicity, 6, 68, 80, 205 n 11, 215 n 59, 216 n 61, n 63

Oakleaf, David, 216 n 65

O'Brien, Maggie, 136

O'Connor, Marion F., 198, 226 n 2

Oedipus the King, 7, 10, 212 n 13; oedipal theory, 7, 207 n 16, 212 n 13

Palmer, John, 52

Pearson, Jacqueline, 207 n 20

Pedicord, Harry William, 225 n 14

Perry, Ruth, 216 n 60

Peterson, Linda H., 222 n 5

Pfister, Manfred, 60, 206 n 9, 214 n 43

Philips, Katherine, 20

Pix, Mary, 20

Poovey, Mary, 6, 205 n 11, 206 n 15

Pope, Alexander (actor), 130

Pope, Alexander, 209 n 4

Pope, Jane, 130

Pope, Maria Ann, 25, 130

punishment, 4, 11, 13, 14, 15, 17, 21, 42, 45-46, 48-51, 64, 65, 69, 94, 105, 106, 119, 120, 189, 191-92, 193, 201, 208 n 21, 212 n 7, 213 n 19, 215 n 49; in *Edwy and Elgiva,* 13, 14, 17, 54, 57-64, 191, 201, 214 n 45, 215 n 47; in *Elberta,* 69, 75-76, 80, 191; in *Hubert De Vere,* 14, 17, 86, 89-93, 191, 213 n 19; in *Love and Fashion,* 121, 124, 126; in *The Siege of Pevensey,* 101, 191, 219 n 20; in *The Witlings,* 36-38, 210 n 16; in *The Woman-Hater,* 151-53, 162, 163, 171-72. *See also* the body, judgment

Purinton, Marjean D., 208 n 28, 226 n 24

Pye, Henry James, 106

Quick, John, 130

race, 16, 18, 21, 168, 207 n 21; in *A Busy Day,* 12, 15, 134, 137, 138, 142-44, 173-74, 222 n 9, 223 n 14; and nationality, 21, 68, 161

Ranger, Paul, 220 n 7

Redmond, James, 206 n 12

Reiman, Donald H., 215 n 50

Reinelt, Janelle G., 10, 14, 156, 206 n 13, n 14, 208 n 27

Reiter, Rayna R., 213 n 20

Rendall, Jane, 216 n 59

Reynolds, Sir Josphua, 23

Roach, Joseph R., 208 n 27

Rogers, Katharine M.: *Fanny Burney,* 4, 5, 6, 199, 205 n 5, 210 n 8, n 17, 226 n 5; *Feminism in Eighteenth-Century England,* 6, 205 n 11; *The Meridian Anthology,* 5, 205 n 9, 207 n 20

Rogers, Pat, 208 n 27, 214 n 35

Rousseau, Jean-Jacques, 218 n 10

Rowe, Nicholas, 179, 212 n 7, 225 n 14

Rowlandson, Thomas, 224 n 39

Rubin, Gayle, 49-50, 213 n 20, n 21

"Rule Britannia," 160-61

Russell, Gillian, 208 n 25

Sabor, Peter, ix, 3, 5, 6, 225 n 1; on *A Busy Day,* 204 n 3, 221 n 1, 222 n 9, 223 n 14; on *Edwy and Elgiva,* 52, 53, 54, 212 n 3, 213 n 25, 214 n 27, n 31, n 32, n 33, n 34, n 45, 215 n 47; on *Elberta,* 66, 67, 215 n 54, n 55, n 56, n 58, 217 n 69; on the gothic, 213 n 17; on *Hubert De Vere,* 83, 84, 89, 217 n 4, 218 n 11; on *Love and Fashion,* 114, 220 n 5; *The Wanderer,* 225 n 2; on *The Witlings,* 25, 209 n 3, n 6, n 7, n 8, 211 n 20; on *The Woman-Hater,* 25, 221 n 1, 223 n 17

Savona, George, 98, 206 n 9, 210 n 13, 219 n 25

Scarry, Elaine, 49, 62, 80, 213 n 18, 215 n 46

Schofield, Mary Anne, 20, 204 n 4, 208 n 27, n 29

Scholes, Percy A., 204 n 2, 218 n 10

Scott, Sir Walter, 152

Sedgwick, Eve Kosofsky: *Between Men,* 50, 213 n 22; *Gothic Conventions,* 48-49, 67, 91, 103, 213 n 16, 218 n 15, 219 n 32

Selden, Raman, 208 n 25

Senelick, Lawrence, 206 n 9

sentimentality and sentimentalism: in comedy, 14, 15, 168, 194; in drama, 19; and motherhood, 67; in *Elberta,* 75; in tragedy, 223 n 28; in *The Witlings,* 170, 173, 209 n 3, 211 n 20, in *The Woman-Hater,* 223 n 28, 224 n 30

sexuality, 14, 49-50, 216 n 67; in *Edwy and Elgiva,* 56-64; in *Elberta,* 70, 86; in *Hubert De Vere,* 87; in *Love and Fashion,* 123, 125; in *The Woman-Hater,* 70, 150, 151, 152, 168

Shakespeare, William, 24, 163, 167, 175, 191, 207 n 20

Sherbo, Arthur, 168, 225 n 7

Sheridan, Frances, 169

Sheridan, Richard Brinsley, 1, 3, 23, 52, 53, 83, 107, 119, 166, 193, 204 n 2, 211 n 17

Show of Strength Theatre Company, 3, *133, 136,* 203, 221 n 1

Shuckburgh, Evelyn Shirley, 53, 196, 214 n 28, 226 n 1

Siddons, Sarah, 19, 20, 183, 184, 186, 188, 190, 208 n 27, 214 n 35; and *Edwy and Elgiva,* 52, 54, 63, 215 n 48; and *The Woman-Hater,* 70, 130, 152

Siege of Pevensey, The, 2, 43, 64, 82, 94-106, 99-101 (figures), 177, 183, 191; compared to *Elberta,* 66; composition of, 44; critical assessment of, 211 n 1, 218 n 20; dialogue in, 103, 197; figures in: Adela, 11, 72, 79, 108, 120, 126, 177, 183, 185, 187, 191, 193, 197, 200, 218 n 20, 219 n 24, n 30; Chester, 11, 126, 185, 197, 199, 200, 218 n 20, 219 n 24; de Belesme, 13, 200, 219 n 24; de Warrenne, 200, 219 n 24; William, 11, 219 n 24; manuscript of, 95; plot, 95-96; sources for, 219 n 22; space in, 97-99. *See also* daughterhood, gothicism, judgment, punishment

Sill, Geoffrey M., ix, 5

Simons, Judy, 211 n 17, n 1

Smollett, Tobias, 54-55, 214 n 37

spectatorship, 7, 8, 207 n 17, 215 n 49, 226 n 22; in Burney's novels, 118, 165; in the comedies, 118; and drama, 161, 176, 186, 207 n 21; in *Edwy and Elgiva,* 17, 63; in *Hubert De Vere,* 17, 92

Stanton, Judith Philips, 166, 208 n 29, 225 n 3, n 9

Staves, Susan, 6, 148, 205 n 11, 206 n 8, 223 n 21

Steadman, Susan M. Flierl, 205 n 2

Steele, Richard, 168, 222 n 7

Straub, Kristina: *Fanny Burney,* 4, 5, 6, 120, 199, 205 n 6, 210 n 8, 221 n 11, n 12, 226 n 5; *Sexual Suspects,* 80, 207 n 21

Streatham Circle, 22-24, 38, 209 n 5, 210 n 15

suffering. *See* punishment

Taylor, John, 167, 225 n 6

Thaddeus, Janice Farrar, 6, 205 n 10, 215 n 56

theater. *See* drama, eighteenth-
century; drama, feminist
Thomson, James, 160
Thrale, Hester Lynch, later Piozzi, 1,
23-25, 43, 52, 210 n 9
torture. *See* punishment
tragedy, 45-51; Aristotlean, 12, 46,
212 n 13; confinement in, 45-46;
"drama of disaster," 86, 90, 99;
domestic, 215 n 52; eighteenth-
century, 12-13, 45-49, 65, 70, 106-
7, 167, 175-76, 212 n 9, 215 n 52,
218 n 20; feminist theory of, 48-
51, 86, 106, 207 n 16, 212 n 13;
Greek, 7, 212 n 13; and narrative,
12-14, 63, 77, 207 n 16; nonfeminist approaches to, 46-47, 208 n
28, 212 n 7, n 9; pathos in, 46;
sentimental, 223 n 28; settings in,
65, 215 n 52; "she-tragedy," 47-48,
208 n 21; by women, 175-92
Troide, Lars, ix
Trotter, Catherine, 20

von Mücke, Dorothea E., 80, 217 n
71

Waddington, Georgiana, 52
Wallace, Tara Ghoshal, 5, 205 n 9,
209 n 4, 220 n 4, 222 n 6, n 10, n
12, 225 n 4
Wanderer, The, 2, 110, 128, 159, 225
n 2; compared to *Elberta,* 66, 72;
compared to *Hubert De Vere,* 218
n 17; Elinor in, 199, 218 n 17;
Juliet in, 22, 66, 165, 166, 218 n
17
Watkins, Daniel P., 162, 208 n 28,
225 n 41, 226 n 22
Weedon, Chris, 131, 221 n 5
White, R.J., 224 n 34
Wikander, Matthew H., 46, 212 n 7
Wilkes, John, 224 n 34
Willingham, Bob, 133, 136
Witlings, The, 2, 22-42, 31 (figure),
84, 89, 108, 109, 111, 115, 125,
140, 168, 169, 170, 171, 173, 193;
Burney as Censoress, 210 n 15;
compared to *Cecilia,* 25, 41; compared to *The Woman-Hater,* 25,
41, 145-46, 209 n 6; composition
of, 22-23, 210 n 14; contemporary
reaction to, 23-25, 209 n 3; critical
assessment of, 209 n 8, 210 n 17;
dialogue in, 28-30, 31 (figure), 32-
35, 39, 194-96, 211 n 17, n 20;
"Esprit Party," 22, 24, 25, 27, 32,
35, 36, 146, 210 n 17; figures in:
Beaufort, 174, 175, 194, 200, 211
n 22; Cecilia, 12, 17, 108, 109,
134, 169, 170, 172, 173, 194, 196,
200-2, 210 n 12, 211 n 22; Censor,
15, 118, 174, 210 n 8, n 16, 211 n
21; Codger, 174, 196; Dabler, 174,
210 n 8; Jack, 174; Lady Smatter,
108, 109, 170, 172, 174, 200-2,
211 n 17, n 21; milliners, 15, 25,
27, 30, 37, 39, 40, 140, 170, 173,
174; Mrs. Sapient, 170, 172, 175,
195, 196, 211 n 17, n 21; Mrs.
Voluble, 170, 195, 196; manuscript
of, 25, 26; plot, 27; production of,
52, 203, 204 n 3; publication of, 5,
205 n 9, 209 n 8; revisions to, 25;
space in, 27-30, 32-35, 40; suppression of, 2, 23-25, 40, 204 n 2, 210
n 9, n 14. *See also* the body, class,
daughterhood, education, judgment,
punishment, sentimentality
Wollstonecraft, Mary, 68, 216 n 62
Woman-Hater, The, 2, 15, 25, 35, 42,
110, 130, 132, 144-64, 168, 171;
compared to *Elberta,* 67, 69-71,
77; compared to *The Witlings,* 25,
41, 145-46, 209 n 6; composition
of, 130, 145-46; critical assessment
of, 222 n 6; dialogue in, 150, 156-
57, 194; figures in: Eleonora, 12,
17, 70, 71, 109, 168, 169, 170,
172, 173, 194, 199, 201, 223 n 28,
224 n 30, n 36; Joyce, 15, 109,
129, 132, 170, 171, 173, 174, 175,
193, 195, 199, 200-2, 222 n 6, 223
n 29, 224 n 30, n 34, n 36; Lady
Smatter, 170, 175, 222 n 6, 224 n
30; nurse, 71, 170, 224 n 30; Sir
Roderick, 170, 174, 202, 222 n 6;
Sophia, 17, 109, 168, 170, 172,
174, 194, 199, 200-2, 223 n 29,
224 n 30, n 36; the Waverleys (Jack
and "Old"), 17, 168, 173, 222 n 6,
224 n 30; Wilmot, 15, 17, 70, 71,

118, 129, 172, 178, 194, 199, 201, 202, 223 n 18, 224 n 36; manuscript, 130, 145-46; plot, 146-47; space in, 150, 157-58, 162. *See also* the body, casting, class, daughterhood, education, gothicism, judgment, motherhood, punishment, sentimentality, sexuality

women. *See* Burney, Frances; daughterhood; drama, eighteenth-century; drama, feminist; education; feminism; madness; motherhood; sexuality; tragedy

Wycherly, William, 126

Yaeger, Patricia, 216 n 65